The test of war

The test of war:
inside Britain 1939–45

Robert Mackay
The Nottingham Trent University

Routledge
Taylor & Francis Group

LONDON AND NEW YORK

First published in 1999 by UCL Press

Reprinted 2003 by Routledge
11 New Fetter Lane
London, EC4P 4EE

Routledge is an imprint of the
Taylor & Francis Group

British Library Cataloguing in Publication Data
A CIP record for this book is available from the British Library.

ISBNs:
1-85728-634-0 HB
1-85728-935-9 PB

Every effort has been made to contact copyright holders for their permission to reprint material in this book. The publishers would be grateful to hear from any copyright holder who is not here acknowledged and will undertake to rectify any errors or omissions in future editions of this book.

Typeset in Garamond by Graphicraft Ltd, Hong Kong.

Contents

CONTENTS

Preface

For all participant states in the Second World War the domestic experience of the war reflected the way in which the conflict widened and intensified. Two separate wars, in Poland and China, spread and ultimately joined in a war embracing the greater part of the globe. The corresponding escalation in the activity of armed forces brought about the mobilization of all possible human and material resources. While it lasted, the war dominated the life of the nations that were involved and most of those that were not. Since Britain was in at both the start and the finish, her people experienced the impact of total war in full measure. The experience was a test of the most comprehensive kind: of the institutions, of the resources, of the very cohesion of the nation. How the nation responded to the test of war is the subject of this book.

Since any book about the Second World War is by definition potentially global in reach, the sub-title of this book is intended to indicate its confinement to the home front in Britain. During the course of the war Britain's armed forces were in action in several continents and oceans but that story in not told here. Reference is made to the changing external context only in so far as this affected government policies and thereby, directly or indirectly, domestic institutions and the daily lives of the people.

My approach has been thematic rather than chronological. I have therefore sought to compensate for the consequent loss of a sense of the passage of time and sequence of events by including in the first chapter a brief overview of the six years Britain was at war.

PREFACE

This book is not primarily concerned with social change and the role of the war in that process; for that, a different focus and a longer perspective would be needed. But I have attempted, in the second and tenth chapters, to record the condition of Britain before and after its ordeal by war.

Books of broad compass like this one necessarily depend on the work of many authors. I acknowledge my debt to them and append a bibliography that (I hope) names them all. I would also like to thank the Faculty of Humanities at The Nottingham Trent University for the time that got the project started and the support that got it finished.

Robert Mackay
1998

Chapter One

.ఎన

Going to war

It is a paradox that when Britain went to war in September 1939, it was, as in 1914, a result of her own ultimatum. For not only was the issue that prompted it on the other side of Europe, where Britain had few interests, but Britain was in a state of military unreadiness, pacifist sentiment was strong, and the government was in the hands of men determined to prevent the country from being drawn into other people's conflicts. "Never again" was the feeling at all levels of society in 1918; and yet, here again, when the memories of that time were scarcely faded, the call to total war went out.

In retrospect, the Second World War and Britain's participation in it has an air of inevitability. But creeping fatalism about another war did not properly begin in Britain until 1935-6. For a decade before then, foreign troubles seemed remote and unlikely to involve Britain directly. On the whole, international politics seemed less threatening than in the early years after the First World War. The League of Nations, established in 1919 to preserve peace through collective security, was steadily increasing its membership and was enhancing its credentials through its role in the settlement of international disputes. Franco-German antagonism, which in the past had been a chief source of instability and conflict, seemed to be giving way to reconciliation: at Locarno in 1925 France and Germany signed agreements that guaranteed the common frontiers of France, Germany and Belgium and committed them to seek arbitration in their disputes. At the same time Germany joined the League of Nations, thereby pledging herself to playing her part in disarmament and the peaceful solution of international problems.

Ten years on the optimists were on the defensive. The whole international atmosphere had deteriorated with the onset of the Great Depression and the resort by states to selfish measures of protection for their economies. This, in turn, had stimulated the rise of political parties advocating extreme solutions to the acute economic problems that democratic governments had failed to solve. In Germany the result was the accession to power of Adolf Hitler's National Socialist Party, followed by walk-out from the League of Nations and, in defiance of the restrictions placed on Germany in the 1919 Versailles Treaty, rearmament and the restoration of military conscription. With a more pugnacious and assertive government in Germany, the departure of Italy from the group of peaceful states was the more worrying. For although Benito Mussolini's rule was an undisguisedly brutal dictatorship, in international affairs Italy seemed not entirely lost to reasonableness and responsibility. In 1935, however, Mussolini shattered this conception when he initiated a war of conquest against a fellow member of the League, Abyssinia. The League's condemnation of Italy had the disastrous consequences of propelling her into a closer relationship with Germany while failing to save Abyssinia and thereby signalling the ineffectiveness of the League in the face of determined aggression by delinquent states. The prospects for an enduring peace looked poorer.

It had been the premise of Britain's defence thinking since 1933 that her most likely enemy in Europe was Germany. This presumption was based more on calculations about Germany's potential industrial and military strength than on a consideration of Britain's interests *vis-à-vis* those of Germany. Yet, at all levels of society, British attitudes towards Germany and the Germans were generally more favourable than towards France and the French, a situation that changed only in the final year of peace. Partly because of J. M. Keynes's telling criticisms of the victors' treatment of Germany at the Paris peace conference in 1919 (*The economic consequences of the peace*), it became generally accepted in the 1920s that Germany had been judged too harshly, that she had legitimate grievances about the details of the terms imposed on her, and that France's attitude to her was punitive and unreasonable. When France responded to Germany's defaulting on reparation payments in 1923 by sending troops into the Ruhr to exact the payments, Britain failed to give France diplomatic support, taking instead an even-handed line that infuriated the French, but which probably represented popular opinion on the matter in Britain. The coming to power of Hitler and the Nazis hardly affected British sentiments towards Germany. If anything, to a general sympathy for German grievances there was now added, at least in the early years after 1933, an admiration for Hitler's success in reviving the German economy and restoring Germans' self-esteem. To be sure, the rough handling of his domestic political opponents was distasteful, and the racial policies were scarcely comprehensible in a modern state, but these were essentially internal matters that should not be allowed to sour relations with Britain. If a sense of fair play disposed most British people to be open-minded about the new Germany, there were special qualities in Hitler that made some rather less impartial. Hitler was outspokenly committed to fighting and destroying Communism. Ever since the Russian Revolution in 1917 and the setting up of the first communist state, conservative elements everywhere reserved their greatest fears for the Bolshevik bacillus that threatened to infect the body politic of every capitalist state. Hitler's unequalled credentials as the enemy of International Communism outweighed any faults he might have had and made his friendship a matter of basic self-interest for capitalist states. Henry "Chips" Channon MP put it this way: "we should let gallant little Germany glut her fill of the Reds in the East and keep decadent France quiet while she does so". Enthusiasts for Hitler existed in France, too, but there the ideological aspect was confused by the country's historically adversarial relationship with Germany. In Britain, people could feel good about Hitler without hearing at the same time the nagging voice of patriotic conscience. Sympathy and admiration for Germany was often coupled in conservative circles with a dislike of France. Paradoxically, for France was Britain's one natural ally, irritation at her obdurate attachment to the letter of the Versailles Treaty was, in the mid-1930s, joined by feelings of distrust as first she made a pact with the USSR in 1935 and then came under the control of the left-wing Popular Front Government in 1936.

In the three and a half years from March 1936 Hitler put these attitudes to the test by mounting a succession of assaults on the provisions of the Versailles Treaty: re-militarizing the Rhineland, incorporating Austria into the Reich, demanding the Sudetenland from Czechoslovakia, annexing the Bohemian and Moravian parts of Czechoslovakia, and finally invading Poland, ostensibly to reclaim former German territory. Britain's response to the first three of these actions showed sympathy for the aims but disapproval of the methods. Hitler's professions on each occasion of a desire for peace in Europe and friendship with Britain kept alive the belief that with goodwill and effort a mutually satisfactory resolution of outstanding issues could be achieved. In the vanguard of believers was Neville Chamberlain, already an influential voice in the Cabinet on foreign and defence policy, who became Prime Minister when Stanley Baldwin stepped down in May 1937.

Chamberlain dominated his Cabinet, and when he set himself as one of his primary tasks the securing of lasting peace, it meant in effect that British foreign policy would be in his hands, reflecting his outlook and methods. Inheriting and accepting the established consensus about the general approach to take with the revisionist states, he soon made it clear that he wanted to quicken the pace: "I am about to enter upon a fresh attempt to reach a reasonable understanding with Germany and Italy, and I am by no means unhopeful of getting results".[1] Chamberlain believed that war was always a catastrophe; "war wins nothing, cures nothing, ends nothing . . . in war there is no winner, but all are losers".[2] He sought to convince the potential disturbers of the peace of this. He acknowledged that beyond a common interest in peace there were legitimate national grievances, but that these were all removable through a process of peaceful re-ordering and adjustment by reasonable men. If German and Italian grievances threatened the stability of Europe, then he was prepared to play a part in bringing about peaceful changes to the Versailles order to help those revisionist states become contented members of the international community and supporters of the rule of law in international affairs. His method was pragmatic and personal: particular problems needed to be isolated and made more manageable, and they should be solved by personal negotiation in an atmosphere of give and take. Personal negotiation was important because it helped to avoid the misunderstandings that so often fed international disputes: "I cannot believe that with a little good will and determination, it is not possible to remove genuine grievances and to clear away suspicion which may be entirely unfounded".[3] Such were the sentiments that underlay the policy of appeasement as it was pursued by Chamberlain and his Foreign Secretary, Lord Halifax. That policy came to naught at the hands of men who saw only weakness in the posture and who were contemptuous of its adherents. Hitler and Ribbentrop, Mussolini and Ciano, were not the "reasonable men" Chamberlain and Halifax hopefully took them to be. At root they were not appeasable; concessions merely encouraged their appetite for more concessions. The realization that this was so gradually turned British opinion against the policy of appeasement, in parliament, in the press, among the opinion-polled public, and finally in the Cabinet itself. The true nature of Hitler's intentions was starkly revealed when, six months after the multilateral Munich Agreement, by which the ethnically-German parts of Czechoslovakia passed to Germany, German troops invaded the diminished state, occupying land that had never been German and whose inhabitants were unmistakably non-German. Bohemia–Moravia was declared a Protectorate and Slovakia an independent state, but in effect both were absorbed by Germany. When Poland was in turn threatened, the mood was determined on all sides in Britain: Poland was a test case as much of Britain's standing and integrity as of the general principle that small nations had the right to exist. Hitler challenged both, and Chamberlain could be in no doubt that even his most loyal supporters through the appeasement years now expected him to stand firm. In his memoirs, Lord Ismay, Secretary of the Committee of Imperial Defence at this time, recalled how he was asked by a friend who was a secretary in the German embassy: "But surely England will not fight for Danzig?" He replied that for public opinion in England, Danzig was "no longer a place but a principle".[4] A less heroic view would not deny the existence of noble impulse but nevertheless put more weight, perhaps, upon the sense of British people at all levels that Britain's power, position and interests would be fatally undermined if one more surrender was made to Hitler. The forceful remodelling of eastern Europe that would follow success in Poland would make Germany the dominant power on the continent. From that position of dominance Hitler would be able to place limits on Britain's own independence.

On 1 September 1939 Germany's armies invaded Poland, making rapid progress against the greatly outnumbered defenders. Even at this stage Hitler was sufficiently misled by Britain and France's behaviour to think that they might stay out. He repeated his assurance that his intentions towards them were peaceful. By the evening of 2 September he had received no ultimatum and might well have begun to think his intuition was sound: the Anglo–French response at this stage went no further than a demand for the withdrawal of German forces. Chamberlain still shrank from the final step; he negotiated for an Italian-brokered conference and made much of the need to act in full consultation with the French. When the Cabinet met at 4.15pm on 2 September Chamberlain and Halifax seemed to be retreating from the demand for withdrawal of German forces as the precondition for a conference. But their colleagues overruled them and it was decided to re-affirm the demand and to add to it a time limit of midnight. At 8pm Chamberlain addressed a crowded House of Commons, but instead of announcing the expected ultimatum, he delivered a lack-lustre and non-committal speech "giving the impression", Duff Cooper recalled, "that even at this late hour Great Britain was going to repeat the surrender of Munich".[5] There was uproar in the House, followed by a deputation of Cabinet ministers to Chamberlain in his room. They warned him that the government would fall if he did not announce the ultimatum the next morning. Chamberlain finally gave up the struggle. The ultimatum was delivered at 9am the next day and at 11am Chamberlain made the now familiar radio broadcast, his voice tired and defeated as he told the nation that it was at war with Germany.

The six years of Britain's war may be divided into five phases that correspond to the contours of military developments, demonstrating thereby the direct, indeed essential, relationship in modern war between the home front and the ongoing clash of arms.

The phases are: the Phoney War, September 1939 to May 1940; Dunkirk, the Battle of Britain and the Blitz, May 1940 to June 1941; the spread of the war and the formation of the Grand Alliance, June 1941 to June 1942; the decline of Axis power, June 1942 to June 1944; the Allies' drive to victory, June 1944 to August 1945.

The Phoney War, September 1939 to May 1940

The expiry of Britain's ultimatum to Germany at 11am on 3 September 1939 did not bring upon London the massive assault from the air that many expected. Nor on Paris, when the French ultimatum expired six hours later. Instead, there was an anti-climax. A strangely unreal period of "non-war" began in which the principal powers formally at war made no serious moves to engage one another in battle. It was to last eight months and acquired various derisory labels: the "bore war", the "drôle de guerre", the "sitzkrieg" and the "phoney war". Such battles as there were took place in Poland during the first three weeks, but without British or French participation; paradoxically so, since it was ostensibly for Poland that the western allies had gone to war.

They made no move to attack Germany at this time, when the bulk of Hitler's army and air force was engaged in subduing the Poles, leaving a mere token force on the French border. France's large army remained ensconced behind the defensive frontier fortification

known as the Maginôt Line and the long-range aircraft of Britain's
Bomber Command confined themselves to a few ineffective attacks
on German coastal targets and leaflet drops over German towns.
The Royal Navy put into operation its blockade plan and the British
Expeditionary Force of four divisions took up its position on the left
wing of French forces close to the Belgian frontier. Meanwhile,
Poland succumbed to the combined onslaught of German and Russian
forces, the latter activated under the secret part of the Nazi–Soviet
non-aggression pact; by the end of September Poland had effectively
ceased to exist, partitioned and annexed by the victors. On 6 October 1939 Hitler made a peace offer to the western allies, appealing to
them to accept the *fait accompli* in Poland and re-open negotiations
on any outstanding issues as a pathway to lasting peace in Europe.
Although they had so far shown little fight, Britain and France rejected
the offer. Steps continued to consolidate the alliance. A Supreme War
Council consisting of the two prime ministers, senior ministers and
service chiefs was established to co-ordinate strategy. An Anglo–French
Co-ordinating Committee was set up to harmonize interallied economic
build-up. But this formal machinery of co-operation was scarcely
used; there was no pooling of economic resources, and military staff
talks did not produce more than the most basic understandings about
dispositions and strategy.

At sea Britain, at least, was more active. German U-boats had struck
major blows at the Royal Navy: in September the aircraft-carrier
Courageous was sunk in the Channel and in October the battleship
Royal Oak was sunk at anchor in Scapa Flow. The Royal Navy struck
back, however. In December 1939 three light cruisers crippled the
pocket battleship *Admiral Graf Spee* in the Battle of the River Plate,
off Uruguay, ending its destructive predations on Allied shipping in
the South Atlantic and Indian Ocean. Magnetic mines were at first a
major cause of merchant shipping losses, but the Royal Navy soon
mastered this problem with the technical counter-measure known as
"degaussing".

For the civilian population this period brought none of the drama
of war but instead the disruption and inconvenience of ARP (Air Raid
Precautions), conscription and rationing. Millions were on the move:
one and a half million people, schoolchildren with their teachers,
and infants with their mothers, were evacuated from cities to safety
in the country areas and another two million evacuated themselves
to bolt-holes of their own. The absence of bombing led to the return
of more than half of the former by Christmas.

In early April 1940 the military pause came to an end with the German invasion and occupation of Norway and Denmark. Anglo-French forces were dispatched to intervene and landings were made at Namsos in central Norway and Narvik in the north. But German forces were too strongly entrenched and after three weeks of fierce fighting the Allied armies began to be evacuated, the last men leaving at the end of May.

This military disaster brought dissatisfaction with Neville Chamberlain's conduct of the war to a head. In some respects, Britain's overall position looked stronger than at the start of the war: shipping losses were declining, aircraft production had doubled, the British Expeditionary Force was now ten divisions and growing. But the mobilization of the economy for war was proceeding only slowly and there was generally little sense of urgency in putting the country onto a war footing. The mishandling of the Norwegian campaign was used by Chamberlain's critics to force his resignation on 9 May. His successor, Winston Churchill, formed a new National Government, inviting into his war cabinet representatives of the other parties.

Dunkirk, the Battle of Britain and the Blitz, May 1940 to June 1941

Almost at once the emergency began that marked the next phase of the war for Britain. German forces swept into the Netherlands and Belgium; the British and French armies crossed the border into Belgium to support the outnumbered Dutch and Belgian armies. By making the main thrust of the attack through the hilly and wooded, and therefore weakly-defended Ardennes region, the German command achieved surprise and a breakthrough was made. Using ten armoured divisions, the German army extended and widened the gap in the Allied line; in the confusion that ensued, Anglo-French forces failed to co-ordinate a counter-attack, a general retreat began and British troops were boxed into a section of the Channel coast near Dunkirk. A decision to withdraw was made and, covered by the Royal Air Force, the greater part of the British Expeditionary Force (together with some French troops, 338,226 in all) was evacuated from Dunkirk by the Navy and assorted other craft. Most of the remaining British troops escaped via Cherbourg. Total British casualties were 11,000 killed, 1,400 wounded and 41,000 missing or taken prisoner. By 22 June 1940 the final collapse of French forces had occurred, leading to an armistice and an agreement between France and Germany by which the country was divided into a northern and western zone occupied by German troops, and a central and southern zone to be administered by a French government based in Vichy. Britain stood alone at this point, apart from the support of its Dominions – Australia, New Zealand, Canada and South Africa. The United States, although it had sympathy with the democracies, had refused to abandon its neutral stance towards the war in Europe. Soviet Russia was meanwhile expanding its control over the Baltic states, and Italy had joined the war on the German side.

Assuming that Britain would now see the futility of carrying on alone, Hitler made a further offer of peace, although naturally on conditions of his choosing. But again Britain would not take the bait, and Hitler reluctantly gave way to the desire of the army leaders to invade Britain. At the threat of invasion, Britain was galvanized into action. Churchill's defiant stance set the tone and at all levels there was a surge of activity to meet the threat. Thousands of volunteers came forward to man the Home Guard and Civil Defence units and productivity in the armaments factories rose. Tough new controls and fiscal measures were introduced and campaigns begun to curb waste, husband resources and increase home food production: steps towards a total war economy. American neutrality continued, but there was a tilt to one side: the "Cash and Carry" arrangement enabled Britain to replace much of the arms and equipment lost at Dunkirk.

The vital prerequisite for a successful invasion being air supremacy, Hitler next attempted to destroy the Royal Air Force. The summer and early autumn of 1940, therefore, was dominated by the Battle of Britain, the crucial clash of the Luftwaffe and the Royal Air Force in the skies over southeast England. By early September it was clear that Britain still controlled its own air space and that the invasion could not take place. Instead Hitler attempted to defeat Britain by destroying the morale of her civilian population. The instrument was again the Luftwaffe, this time in the form of fleets of bombers, unloading huge quantities of high explosives and incendiary bombs onto London and selected other cities during the period from early September 1940 to late May 1941. The "Big Blitz" caused great devastation and loss of life but failed seriously to dislocate Britain's war economy or to bring about a collapse of public morale.

In tandem with the air assault was the campaign of the U-boats against Britain's food and raw materials imports. The Mediterranean and the Channel were closed to merchant shipping for a time and the Atlantic shipping routes became hazardous. Shipping losses rose throughout 1940 and stayed at a high level in the first half of 1941. American help in the form of the Lend–Lease Bill buttressed Britain's position: from March 1941 the flow of American arms and food was no longer limited by Britain's capacity to pay. Also, the United States began naval escorts of its own and British shipping in the western Atlantic and shipping of any nationality going to and from Iceland, which it had occupied in July 1941. In effect, since its ships had orders to shoot at surface or submarine raiders, the USA was fighting an undeclared war in the Atlantic, to Britain's benefit.

The defensive character of this phase nevertheless saw the beginnings of some offensive action by Britain against the German–Italian Axis. Bomber Command began the strategic bombing of Germany, striking at many cities in the industrial Rhineland and at Berlin itself. But daylight raids became too costly in planes and crew and the consequent switch to night bombing was at the expense of accuracy. In the Mediterranean the Royal Navy and Royal Air Force combined to disable three Italian battleships at Taranto, and at Cape Matapan British warships sank three heavy cruisers without incurring losses. British forces commanded by General Wavell moved from Egypt against much more numerous Italian forces in Libya, defeating them and occupying the port of Tobruk. It was a short-lived success: a German division commanded by General Rommel landed to reinforce the Italians and rapidly drove the British army back to the border with Egypt. Mussolini's invasion of Greece from neighbouring occupied Albania drew British forces from Egypt and Crete to its aid. This in turn drew German forces into Greece and Yugoslavia, compelling the small British contingent to evacuate to Crete; there it came under renewed German attack and was obliged to withdraw to Egypt. In the retreat 12,000 troops were left behind, to become prisoners, and a significant quantity of equipment and transport was lost.

Global war and Grand Alliance, June 1941 to June 1942

A new phase of the war began with the German invasion of the Soviet Union in June 1941 followed at the end of the year by the entry into the war of the United States. From this point on Britain had allies and the prospect of ultimate victory opened up. The Russians were offered immediate help: convoys began on the Arctic route to Murmansk and supplies were brought in via the Persian Gulf through Iran, which together Anglo–Russian armies occupied. Precipitated into the war by the Japanese attack on her Pacific base at Pearl Harbor and by the gratuitous German declaration of war, the United States linked up with Britain and the USSR to form the core of the Grand Alliance. But for Britain there were in the short term further military setbacks. In the Far East Japan began a new expansionist drive through military conquest. In succession the British possessions of Hong Kong, Malaya, Burma and Singapore came under Japanese occupation. Britain's imperial position in Asia up to the Indian border was demolished. Meanwhile, in North Africa Axis armies resumed the offensive, capturing Tobruk and taking 33,000 prisoners, then driving British and Commonwealth forces back into Egypt. In the Battle of the Atlantic the improved position on shipping losses during the last quarter of 1941 was not sustained; in the first half of 1942 four and a half million tons of Allied shipping were lost, 70 per cent to U-boats. This was a result of several factors: the need to ship supplies to the Soviet Union on the Arctic route created many more opportunities for Admiral Raeder's U-boats to attack convoys in the favourable conditions that the long daylight hours gave from spring onwards; the Americans transferred part of their Atlantic fleet to the Pacific to wage war against Japan, with a consequent reduction in the strength of convoys in the west; the Germans' increased submarine production enabled them to multiply their attacks. During 1942 the strategic air offensive against Germany was intensified; the new head of Bomber Command, Sir Arthur Harris, staged thousand-bomber attacks on Essen, Cologne and Bremen. By this time some of the aircraft were of the superior new four-engined types: the Lancaster, the Stirling, and the Halifax. There was improved navigation through new technical devices and the creation of Pathfinder Force, which marked out the targets for the bombers. But despite spectacular individual successes this onslaught failed to check the rise in Germany's armaments production or to crack the morale of her people. And the cost to Britain in human and material resources was heavy.

Lack of military success abroad and the austerity of life under the total war economy at home led to a fall in the popularity of the government and challenges to Churchill's leadership, although not enough to bring about political change. An additional source of discouragement was the renewal, albeit brief, of German bombing in the spring and summer, aimed with some success at Britain's ancient cathedral towns.

The decline of Axis power, June 1942 to June 1944

The next phase began with the resurgence of American power in the Pacific. After the naval victories of Midway and the Coral Sea, the United States went over to the offensive, making landings in the Solomon Islands in August and New Guinea in September. Then, in North Africa General Montgomery's 8th Army attacked the German–Italian position at El Alamein. At the conclusion of an enormous tank battle Rommel's Afrika Korps was in full retreat, leaving 30,000 prisoners and with only one-sixth of its tanks intact. Almost immediately a major Allied offensive, codenamed Operation Torch, began with successful landings in French North Africa. The subsequent drive against the Axis armies from east and west culminated the following May in total victory. About 240,000 prisoners were taken, over half of them German, and Allied power extended across the entire North African littoral. Meanwhile, on the Eastern front the Russian armies inflicted a major defeat on the Germans at Stalingrad. Losing 500,000 men in the battle and a further 100,000 as prisoners of war, the German armies in Russia were thrown on the defensive and their long westward retreat began.

Following up their success in North Africa, British and American forces further strengthened Allied power in the Mediterranean by invading Sicily in July 1943. Mussolini's dictatorship collapsed and Italy sought an armistice. The Italian surrender followed and the mainland was occupied to a line north of Naples. Further progress was slow and costly because of the large numbers of German troops that had been moved in to shore up the position.

In the air war the strategic offensive against Germany continued with greater intensity, becoming a combined RAF–USAAF operation from January 1943. The war at sea turned in the Allies' favour in the second half of the year, largely because of improved British radar techniques and the deployment of escort carriers and American long-range aircraft. In the Pacific theatre the steady erosion of Japan's empire continued with the liberation of the Aleutian Islands, landings in the Gilbert Islands and the opening of the assault on the Marshall Islands.

From the end of 1942 the big topic in British politics and in the media was reconstruction, or planning the shape of post-war Britain. The debate was given a stimulus by the publication of the Report on Social Insurance and Allied Services, which became known, after its chairman, as the Beveridge Report. In the meantime the social life of Britain absorbed the impact of nearly one and a half million foreign troops, mostly American, who came to be stationed in Britain as part of the preparation for the Allied liberation of mainland Europe scheduled for mid-1944. From January to March 1944 the inhabitants of London, Hull, Bristol and South Wales experienced a renewal of air raids, although these were less frequent and intense than those of the Big Blitz of 1940–41.

The Allies' drive to victory, June 1944 to August 1945

Operation Overlord, marked the beginning of the final phase of the war. The Soviet leader Stalin had wanted a second front in Europe to take place much earlier to relieve the intense German pressure on the Soviet Union. But because of Churchill's wish to avoid making the assault before adequate preparation had been made to ensure its success, and because of the time it took for American military power to be built up, Allied activity in the West had been confined to the North African and Mediterranean campaigns, together with the war at sea and the bombing of Germany. The consequent delay to Overlord was resented in Moscow and was a source of strain and mistrust in the Grand Alliance. In early June 1944, under the command of General Eisenhower, 20,000 Allied troops were landed on the Normandy coast and, against fierce opposition, established the beachheads from which the following armies began the slow drive inland. In the last week of August Paris was liberated and by mid-September all of France was in Allied hands. But the progress of the armies slowed against the stiffening resistance of the enemy in the Low Countries and the Rhineland. A plan by Montgomery to cross the Rhine by a thrust through Holland supported by advance airborne landings miscarried, with heavy casualties to the parachute troops at Arnhem. On the Italian and Eastern fronts, too, German armies did not easily give ground. The advance was inexorable but it was fully 11 months after the Normandy landings before German resistance finally collapsed and the war in Europe ended. By that time, Britain's armed forces were greatly outnumbered by those of the United States and inevitably, the greater salience of American manpower and resources in the combined effort meant that Americans also dominated the command and the strategy. In Asia the American dominance was still more marked. Even in Burma Britain was unable to do things its own way, although it was a British army under General Slim that expelled the Japanese in May 1945. The Royal Navy took part in the

13

combined attacks on the Ryukyu Islands from March 1945 and against the home islands in the weeks before the dropping of the atomic bombs, which precipitously brought about the Japanese surrender in August.

At home the long drawn-out nature of the war's final phase produced a degree of war weariness and apathy. In the southeast corner of England the dangers of war were renewed in the V-weapon attacks that began in June 1944 and which ended only in March 1945. By that time the wartime coalition had worn very thin and the political parties had begun to prepare for the renewal of adversarial politics. In the General Election held on 5 July 1945 the Labour Party, led by Clement Attlee, was elected to power with a large overall majority, ending the long period of Conservative domination of British government. To Labour fell the task of reconstructing a battered and exhausted country and at the same time meeting the social expectations that the war had raised.

Notes

1   K. Feiling, *Neville Chamberlain* (London: Macmillan, 1966), p.324.
2   Ibid., p.300.
3   N. Chamberlain, *The struggle for peace* (London: Hutchinson, 1939), p.74.
4   *Memoirs of Lord Ismay* (London: Heinemann, 1960), p.96.
5   D. Cooper, *Old men forget* (London: Rupert Hart-Davis, 1953), p.259.

Chapter Two

જી

Britain on the eve of war

There were good grounds for describing Britain as a Great Power still in 1939. The British Empire took up one-quarter of the globe; the Royal Navy was matched in size only by that of the USA; in Europe, as the pecking order at Munich indicated, only Germany had as much clout as Britain. From the standpoint of the last decade of the twentieth century, however, the decline of Britain as a power in the world seems too obvious to merit much comment. It is equally clear that it is a long story, beginning probably before the First World War. The long view points to the fundamentally damaging effects of that war on Britain's power and economic position: the loss of overseas markets for her products, the reduction in assets held abroad, the greatly enlarged National Debt, the increase in nationalist activity among the peoples of the Empire. At the same time, the war had shown Britain able to mobilize itself for an unprecedented test of its strength. There had been no previous war in which the energies of the whole nation were in some degree drawn upon. The key institutions of the state, the armed forces, the civil service, local government, the legal system and the parliamentary system itself were subjected to a sustained trial of their resilience and vitality. The sinews of the economy – industry, agriculture, the transport and energy infrastructure and the merchant marine – had to do more with less. And for four years the war had placed extraordinary strains on the bonds of civil society by exposing millions of citizens to death or injury, curtailing freedom of speech, removing the rights of capital, labour and property and imposing all manner of austere regulation on daily life. The strain had shown from time to time, and ministers fretted about the people's morale. But things did not fall apart and the nation, though war weary, stayed resolute and united to the war's end.

While the war had highlighted some of society's defects and given an impulse to social reform, victory seemed to imply that, for all its faults, the social and political order was basically sound. The test of war had been surmounted; Britain had shown itself to be a remarkably stable, cohesive society, coming through without the political turmoil that took place towards the end in many countries.

National complacency about the inherent strength of British society was one of the more dangerous consequences of the experience of the First World War, however. The world of 1939 was already much changed from that of 1918; Germany was again bursting with economic and military strength; many of Britain's allies of 1914–18 were either with Germany or indifferent towards her revisionist policies; the instruments of war were substantially different. An observer contemplating another trial like that of 1914–18 in the changed circumstances of 1939 might have wondered whether this time Britain would be strong enough.

The economy

While the economic strength of the USA, Germany and Japan continued to grow in the decades before 1939, for Britain this was a period of steady relative economic decline. In terms of world trade the trend was clear: her share was 14.15 per cent in 1913, 10.75 per cent in 1929 and 9.8 per cent in 1937.[1] The years of the Depression compounded the older problem of over-reliance on the export of textiles, coal and ships, for which demand was not increasing or which other countries could make more cheaply. Production in these old staple industries was drastically cut back and for the first time "invisible" earnings from shipping, banking, insurance and overseas investments failed to bridge the gap between the value of imports and the value of exported manufactures. The worst seemed to be over by the mid-1930s when there was a slight recovery, but the pre-1930 levels of exports were still not reached and the fall resumed in 1937, Gross National Product peaking at about the same time. Britain did have the advantage of access to cheap food and raw materials from the Empire, and trade within the Sterling Area mitigated the difficulties of shrinking world trade.

If the continuing weakness of Britain's trading position can hardly be disputed, an examination of her industrial health in terms of her fitness to wage a modern total war produces a less clear-cut picture.

Between the wars the structure of industry had begun to change: the old staple industries contracted and the newer industries began to grow quickly. This belated shift from the old to the new was recognized as crucial to national security, but both would be needed against an advanced enemy, coalmining, steel-making and shipbuilding as much as the chemical, aircraft and electrical engineering industries.

The coal industry, struggling to come to terms with the stagnation of demand for coal at home and abroad, had raised output per manshift by 19 per cent between 1913 and 1936 but this compared with 81 per cent in Germany, 117 per cent in Holland, 73 per cent in Poland, 51 per cent in Belgium and 25 per cent in France.[2] It reflected a failure to modernize as quickly as other countries despite high output in new mines opened in Yorkshire, Nottinghamshire and Scotland and a general improvement in the proportion of coal cut by machine and conveyed mechanically. Modernization was difficult and slow in an industry handicapped by a structure more appropriate to the nineteenth century than the twentieth, and by the similarly time-bound attitudes of owners, managers and workers. The age of economic rationalization had passed it by, for in 1939 there were 1,700 mines of which 466 employed fewer than 20 people. Thus 46 per cent of the mines accounted for less than 3 per cent of the workforce and 2 per cent of the output of coal.[3] The Royal Commission report of 1926 had recommended amalgamations and closure of technologically backward and geologically difficult mines; but owners resisted, and governments failed to compel such rationalization, so that by the end of the 1930s there had been only 90 voluntary amalgamations, which still left over 950 separate companies. Three-fifths of British coal output, moreover, still came from the areas of low productivity. The industry hadn't enough engineers and those it did have were not adequately trained. Whereas in Germany there were over 200 places annually for mining engineering concentrated in four mining colleges, in Britain there were a third of this number scattered among fourteen non-specialist institutions. As for the miners, in Germany two years' systematic part-time training was normal; in Britain they learned on the job. Labour relations were probably the worst in the whole of British industry, set in an adversarial mould in the 1840s and hardly changed since. Just as managers acted largely in ignorance of modern practice in "scientific management" so, too, the miners through their unions adopted luddite attitudes to mechanization and other attempts to change established methods. Despite an average unemployment rate in the industry of 25 per cent, strikes remained endemic. In the 1935-9 period, with only 6 per cent of the insured workforce in the country, it had 64 per cent of the disputes and accounted for 52 per cent of the days lost by all industry.[4]

Just as coal would be needed to forge the engines of war so, too, would ships be needed to wage it. And like coal, shipbuilding had suffered a steep fall in demand during the slump, with a consequent contraction of the industry. It had fallen behind its foreign rivals in improving cost efficiency, in specializing and concentrating production, and in building newer types of ship. There were, in any case, several features of the industry that made it ill-equipped to exploit the improvement in the market in the mid-1930s. Its domination of the world markets between 1880 and 1914 had produced a complacency among most who worked in the business that impeded the adoption of new technology and methods of organization and management appropriate to meet the standards being attained in the USA, Japan and Germany. Many of the shipyards were still run by descendants of the original founders, family name often counting for more than managerial competence or understanding of the requirements of a modern industry. Investment in research and development was pitifully small and the amount and level of technical education for the trade was inadequate. Traditional reliance on craft skills learned on the job had also helped to create the problem of proliferation of crafts, which in time acquired their separate unions, some 90 already by 1914, each jealously guarding its bit of the work process from encroachment by the others, or modification by the management. Vickers–Armstrong, one of Britain's largest naval shipbuilders, trying to meet new contracts under the rearmament programme, reported in November 1936 that delays were being caused by the refusal of workers belonging to two of the larger unions, the AEU and the ETU, to work further overtime.[5] In April 1937 the Defence Requirements Committee received a report from the Admiralty on delays expected from a strike of apprentices on the Clyde and a strike at Beardmore's yard that had for six months held up production of the new "Tribal" class of destroyers.[6] And this was at a time when the contraction and dispersal of the workforce over the years since 1920 had left it with shortages of key skilled workers, itself a factor threatening the pace of rearmament. Corelli Barnett summed up this parlous state of affairs thus:

> Britain entered the Second World War in 1939 with a shipbuilding industry that was a rusting, partly dismantled and partly unmanned hulk of essentially Victorian technology; and, on the whole, no less rusting were its management and workforce and their operational methods.[7]

Britain's iron and steel industry had once been the world leader in output, export share and innovation. That position was already lost, however, before the First World War. Since then, there had been a short period of expansion and profit, then the devastation of the Depression and finally, from 1935, a rearmament-assisted recovery that had the industry working at full capacity. But in its international competitiveness and its potential for total war, it was a weak and backward industry in many respects. Like coal and shipbuilding, it still carried the burden of its Victorian legacy. Over half of the output came from small works using outdated plant; only five large modern integrated works were operating in 1939. Productivity was low: the average British plant used almost twice the number of man-hours needed to produce one ton of steel in the USA. The steel produced in small, obsolescent works was of inferior quality, moreover, to that attainable in the modern ones. In terms of management expertise, scientific and technical training, and investment in research and development, the industry as a whole was at least a generation behind its counterparts in the USA, Germany, France and Belgium. The significance of the backwardness and inefficiency of the British iron and steel industry had already shown itself in the rearmament programme. Delays in the delivery of structural steel held up construction of new warships, naval equipment and factories, airfields and sector stations. As early as 1936–7 the delivery time for steel was six months.[8] One consequence of this was the resort to suppliers in the USA, Czechoslovakia and, alarmingly, Germany for both general and special steels. In short, the industry was unable to cope with the modest extra demand that rearmament had created by 1937. It remained to be seen whether the belated investment in large modern plant which began in that year would be adequate for the huge needs that assuredly lay ahead.

It was in the newer industries that expansion had taken place in the 1920s and 1930s and it was here that Britain's capabilities stood comparison with those of her rivals. The chemical industry, making strategically important products such as explosives, heavy and fine chemicals, dyestuffs, plastics, industrial gases and fertilizers, had become as technically efficient as any in the world, owing largely to the successful mergers that had given birth to Imperial Chemical Industries Ltd. British oil refining, however, had been declining throughout the 1930s and an increasing proportion of British petrol consumption depended on imports from refineries abroad.

The motor industry was a major growth sector and had become a powerful agent of the modernization of mechanical engineering in general, and of the advance of mass production methods and inter-changeability of parts. In addition, it had stimulated the expansion or modernization of strategically important industries such as oil refin-ing, metallurgy, electrical goods, glass and rubber.

In view of the general expectations of the shape of future war, there could have been no more vital industry than that of aircraft production. Yet it is only a slight exaggeration to say that as late as 1935 Britain did not possess such an industry. What it had at that time was a scatter of firms designing and making engines and airframes, mainly for light aircraft. Most of these were operating on a small scale; even the largest firms like de Havilland, Hawker and Handley–Page employed fewer than 2,000 workers. There was no central research institution for the industry; it depended rather on the work of the National Physical Laboratory and the Royal Aircraft Establishment at Farnborough. Most developments in relevant tech-nology took place abroad. In design, too, the important innovations were made at Lockheed, Douglas, Junkers, Heinkel and Dornier. The backwardness of the British industry was symbolized by the persist-ence of obsolescent bi-plane designs for civil and military aircraft, when elsewhere monoplanes had become the norm. When Baldwin's government decided in 1935 to meet the German threat by a massive expansion of the RAF, the indigenous capacity to carry it out was simply not there; it had to be created. This was done partly by adding new plant to the existing plant of the aircraft firms, partly by building so-called "shadow factories", to be operated by motor manufacturers, some of whom, like Austin and Morris, had experience in large-scale series production. It was a huge investment in new technologies, paid for by the state and carried out under its overall supervision. Immense problems beset it from the start. The human resources were initially only 30,000 and very few of these were highly-skilled. There was a small number of graduate aeronautical engineers but a dearth of personnel with general engineering competence. No one in the industry had experience of directing the mass production of engines and airframes, let alone of planning and setting up the plant that would produce them. And the national shortage of skilled shop-floor labour was nowhere more sharply felt than in this industry, plunged almost overnight into a process of transformation from cottage industry into mass production giant.

By the time war came Britain had achieved this miracle: in 1939, 8,000 aircraft of all types were produced, which almost matched Germany's 8,300. With Hurricanes, Spitfires and Wellingtons, world-class military aircraft were at last being made in Britain, and yet others were in blue-print. The trouble was that it was achieved at an unsustainable cost. Such were the deficiencies of the home machine-tool industry that the new factories could only be tooled through the importation of large amounts of machine-tools from abroad: 7,765 tons in 1935, 20,058 tons in 1936, 31,591 tons in 1937. The arming and instrumentation of the new aircraft, likewise, was made possible only by the purchase of foreign-made weapons and instruments such as Browning machine-guns and altimeters from the USA, track-recorders from Austria and dashboard clocks from Switzerland. While it is true that progress had been made by 1939 in setting up home manufacture under licence of the sort of tools and components that had to be imported at the start of the rearmament programme, it was more than probable that the planned expansion of the programme would require continued reliance on foreign-made equipment.[9] This way of rearming played havoc with the national finances. The balance of payments went from surplus into massive deficit, and gold and currency reserves shrank. Expert opinion, i.e. the Treasury, held that spending at the 1939 rate would bring national bankruptcy no later than 1942. Moreover, the sustainability of an expanding programme was questionable in another sense: the aircraft industry had already soaked up all the available skilled labour in the country, and additional recruits in worthwhile numbers were unlikely to be delivered by Britain's neglected and deficient technical education system.

After a slow start compared with other industrialized countries, Britain's electrical engineering and electricity generation industries had almost caught up by the end of the 1930s. The creation of the Central Electricity Board and the establishment of the National Grid had helped to eliminate inefficiencies and reduce costs. That its modernity and innovativeness was strategically important was demonstrated by the series of discoveries that made radar possible in 1936. Even so, it was a less than ideal situation that large amounts of electrical goods were still imported from Germany and Holland.

In peacetime the capacity of a nation to feed itself from home production has little bearing on the question of national power; in wartime, however, when external sources are disrupted, the agriculture industry assumes a vital role. Through massive state intervention during the 1930s British agriculture was able to survive the fall in world prices and the intensification of foreign competition. At the same time, it had become more efficient in terms of size of yields, output per person and growth of mechanization. Although the long-term contraction had not been halted and there had been a loss of arable farming to livestock production, Britain's agricultural industry on the eve of war was sufficiently healthy to be able to respond to a sudden increase in demand for its products.

Looked at as a whole, British industry, at what turned out to be the end of the Depression, presents the observer with a picture of vigorous diversification and technological advance alongside contraction and stagnation, pockets of modernity in a scene that still retained many features of the previous century. Although failing to close the gap with the best of its foreign counterparts, it was in general more efficient than it had been, as is shown by the big increases recorded in the interwar period in total industrial output, output per head and product per man hour, despite shorter hours of work. The advance of a "modernizing" outlook among industrialists is to be seen in the steady growth over the same period of the number of firms spending money on research and development, and in the increase in the global amount spent in this way; again, nowhere near matching levels in the usa and Germany but a move in the right direction, nevertheless. Relations between employers and organized labour were generally more amicable and constructive than had been the case in the past. What remained to be seen was how far the years of contraction and stagnation had limited the ability to revive the old industries and expand the new. For, as the rearmament effort had already indicated, in all the key industries there was a shortage of skilled workers. The inadequacy of technical and scientific education in Britain, compounded by the withering away of apprenticeships in trades hit worst by the Depression, had by the end of the 1930s created the paradox of skills shortage amidst mass unemployment. This situation was described in a Ministry of Labour report to the Defence Policy Requirements Committee in June 1936:

There is a widespread shortage of fitters, turners, capstan setters and operators, machinists, toolmakers, millers, universal grinders, coppersmiths, sheet-metal workers, welders and aircraft riggers. In all divisions, with the exception of Wales, there is an unsatisfied demand for all classes of skilled operatives . . . In many areas the shortages are greatest in the branches concerned with armament work. Although in all divisions, with the exception of the South-Eastern, there is an apparent surplus of skilled labour, much of this surplus consists of men of poor industrial quality . . . Inability to read blue-prints and/or work to fine limits makes many of them not really acceptable to employers.[10]

As in 1914, the national aversion to things technical was revealed as a source of weakness, threatening the very existence of the nation, for, as then, the enemy had no such cultural handicap.

The role of the State

The increasing role of the State in the institutions of society and in the lives of ordinary citizens is a distinctive feature of Britain's twentieth century history. Although there had been a reaction after 1918 against the strongly interventionist hand of government that had been deemed necessary for victory in the war, and accordingly nearly all the "public sector" was dismantled, by the end of the 1930s there was general acceptance among employers, trade unionists, government officials, ministers and their economic advisers that some sort of mixed economy of nationalized and privately-owned enterprise was both necessary and desirable. It was also generally thought that the regulatory role of the State in the health and welfare of the nation would grow and that this was on the whole a good thing. As a proportion of national income, social welfare spending stood at 13 per cent in 1938 compared with 5.5 per cent in 1913, a trend also reflected in the rise in the standard rate of income tax: 27.5 pence in 1939 compared with 6 pence in 1913. To a large degree government intervention in economic matters came from the seriousness of the economic crisis of 1931 and the slump that followed it; governments everywhere were intervening to protect the nation's economy and it would have taken near-religious conviction in the inherent efficacy of free-market forces to have resisted this trend and done nothing. In any case, the balance of political forces in Britain during the 1930s

23

made intervention more likely than it had been previously; the party most committed to free trade, the Liberal Party, was in rapid decline, which made those parties who for different reasons had no ideological objection to intervention, the Conservatives and Labour, the only real contenders for power. So it came about that "protection", "subsidies" and even "nationalization" increasingly entered the discourse of the ruling establishment and took concrete form in the pre-war decade.

In agriculture, the Agricultural Marketing Act (1931) opened the way for the setting up of Marketing Boards for milk, potatoes, hops and bacon that guaranteed minimum prices for producers, and in 1932 acreage subsidies were begun for oats, wheat, barley and sugar beet. Government intervention in industry also came through the exercise of fiscal and legislative power. From June 1932 nearly all investment abroad was prohibited so that capital was diverted into investment in home industries such as house building. The Housing Act of 1930 provided subsidies to local authorities for slum clearance and the 1934 Special Areas Act offered inducements to enterprises to move to depressed areas and to unemployed workers to move to more prosperous areas. Protection to home industry and agriculture was attempted through the setting up of tariffs and a system of trade agreements with the Dominions and quotas with Crown Colonies. To stimulate economic activity at home, the Treasury effectively took over the regulation of credit from the Bank of England and adopted a cheap money policy, which meant that the bank rate remained at only 2 per cent from June 1932 to the outbreak of war. In addition, exchange control came directly under the Treasury through the establishment of the Exchange Equalization Fund in 1932. With assets of £150 million the Treasury was able to counter speculation in sterling and unusual capital movements, thereby keeping the exchange value of the pound to a preset level. Finally, some important enlargements of the "public sector" took place, building on the earlier bases of the Forestry Commission, the BBC and the Central Electricity Board. The chaos of unregulated competition for passenger transport in the capital was at a stroke replaced by the orderly, co-ordinated service that came with the setting up of the London Passenger Transport Board in 1933. In 1938 mining royalties were nationalized, a first step towards nationalization of the coal industry. Just one month before the outbreak of war parliament passed the British Overseas Airways Bill, bringing into being a state-owned corporation, the BOAC, formed by buying out and merging

British Airways and Imperial Airways. Here it was a case of subsidizing a home-grown air transport industry or doing without one, for all the foreign competitors were heavily subsidized by their governments. There was a large measure of consensus that certain sectors of industry, particularly the large utilities that required big capital sums and which served the public welfare, ought to be public rather than private monopolies. BOAC was fairly typical of the favoured form nationalization took in Britain: the Public Corporation, controlled by a Board which, apart from an obligation to meet fixed-interest charges on capital, had the single task of providing the optimum public service from the revenues raised from direct charges to consumers. In short, the public interest replaced the profit motive as the driving principle. Paradoxically, it was under Conservative or Conservative-dominated governments that these measures of "state socialism" had taken place.

For millions of citizens the most direct contact with the State came through education and the operation of social welfare. All but 6 per cent of children received their education in schools financed entirely or partly from public funds administered through the local authorities. Under-financed would be a more accurate statement, for there was no concealing the failure of the provision to meet the children's or, indeed, the nation's needs. Educational thinking had long come to believe in the necessity for all children to transfer to senior schools at 11 (a recommendation of the 1926 Hadow Committee in its Report on *The Education of the Adolescent*). However, economic stringency in the interwar depression years had slowed the implementation of this change despite the general recognition of the importance to the infrastructure of a modern industrial society of maximizing the intellectual resources of its people. At the end of the 1930s 36 per cent of children over 11 years of age were being educated in elementary schools (the schools in which they started at 5) that could not offer "advanced instruction". Secondary education proper took place in the grant-aided grammar schools, which could cater for only one in five children. Since they charged fees the only chance of getting into these schools for the average working-class child was to win a free-place scholarship by passing an examination at the age of 11. Depending on locality and gender (for there were overall fewer places for girls), only about 10 per cent of the age cohort gained a free place. This was a marked improvement on the position of 20 years before, but the intellectual wastage of the majority, who left school at 14 with little more than basic skills, was nonetheless a national calamity. Economic constraint hampered attempts to modernize school buildings, so that "slum schools" were as much a feature of the time as slum houses. Budgets for new apparatus and equipment were held down, the training of teachers was under-resourced and teachers' salaries were depressed. For 20 years the promised raising of the minimum school leaving age to 15, which implied secondary education for all, was repeatedly postponed. Scheduled at last for the start of the new school year in September 1939 it was put off yet again because of the outbreak of war. Unsurprisingly, the school system did not lend itself to channelling more than a small fraction of the nation's keenest minds into the universities; only four or five out of every thousand elementary-school pupils got there, despite the launching in 1919 of State scholarships and local authority grants. The university system expanded only a little between the wars, with the founding of Reading University and five university colleges (at Nottingham, Leicester, Hull, Southampton and Exeter). Even these new institutions catered, like the old ones, mainly for a narrow privileged class, notwithstanding the fact that over half their costs were met from general taxation.

For at least three generations commentators had drawn attention to the defects of the English educational system, warning in particular of the threat to the country's industrial and economic strength of its neglect of scientific and technical education compared to its European competitors. In 1937, while more than 90 per cent of School Certificate candidates offered English, mathematics and French, only 35 per cent offered chemistry, 27 per cent physics and 10.3 per cent physics-with-chemistry. The extent of the neglect was partly masked by the disproportionately better performance of Scotland's schools and universities, but not enough to conceal the threat it posed to the very security of the nation on the eve of a war in which the fruits of the intellect would undoubtedly count for as much as the people's valour.

Following its beginnings in 1908, social welfare provision had been extended in a piecemeal fashion, using the insurance principle to cover sickness, unemployment, old age and the care of widows and orphans. But it was too uneven and incomplete to be called a system. By 1939 all wage-earners were covered but not their dependants, and salary-earners had to make their own insurance provision. Because health benefits were administered by private companies, the "Approved Societies", it was a matter of chance whether an individual received just the basic services of the "panel" doctor or additional benefits such as eye and teeth care that the larger, better-run companies provided. Worst of all, "bad risk" cases were usually refused by the Approved Societies and so their insurance was administered by a Local Insurance Committee. This invariably meant that those whose needs were greatest got the minimum benefit.

In the age of total war, when the home front was almost as dangerous as the battlefield, the absence of a public hospital system in Britain must be seen not just as a scandalous social deficiency but also as a national weakness. The establishment in 1919 of a Ministry of Health to integrate all the public medical services, and the passing of the Local Government Bill in 1929, enabling local authorities to take over Poor Law infirmaries and make them into municipal hospitals, had provided the framework, but by 1939 only 36 county boroughs and 10 county councils were providing a general hospital service. The number of beds fell greatly below the need, yet only 4,000 more were added by local authorities in the 1930s. They did provide an uneven patchwork of specialist hospital services such as isolation and tuberculosis hospitals and clinics for maternity, child welfare and venereal disease; but voluntary hospitals constituted one-third of all hospitals and another sixth were Poor Law infirmaries. It followed that a disproportionate part of hospital funding was raised from voluntary donations.

Because of its size and persistence throughout the interwar years, unemployment was another significant way in which millions of British people were drawn into a closer relationship with the State. In order to manage the difficulties arising from more than 10 per cent of the working population being without paid work and from the compounding problem of long-term unemployment, governments resorted to rationalizing legislation like the Unemployment Insurance Acts of 1934-5, which brought more workers within the scope of unemployment insurance and set up the Unemployment Assistance Board to assess the means of, and dole out benefits to, those insured workers who had exhausted their 26 weeks of employment benefit. As with the extension of health insurance, the struggle to deal with the problem of unemployment incidentally resulted in a more uniform "national" system, the central government increasing its role in formulating policy and funding its implementation. In this sense power was moving away from local government and towards the centre; for as more of the expenditure on local services was met from government grants (41 per cent in 1939), and as the share of spending coming from locally-levied rates diminished, so the autonomy of local authorities was reduced. This was masked from the ordinary citizen, whose day-to-day experience rather suggested the opposite. For the ambit of local authorities' activity was growing, and whether it was in connection with health, education, housing or the utilities of water, gas and electricity, it was with local officials that people typically had to deal. Although its period of greatest trial was about to start, the trend of the interwar years and the battles between central and local government over welfare and education spending showed that municipal power and influence was nevertheless retreating before the encroachments of Westminster. From the standpoint of the ordinary citizen this shift was of less account than the fact that the role of government, central or local, in his daily experience was larger on the eve of the Second World War than had been the case before the Great War. This reality was symbolically underlined in May 1939 when the government, breaking all peacetime precedent, introduced compulsory military service. By contrast, in the First World War, such a measure came only after 18 months of the fighting had gone by; the distance to government designed for total war would be much shorter this time.

Politics and national cohesion

The government that brought in conscription still bore the title "National", although the bitter opposition to the measure by both the Labour and Liberal parties is a reminder that adversarial politics had not ceased. The idea of a National Government had worn pretty thin after eight years, especially after Chamberlain became Prime Minister in 1937. In all but name the government of Britain was Conservative. The Conservative Party had its divisions but its inclination to loyalty towards the leadership prevented dissident groups, such as those who opposed appeasement, from co-operating with opposition parties. The Conservatives and their allies held over two-thirds of the seats in the House of Commons, but this was a misleading representation of how they stood with the electorate, for at the last general election of the pre-war period, in 1935, nearly 10 million people voted for opposition candidates as against the 11.75 million who voted for "National" candidates. By-elections after 1935, moreover, tended to go against the government. There was no real threat from the opposition however. The chief contender, the Labour Party, had decided against participation in some sort of popular front such as had brought the Left in France and Spain to power. Although its performance in 1935 had partially restored its parliamentary position and there were some subsequent by-election gains, Labour's recovery was painfully slow. The continuing decline of the Liberals did not translate into support for Labour and on the eve of war the gap between them and the Conservatives was still too wide to suggest an early return to power. Nor did Labour look ready for power. On the big domestic issue, unemployment, it had no credible alternative policies to those of the government, and on foreign affairs and defence it appeared confused, misguided and, by 1939, simply wrong. The parties of the far Right and Left, so salient in the politics of many European states in the 1930s, never became significant forces in Britain. Mosley's British Union of Fascists and the Communist Party of Great Britain, despite the publicity they derived from their staged confrontations and vociferous support for opposing sides in the Spanish Civil War, remained small, fringe affairs outside the mainstream of British politics.

Also in contrast to their continental counterparts, the trade unions were remarkably unmilitant. The débâcle of the General Strike and the subsequent catastrophic decline in union membership, to 4.4 million at its lowest point in 1933 (it had reached a peak of 8.3 million in 1920), weakened the bargaining power of organized labour. Its methods consequently became defensive and non-confrontational. Membership gradually rose as the recovery began in the mid-1930s but there was no return to the aggressive unionism of the 1920s; instead the TUC's reformist and constitutional approach to improving the welfare of working people became characteristic of organized labour as a whole; and although union leaders continued to have aims whose fulfilment required political change, they tended to channel these through the Labour Party and the TUC.

This brief survey of the political scene at the end of the 1930s shows more stability and consensus than issues of the time might lead one to expect. Was Britain not, then, the "bitter society" or "divided nation" that some writers have suggested it was in this decade?

A sense of belonging to a single community called "the nation" derives in any one instance from the meshing of a multiplicity of factors, such as territory, race, language, religion and law. These factors typically have been present together over a long period of time and therefore have a strength and resilience that enables them to survive the shocks of potentially destructive events like defeat and invasion, partition and loss of territory, or the imposition of an alien system of government and law. Britain was more fortunate than most in being spared such trials (unless one counts the creation of a sovereign Ireland) over the whole of its modern history. It has already been suggested that the First World War showed British society, after more than a century of the upheaval associated with rapid industrialization, to have a high degree of social cohesion. It had nevertheless highlighted rather than obscured the weaknesses of British society – the poverty, the inequality, the injustice – and reconstruction and reform was on the agenda of politics even before its ending. The implication was that for Britain to remain a united kingdom the defects that the war brought into focus had to be remedied. Could a nation that had pulled together through the strains of total war retain its social cohesion in the context of continuing gross inequalities of wealth and life chances? And would toleration of such inequalities be possible in a time when most people had some basic education and when mass circulation newspapers and magazines, the cinema and the radio made them much more aware than previous generations of differences in living standards and how these might be altered?

Twenty years on, an objective observer might have drawn mixed conclusions about what had been achieved and whether the health of the nation had improved. Although the worst of the Depression was over, there were still 1.3 million people registered as unemployed (i.e. 12 per cent of the insured population). Also, these national figures conceal the huge regional differences in unemployment levels. People living in the towns of the southeastern part of the country, where the new consumer goods and services industries were growing, were much less likely to become unemployed than those living in Wales, Northern England, Scotland and Northern Ireland, where the combination of the falling demand for the products of the old staple industries of coal, textiles, steel and shipbuilding and the absence of new industries to take their place, gave rise to unemployment levels of 16 to 24 per cent and locally, e.g. Rhondda, as high as 35 per cent.[11] In contrast, the percentage of the industrial population out of work in prosperous Deptford was 7 per cent. Another dimension to this regional difference was the nature of the unemployment: in the areas of decaying staple industries there was much long-term unemployment; in the areas of the new industries, hardly any. Using the same places as examples, the figure for long-term unemployed as a percentage of the total unemployed was 63 per cent in Rhondda, whereas in Deptford it was only 6 per cent.

Government subsidies to the "Special Areas", created in 1934, were on too small a scale to make a noticeable improvement. And ominously, the overall numbers of unemployed had begun to rise again in 1938 despite the extra activity that came with rearmament; unemployment was still, in 1939, a major unsolved problem.

It was also the main factor preventing people from escaping from other social evils such as poverty, bad housing, ill health and poor nutrition. For although average real incomes rose between the wars and this, together with the availability of "cheap money", enabled millions of families to improve substantially the material conditions of life in terms of housing, food, clothes, consumer goods and leisure activity, the averaging statistics conceal the reality of the life of the undernourished families of the unemployed in the urban slums of the decaying regions. The majority of people were in work; the 1930s were for them a time of expanding access to houses with bathrooms and gardens, a more varied diet, paid holidays and the vast range of mass-produced goods, from leisure clothes and sports equipment to radios, three-piece suites and even motor cars. While it is true that the standard of living of the family of a man "on the dole" in 1939 was higher than that of an unskilled labourer in work in 1913, this slight improvement did not suffice to counter the feelings of relative deprivation experienced by those who did not share in the good things of life enjoyed by the employed and their families. Feelings of bitterness and marginalization among the unemployed, especially the long-term unemployed, were an understandable consequence of this situation and often led to a general resentment towards a society that not only denied them the dignity of work but compounded the offence by imposing on them a means test. This required applicants for unemployment assistance (40 per cent of the unemployed in 1939) to disclose the income and savings of all members of their household before payments would be made. A more perfect means of promoting family discord and disintegration could hardly have been devised.

The contrast between the situation of those in and those out of work should not be allowed to obscure another aspect of social conditions that average figures do not reveal: the persistence of poverty in large families and among the low paid, the elderly, and the sick. This was highlighted in the many social surveys conducted in the 1930s, such as B. S. Rowntree's *Poverty and progress* (in York), H. Tout's *Standard of living of Bristol*, and J. Boyd Orr's *Food, health and income*. And even though the definition of poverty

31

was a more generous one than that used by their Victorian and Edwardian predecessors, it remained a major blemish on the idea of one nation that, according to the findings of these unimpeachable investigators, at best 10 per cent, at worst 31 per cent of the population fell below the poverty line.

Resigned acceptance was the consequence, rather than a growth of militancy. As we have seen, the political parties advocating extreme solutions to the country's ills failed to recruit significant numbers of supporters. Nevertheless, when so many people were failing to share in the general rise in prosperity, their dependability in the event of a call to bear the sacrifices of another total war was a question that in 1939 was exercising the minds of the political elites; for, as the First World War had shown, divided nations were losers. By the 1930s, moreover, in the Celtic fringe the idea of the nation as an appropriate term for the people of Britain was being questioned. Nationalist parties appeared in Wales and Scotland during the 1920s and, under the differential impact of economic recession, steadily grew in the following decade. Plaid Cymru and the Scottish National Party were of a generally pacifist orientation and were hostile to the idea of a government in Westminster introducing military conscription in Wales and Scotland. These parties fell a long way short of speaking for most Welsh and Scottish people but their mere existence introduced an element of uncertainty about the reliability of Wales and Scotland in a future war.[12]

There was uncertainty, too, about the significance of pacifism. For the majority of the British people, involvement in another war so soon after the terrible war of 1914–18 was unthinkable. That pacifist sentiment should be widespread in the years that followed that slaughter is understandable enough: few families had been spared the pain of premature death of loved ones. Anti-militarism became a significant popular attitude fed, at least among the book-reading sections of the public, by a succession of books, some of high literary merit, that focused on the huge waste of human life and resources in the war, the incompetence of the commanders, the profits made by the arms manufacturers, the loss of civilized values and the general futility of war in human endeavour.[13] By the mid-1930s fear of future war took on an extra dimension: the expectation that it would include massive destruction of life and property by aerial bombardment. The Conservative Party leader Stanley Baldwin pessimistically expressed the view in 1932 that "the bomber will always get through", and the evidence of the destructive power of bomber aircraft accumulated relentlessly in the thirties decade: Shanghai, Guernica, Barcelona. Fear of bombing was stimulated by popular fiction with titles such as *Invasion from the air*, *The poison war*, *Air reprisal*, *The gas war of 1940* and *The shape of things to come*, the last of which made an even greater impact on the popular imagination when released as a feature film in 1935. Pacifism might take the formal shape of membership of institutions and societies of pacific intent, such as the learned David Davies Institute, which promoted research into the causes of war; the League of Nations Union, committed to achieving disarmament and universal acceptance of the abandonment of war as a means of settling international conflicts (over a million members at its peak in 1931); the No More War Movement (mainly socialist, founded in 1921, 3,000 members in 1927); the Fellowship of Reconciliation (Christian pacifist, founded in 1919). In 1933, at Oxford university, the Union, after a debate in which the principal speaker was the pacifist Professor C. E. M. Joad, passed by a large majority a resolution that it would "under no circumstances fight for King and Country". The next year Canon "Dick" Sheppard, a popular radio preacher, founded the Peace Pledge Union. Within two years, 100,000 people had pledged themselves on postcards not to fight in a war. In 1935, a "Peace Ballot" organized by the League of Nations Union, to which 11.5 million people responded, showed a ten to one majority in favour of multilateral disarmament and collective security. Alternatively, anti-war attitudes were expressed in support for political parties. The Labour Party and the Liberal Party both adopted the policy of disarmament and collective security through the League of Nations and in 1932 the Labour Party chose a thorough-going pacifist, George Lansbury, as its leader.

Anxiety in the ruling establishment about the Celtic fringe and pacifism could be assuaged a little by the comforting knowledge that there was at least one unifying institution that by all appearances was in robust health: the monarchy. As a symbol of the nation and as an important element in its sense of identity, the monarchy was undoubtedly a remarkable success. There can be no question of its popularity: the big "royal events" of the interwar period, even allowing for official stage-management, showed that none of the bitterness of the Depression or talk of class war attached itself to the Crown. George V's Silver Jubilee in 1935 turned into a demonstration, surprising even to the king himself, of popular affection for this father-figure of the nation, the personification of its ideal of devotion to duty, who yet shared the tastes and concerns of the ordinary citizen.

George V had, perhaps unconsciously, fed this image of himself through his Christmas broadcasts to the people of Britain and the Empire, begun in 1932. These talks placed the "common allegiance" of the people on a more intimate basis, while enhancing the magic of monarchy and reinforcing its symbolic strength. The abdication and withdrawal from public life of Edward VIII in 1937 failed to weaken the monarchy as some abroad had forecast, especially as the new king, George VI, so perfectly reproduced the popular pattern established by his father. An upright, modest and hard-working man devoted to his charming wife and young daughters, he was at once accepted as a worthy holder of the position, the near-ideal embodiment of the nation. Certainly, official efforts were made to represent the monarchy as a symbol of national unity – the co-operation of newspaper owners, the newsreel companies and the BBC could always be relied on here – but in reality public opinion did not need to be manipulated: the monarchy was genuinely popular and this popularity was as much as anything a reflection of a real, underlying sense of national unity. That the institution of monarchy was in good heart in 1939 was an indicator of a high degree of social cohesion. There was no more precious attribute than this for the trial that lay ahead.

Royal speeches invariably contained references to the worldwide empire of which Britain was the centre; and politicians continued to speak of the British Empire as if British power corresponded in some way to the impressively large amount of the world map that was coloured red.[14] In more ways than one, however, the reality was different. In the first place, the inclusion of the white Dominions masked the fact that these were effectively independent states. This was precisely defined and enacted in the 1931 Statute of Westminster; from that point the imperial government had no sovereign power over the Dominions. The monarch remained titular sovereign but in practice was a mere figure-head and the governor-general he appointed to each Dominion was first chosen by the Dominion government. Even before this, the very word "empire" had become an anachronism and while some, like Winston Churchill, continued to speak of "The British Empire", other terms were already in use that attempted to reflect the evolution of the institution, such as "The British Commonwealth of Nations", and "The Imperial Commonwealth of Nations". The real significance for British power of the developments formalized in the Statute, however, was that the Dominions were free to have their own foreign policies. As the Czechoslovakian crisis of 1938 showed, Britain could no longer assume support for her foreign policy from the Dominions; a common policy was not impossible but it had to be negotiated. This change happened, moreover, at a time when Britain's diplomatic and strategic choices were greatly narrowed: the USA was isolationist and neutralist, Italy and Japan had moved into the revisionist camp and Russia was no longer a trustworthy potential partner in a power balance. Britain's choice of possible allies was reduced to France and the Dominions and colonies of the Empire. As Britain's foreign policy became more closely associated with that of France and thereby with French commitments in central Europe, tension appeared between London and the Dominions. Although, as the European crisis deepened after Munich, the Dominion governments became more supportive towards Britain, the weakness in Britain's position implied by notes of discord in the Empire was not lost on the dictator governments in Berlin, Rome and Tokyo. As far as the colonies were concerned Britain could in theory speak with one voice and no-one could doubt the value of the resource potential of that vast aggregate in time of war.[15] But here, too, paper strength was misleading. In several parts of the Empire nationalist sentiment was increasing and the pressure for self-rule becoming such as to put into question the reliability of the colonial peoples in the event of war and a call to rally to the flag. This was especially the case in India, the most important in terms of manpower resources and strategically vital because of its position commanding the sea-routes from Britain and Africa to southeast Asia and Australasia. The Government of India Act of 1935 was an attempt to establish a degree of political devolution consistent with perceptions of India's capacity for self-rule and with the needs of imperial defence. Its rejection by the two main nationalist movements, the Indian National Congress and the Muslim League, meant that India was still politically unstable on the outbreak of war, a question mark standing over its role in the conflict that was beginning.

Ready for war?

Absolute readiness for war is probably an unattainable ideal for any country, not least because of uncertainty about the exact circumstances in which a future war might take place. Which states will be allies, enemies or neutrals is one element of unpredictability; the point in time when hostilities will begin is another. Full provision for every contingency has to give way to informed calculation about which are more likely and which can be regarded as of too low a risk to be worth the allocation of resources. It is true, of course, that governments have some power, through the skills of statesmen and diplomats, to narrow the range of possibilities. Not that this game is without its surprises, however. Right up to the final crisis Britain imagined a German–Soviet *rapprochement* was impossible and, for its part, Germany confidently expected to have Italy at its side when war came. Both were deceived. Autocratic governments are popularly supposed to have advantages over democracies in gearing up the nation for war, and it is undeniable that the democratic process, which favours the consideration of competing claims on the national purse, can hinder provision for the contingency of war, typically trimming defence budgets and delaying their implementation. A recognition of what seemed politically possible caused Baldwin and Chamberlain to limit the size of the defence budgets and the scope of defence commitments. By comparison, Hitler was untroubled by such considerations, any likely opponents of his preparations for war being silent or silenced.

Bearing in mind, then, that no state is ever really ready for war and that democratic states are typically least ready, how well did Britain's preparations measure up as her leaders took her to the testing ground?

The uncertain value of the Empire was, as we have seen, a significant consideration in any estimation of Britain's power and was a factor in the formulation of the policy of appeasement. The Empire was also at the centre of Britain's strategy of defence; alongside the need to consider the defence of Britain itself, there was always the concern for the security of the sea-routes to the Middle East, India and the Far East, the vulnerability of India to invasion from the north, and the threat to Malaya, Singapore and Hong Kong posed by an expansionist Japan. When from time to time defence needs were reviewed, the global nature of the subject was always apparent and was increasingly seen as problematical. The problem boiled down to finding the resources to meet the possible threats from revisionist states, against a background of a declining industrial base and reduced scope for help from rich and powerful allies. Unfortunately, the solution ran foul of the Treasury's orthodoxy on the best way to respond to the economic recession: cuts in public expenditure. The armed services (though in this they were not alone) were repeatedly subjected to penny-pinching reviews of their manpower and equipment, the lowest point being reached in 1932-3 when the defence estimates, which had been £604 million in 1919–20, were pushed down to £102.7 million.

There were, it is true, siren voices, notably that of the dissident Conservative MP Winston Churchill, preaching a different wisdom. In May 1932 Churchill spoke out against the government's £7.3 million reduction in defence spending for the year 1932–3.[16] This laid him open to the charge of inconsistency, since as Chancellor of the Exchequer between 1924 and 1929, his own very orthodox policy had starved the armed forces of money. But by 1933, given what was happening in Germany, his new line made more sense. From the moment the Nazis came to power and reports of Germany's rearming were confirmed, he urged rearmament on the government. In March and November 1933 he warned of Germany's superiority over Britain in the air and of the acceleration of German rearmament.[17] Churchill's attacks, though focused on armaments spending, in effect raised the issue of the whole direction of British defence policy. The traditional policy was one of freedom from binding alliances and of reliance on the Royal Navy as the mainstay of imperial defence, with the small professional army being kept largely for policing the Empire. The exigencies of the First World War forced a radical departure from this tradition: conscription was introduced and ultimately millions of British soldiers participated in land warfare in Europe. This experience implied that the traditional policy needed to be reviewed. Was a permanent alliance with France more likely to preserve the European peace? Was a large peacetime conscript army, which all European countries had, a better way of providing for Britain's security? All post-war governments had avoided confronting these questions and, almost by default, Britain had resumed the old ways, ministers glibly citing the League of Nations and the RAF as new factors of security, when in reality the commitment to both was feeble.

Churchill was unpopular with most of his party and regarded as a warmonger by most members of the other parties. Few wished to hear what he had to say on defence and foreign threats, more perhaps from a wish to believe he was wrong about the growing danger of war than from a realistic appraisal of the situation. Increasingly, however, informed opinion among service chiefs and senior civil servants was moving closer to Churchill's view that Britain was seriously under-armed and that steps were needed to remedy her growing weakness relative to other powers. In October 1933 the chiefs of staff concluded that the British army would be able to provide no more than two divisions for intervention in Europe in the event of an outbreak of war and that these could not be reinforced for many months.[18] The following February, the Defence Requirements Committee, consisting of the chiefs of staff and the permanent under-secretaries of the Foreign Office and Treasury, reported that an extra £97 million would need to be spent over the following five years to remedy the worst deficiencies in the armed services.

Here, then, was a political problem for the government: expert opinion was advising rapid reversal of the preceding years' policy of defence cuts, but public opinion seemed unready for it. Such a policy could produce the sort of arms race that took place before the First World War, and, so many argued, made that war more rather than less likely. A former Deputy Secretary to the Cabinet, in a letter to an American correspondent, put it this way: "At present the mood here is most pacific especially among the youth of the country . . . And one of the perplexities of those statesmen who think we shall have to re-arm is how to bring the country to that point".[19] In 1935 Britain was governed by a Conservative-dominated National Government, originally formed in 1931 under the premiership of Ramsay Macdonald to deal with the economic crisis. Reduction of defence spending had been an important part of its strategy for achieving a balanced budget. Yet it was the purse-keeper himself, the Chancellor of the Exchequer Neville Chamberlain, who found a solution that met both political and financial requirements. He argued that the proposed upgrading of all three armed services would not only be impossible to finance without resorting to special borrowing; it was based on a misconception of the appropriate means for security in the modern world. "Our best defence", he said, "would be the existence of a deterrent force so powerful as to render success in attack too doubtful to be worth while . . . this is most likely to be attained by the establishment of an Air Force based on this country of a size and efficiency calculated to inspire respect in the mind of a possible enemy."[20] Accepting that public opinion was not ready for the introduction of the idea of a larger army for intervention on the continent in the event of war, the Cabinet endorsed Chamberlain's proposal; the army was not increased and the Royal Air Force's 43 squadrons were almost doubled to 84. In this cautious way Britain belatedly began the process of facing up to the unavoidable fact that in an increasingly threatening world, reliance on a presumption of at least ten years of peace ahead and on the effectiveness of international institutions like the League of Nations for the settlement of disputes, was to take risks with the nation's security. Although Labour and Liberal Members opposed the new programme as jeopardizing the prospects of international disarmament and likely to lead to an arms race, the government had probably judged correctly what the public would accept. A year later in 1936, in the campaign for the general election, the Conservative manifesto reaffirmed that "The League of Nations would remain . . . the keystone of British foreign policy". It acknowledged the need for a measure of rearmament to fill gaps in the national defence; but the Conservative leader Stanley Baldwin felt it necessary to address the International Peace Society on 31 October and say, "I give you my word that there will be no great armaments". These were the words of a shrewd politician judging accurately the public mood. Several years later, when war had come, Baldwin was charged with abdication of responsibility in failing to rearm Britain sooner. It has to be borne in mind, however, that throughout the 1931–9 period, outside Westminster there was no pressure on government to speed up rearmament and even in parliament such urgings became significant only after 1935. If it was the case that Baldwin concealed an intention to rearm in order to make sure of electoral victory, then, political morality apart, it was ultimately better for Britain's security that those in charge of her affairs were not under the delusion that disarmament by Britain would make the likes of Mussolini and Hitler behave reasonably.

The programme embodied in the Defence White Paper of 1936 was for the first time aimed at enabling Britain to fight a major war against the most likely enemies. It proposed a two-power standard for the Royal Navy such as would permit simultaneous defence of Britain's Far Eastern interests and war with Germany. By 1939 the RAF would have 1,736 front line aircraft, including nearly a thousand bombers, with adequate reserves.[21] New orders and subsidies to firms would expand the country's war-goods capacity and enable reserves to be built up in peacetime, sufficient to cover the period of conversion to full war production after the outbreak of war.

The naval chiefs had insisted that the navy could not cope simultaneously with the defence of Britain and challenges in the Mediterranean and the Far East. Fortunately, by 1939 relief had appeared in two of these areas: drawing closer to France meant that the burden of countering Italy in the Mediterranean could be largely borne by the French navy and, thanks to President Roosevelt, the US Pacific Fleet was moved to its West Coast stations, thereby keeping a check on the Japanese.[22] Even so, a decision was made in the early summer

39

of 1939 to move to a two-ocean standard; Japanese naval strength would be countered by the creation of a separate Far East fleet. Although this scheme had yet to be realized, the Royal Navy was in a reasonably healthy state in September 1939. It had 12 battleships and battle cruisers, 6 aircraft carriers, 35 fleet cruisers, 200 fleet or escort destroyers and 57 submarines. Among these there were some antiquated craft (the newest of the capital ships, the *Nelson* and the *Rodney* were completed in 1927) and ideally the complement of aircraft carriers ought to have been greater, but on the whole the favoured treatment the navy had received even during the years of defence cuts had secured it the capital expenditure and modern equipment it needed. In any case, it was greatly superior to the German navy. The Germans had almost as many submarines but the Admiralty was confident that with Asdic, its submarine detection device, the Royal Navy could neutralize any threat from them.

The attempt to match German air strength in order to deter Hitler from contemplating a bombing campaign against Britain was by 1938 looking like a pipe-dream. Although the funds were there and the fighting manpower was expanding rapidly in both the regular force and the new Royal Air Force Volunteer Reserve, the absence of a large aircraft industry meant that much more time would be needed to build the factories and divert resources and workers from other industries into aircraft production. The RAF's official doctrine remained one of deterrence through "massive retaliation" but in practice in the final year of peace the resources were switched to air defence, i.e. fighters, anti-aircraft guns and radar. This was in part the result of Treasury pressure, for fighters were much cheaper to make than bombers, but more because of the realization that the bomber gap could not be closed in the short-term and in the meantime Britain, with inadequate air defences, was vulnerable to attack from the massed bombers of the Luftwaffe. The prime movers in this reorientation were Sir Thomas Inskip, who was appointed Minister for the Co-ordination of Defence in 1936, and his Permanent Under-Secretary Warren Fisher. Monthly output figures of aircraft increased from 161 in January 1938 to 348 in September and 712 in March 1939. This was mainly owing to the higher proportion of fighters in the totals, but this was just as well, for it meant that in September 1939 Britain's air defences were in much better order. Although German output levels were not yet being matched, Spitfires and Hurricanes were coming off the production lines in sufficient numbers for the objective of destroying an incoming German bomber force in the air to be realizable. In addition, there was the building of a chain of radar stations from the Northern Isles to the Isle of Wight. The system was not quite complete and in 1939 still lacked the supplementary network for the detection of low-flying aircraft, but the chances of a surprise bombing of London were less than they had been a year earlier and were steadily reducing. The consequence of the switch to air defence, of course, was as wide a gap as ever in offensive capability, even allowing for the much-exaggerated notions held in high places of the Luftwaffe's bombing power. Britain's bomber fleet was growing but to little point when only a quarter of the planes had a long enough range to attack Germany from Britain, and even then not beyond the Ruhr. The two-engined Blenheims, Whitleys, Hampdens and Wellingtons with which Britain started the war were in varying degrees obsolescent and their replacement by the longer-range four-engined Stirlings, Halifaxes and Lancasters could not begin for two years. In short, although deficiencies were being steadily made good, Britain was some way short of readiness either for defensive or offensive war in the air in September 1939.

The years of rearmament from 1935 had scarcely affected the British army except to confirm it as the poor relation of the navy and air force. Its principal role remained imperial defence, which increasingly had meant keeping order in restless parts of the Empire such as India, Palestine and Egypt. After Munich, however, a limited continental commitment was made, the chiefs of staff and the government recognizing that supporting France directly safeguarded Britain, especially after the effective loss of Czechoslovakia's 35 divisions. In February 1939, a target was set for a 32 division army, 6 regular divisions and 26 Territorials. The Territorial Reserve Army was a second-line force of part-time militia and volunteers originally set up in 1907. From 1937 the government had begun to upgrade it through enlargement and re-equipment; during and immediately after the Munich crisis over 20,000 men enlisted, bringing within view the doubling in size represented by the 1939 target.[23] The introduction of military conscription in May 1939 implied that Britain intended to equip itself with the mass army all other major states, with the exception of the USA, thought necessary in peacetime. As in the First World War, it was to be an *ad hoc* affair associated with an emergency rather than an evolution towards the continental model. Naturally, it would take time to produce a large force, trained, equipped and ready for action. The four-division expeditionary force that was sent to join France's 94 after the declaration of war consisted entirely of long-service regular soldiers. At least it was a reasonably modern force; all units in the British army were mechanized or motorized. On the other hand, its commanders' strategic thinking was unimaginatively defensive. To a large extent it had to be, for the strategy of the French was defensive, and as by far the greater part of the combined force would be French, Britain was in no position to challenge this orthodoxy. But in any case, the years of managing on low budgets seems to have stifled the development of the original thinking associated with Major-General J. F. C. Fuller, Captain B. H. Liddell Hart and Major-General G. le Q. Martel, especially in the use of tanks to restore mobility to warfare. Britain had 1,100 tanks in 1939, which, added to France's 2,200 denied the Germans a numerical advantage. Most of these were light or medium tanks, however, Germany having a preponderance in heavy tanks. Also, like France (and unlike Germany), Britain had yet to appreciate the possibilities that lay in concentrating tanks into armoured divisions. Such tanks as she had were dispersed among the infantry divisions, underlining their role as infantry support.

Inter-service rivalry and imperfect comprehension between officers and politicians seem to have been endemic historically in most countries. In this Britain was no exception. It was a significant development between the wars, then, that this debilitating tendency was substantially reduced. The key factor was the revived Committee of Imperial Defence, together with its sub-committees, and the creation of the Imperial Defence College. It was an advantage that the leaders of the military and political elites were largely drawn from the same social stratum, but the new institutional arrangements brought much-needed mutual knowledge and understanding. Officers who served on the CID or who graduated from the IDC had more experience and a broader understanding of the context of the armed forces' role than their predecessors. The chiefs of staff sub-committee did not entirely prevent inter-service rivalry and suspicion but undoubtedly went a long way towards producing compromise and consensus among the service chiefs in their dealings with the politicians.

This broad picture of Britain's armed forces as war began suggests a degree of mismatch between her fighting capacities and her Great Power status. Rearmament and modernization had begun late and proceeded too slowly to make up the deficiency. The expansion and equipping of the three armed services in the last six years of peace is a story of inconsistency of purpose and lack of strategic vision. Although the total spending on rearmament increased from £37.2

million in 1934 to £273.1 million in 1939, this was only just over half the rate of increase in German defence spending and it was not enough to furnish the RAF with the bombers it needed for a viable offensive capability, or the army with sufficient anti-aircraft and anti-tank guns for its presumed role against the Luftwaffe in England and the Wehrmacht in France. Priority had for years gone to the navy and air force and yet the ability of the latter effectively to defend Britain itself, let alone take the offensive against the enemy was in doubt, as the forays of Goering's bombers were soon to show. Unprepared for a role in land warfare, half-prepared for war in the air, only for naval warfare was Britain equipped like a Great Power and ready for action.

The building up of industrial capacity to sustain the supply of equipment and munitions began with the creation of a Director-General of Munitions Production in 1936.[24] New Royal Ordnance factories were established and subsidies made for the building of private arms factories. In 1938 the "shadow factories" scheme was begun and aircraft factories were enlarged to take on the new orders for aircraft. But as has been shown, the smallness of the machine-tool industry and the serious shortage of skilled workers set limits to the pace of expansion and to the prospects for future growth. This was a product of long-term neglect for which the government had only the solution of buying in what was needed from abroad. Quite apart from the implications of this for the balance of payments, it was a solution that could quickly founder in the disruption of ocean transport to be expected in wartime. By September 1939 things were moving in the right direction on all fronts but plainly, almost everything would have been in a greater state of readiness had the government shown more foresight. As it was, even in 1939 it seemed unmindful of the need for dispatch, as the leisurely pace of the conscription scheme showed. It applied only to men aged 20 and 21, registration did not begin until June, the first conscripts were called up in July and were to serve for only six months preparatory to the call-up proper, scheduled for 1941 at the earliest. Even granted the particular sensitivity of the conscription question in Britain, to presume that there was this amount of time to play with was surely remiss.

In other areas of contingency planning the government can be credited with some foresight or, at least, the willingness to use hindsight. The First World War had shown the damaging effects to industrial and agricultural production that could result from unrestricted recruitment of able-bodied men into the armed forces. Many categories of skilled worker would not be called up anyway, but the government did not want any of this precious group to be "lost" through volunteering. In 1938, therefore, it published a Schedule of Reserved Occupations and followed it in January 1939 with a handbook, sent to every household, cataloguing the various full-time and part-time war jobs.

The earlier conflict had also revealed that the demands of total war could not be met without major administrative changes. In anticipation of this need in a future war, the secretariat of the Committee of Imperial Defence, under the direction of Sir Maurice Hankey, was set to update the "War Book". This meant that by the outbreak of the Second World War there was, ready to hand, a carefully worked-out plan for the organization of government and administration. Under this scheme, large sections of various government offices were to move out of London to designated provincial bases ("Plan Yellow"), and there was even a plan, known as "Black Move", for the government itself to leave if the capital's destruction seemed imminent. A shadow system of war-government was also devised that envisaged four new ministries: Economic Warfare, to organize the blockade of the enemy; Shipping, to control the use of the merchant marine and direct the building of more merchant ships; Food, to ration supplies and encourage food economy; Information, to sustain the morale of the home population, to undermine that of the enemy, and to solicit the support of the neutral states. In addition, there was the Ministry of Supply, which was actually in being before the outbreak of war. This was not, however, a sign of percipient preparedness, for the decision to create it, taken reluctantly by Chamberlain over three months earlier, was implemented only in July with the appointment of the minister. The choice, moreover, fell on the National Liberal Leslie Burgin, whom A. J. P. Taylor describes as "another horse from Caligula's well-stocked stable".[25] Burgin, to pursue the allusion further, fiddled while Rome burned, taking a month after his appointment to set up his office and, in one of his first actions, appointing an Industrial Advisory Panel that consisted entirely of businessmen to the exclusion of trade unionists. Some of the government's critics had been advocating the creation of a ministry with powers to oversee the entire war economy. It was not yet thinking along these lines, however: the remit of the new ministry was not much wider than that of the Ministry of Munitions in the First World War, that is, it had no responsibility for the requirements of the navy and air force, which retained their independence.

When statesmen repeatedly forecast, as Baldwin and Chamberlain did, that a future war inevitably meant assault on the civilian population by the enemy's bombers, it behoved them to make some provision to mitigate the effects. While strategic policy passed from deterrence to air defence the government began serious work on civil defence from as early as 1935, that is, before the threat from Germany had become clear. The whole question of civil defence became virtually one of what to do about the expected air bombardment. The Committee of Imperial Defence calculated that the first attack would last for 60 days and that the total number of casualties might amount to 600,000 killed and 200,000 injured. Between 1,000,000 and 2,800,000 hospital beds would be needed and there would have to be mass burials of the dead. An Air Raid Precautions (ARP) Committee was set up under the Home Office with a brief to educate the public, to devise warning systems, and to plan for the survival of essential services, repair of bomb damage and maintenance of public order. This involved the training of air-raid wardens, policemen and doctors, the recruitment of volunteers, and the preparation and distribution of handbooks for the public. The Air Raid Precautions Act of 1937 required local authorities to organize ARP in their areas, the government meeting nine-tenths of the cost. The system, such as it was, was tested during the Munich crisis, although the resort to the inadequacies of slit trenches in parks showed there was still a long way to go. After Munich, in October 1938, the new Lord Privy Seal Sir John Anderson, a prominent civil servant, was put in charge of civil defence and under his dynamic leadership new arrangements were devised and put in hand, including the preparation of emergency, fire and transport services and the ordering of 2.5 million family-sized corrugated-steel air-raid shelters for erection in the gardens of people's houses. The "Anderson" shelter measured 6ft by 6ft by 4ft 6 in; reinforced above with the earth that had been removed to set it half into the ground, it could accommodate four adults (six in an emergency) and, according to tests, would provide good protection from everything except a direct hit. It cost £5 but was free to families whose annual income was less than £250. During the Munich crisis 38 million gas masks had been distributed to regional centres, although there was no version suitable for babies and small children. This lack was remedied by the invention of a gas helmet, the oxygen supply to which came from a hand-operated bellows. The entire population was thus equipped to survive the gas war that officialdom expected. Finally, under the Civilian Defence

Act of July 1939 the government took powers to requisition suitable buildings for use as public air-raid shelters and imposed on owners of factories and shops an obligation to adopt their own ARP measures. By the outbreak of war the civil defence services had reached their target of 1.5 million recruits, two-thirds of them unpaid part-time volunteers, the remainder paid full-timers. The provision of shelters was well short of the target, however, which placed an extra importance on the elaborate plans for evacuation of people from the places thought to be most at risk from bombing. It took the Munich war scare to bring some urgency to this planning, for although Home Office officials had been working on the matter for some years before, no national scheme had by then emerged. An improvised arrangement was produced at the end of September 1938 for the evacuation of London schoolchildren; it was fortunate that it was not put to the test. Thereafter, the daunting task of working out a scheme for the sudden mass movement of perhaps five million people was purposefully addressed, mainly by Walter Elliot's staff at the Ministry of Health. The result was a national plan that zoned the country into evacuation, neutral and reception areas, and set out procedures for the evacuation of infants with their mothers, and schoolchildren with their teachers, from cities to billets in private homes in the rural areas. A typically British touch was the non-compulsory nature of the evacuation, although at the billeting end it was clear that the Englishman's home was no longer the castle he thought it to be. Hospital patients were also to be evacuated from the big cities or, if non-urgent cases, simply discharged, in this case in order to free beds for the expected inrush of casualties once bombing started.

Looked at together, the various measures for civil defence taken by the government in the last year of peace amounted to a creditable effort and an efficient use of resources, considering the size of the problem and the simultaneous demands on resources being made by the rearmament programme. If fault is to be found, it is in the thinking behind the government's foreign and defence policy that produced this situation of a Great Power entering what might turn out to be a major war in a state of only partial readiness. For embedded in that thinking was the belief that war was avoidable and therefore need not be properly prepared for. The realization that this might not be so came too late for the best chance of stopping the aggressor to be taken and inevitably made the attempt to make up for lost time something of a hasty improvization.

Notes

1 P. Kennedy, *The rise and fall of the Great Powers* (London: Fontana, 1989), p.409.
2 S. Pollard, *The development of the British economy*, 2nd edn (London: Edward Arnold, 1969).
3 C. Barnett, *The audit of war* (London: Macmillan, 1986), p.66.
4 H. Wilson, *A new deal for coal* (London: Contact, 1945), p.33.
5 CAB 16/141, DPR 140, 6th Report by Admiralty, Nov. 1936.
6 CAB 16/141, DPR 184, 11th Report by Admiralty, April 1937.
7 Barnett, *The audit of war*, p.112.
8 Ibid., p.89.
9 Machine-tools made in Britain in 1935, 20,000; in 1939, 35,000. Pollard, *The development of the British economy*, p.312.
10 CAB 16/140, DPR 96.
11 The Pilgrim Trust, *Men without work* (London, 1938), pp.12–14.
12 The SNP's best pre-war performance was 16 per cent of the vote in the eight seats it contested.
13 E.g. E. M. Remarque, *All quiet on the western front* (1929), R. C. Sherriff, *Journey's end* (1929), Ernest Hemingway, *A farewell to arms* (1929), Henri Barbusse, *Under fire* (1916), Siegfried Sassoon, *Complete memoirs of George Sherston* (1928–1936), Robert Graves, *Goodbye to all that* (1929), Philip Noel-Baker, *Hawkers of death* (1934), C. S. Forester, *The general* (1936). The first three of these titles were also made into feature films.
14 500 million people, a quarter of the world's population, lived in the British Empire.
15 Some of the richest sources of raw materials in the world were within the British Empire: gold and copper in Africa, oil in the East and West Indies and Burma, tin and rubber in Malaya.
16 W. S. Churchill, *The Second World War,* vol. I *The gathering storm* (London: Cassell, 1948), p.66.
17 Ibid., pp.66, 77.
18 M. Howard, *The Continental commitment* (London: Maurice Temple Smith, 1972), p.104.
19 T. Jones: letter to Abraham Flexner, 1 March 1934, in *A diary with letters* (Oxford: Oxford University Press, 1954), p.125.
20 M. Howard, *The Continental commitment*, p.109.
21 To get this expansion into perspective: in 1936 Germany made 5,112 aircraft, Britain 1,877.
22 J. Gooch, *Armies in Europe* (London: Routledge, 1980), pp.220–21.
23 The strength of the Territorial Army was 186,421 in October 1938. Source: Statistical Abstract of UK, 1938, p.170.

24 The first holder of the position was Engineer Vice-Admiral Sir Harold Brown.
25 A. J. P. Taylor, *English history 1914-1945* (Oxford: Oxford University Press, 1965), p.444n.

Chapter Three

۶

Politics

There was a general expectation that the outbreak of war would bring about an end to party government and its replacement by a cross-party coalition; the First World War had taught that nothing less than this was needed for the organization of the nation's resources for victory. But it was not to be. Chamberlain responded to the expectation by offering places to the opposition Labour Party in a re-constituted government. The offer was genuine enough but Chamberlain was relieved when it was refused, for he did not relish the prospect of working with those whom he despised and whose criticism of his failed appeasement policy he could not forgive. Personal animus against Chamberlain was part of the explanation for Labour's refusal but there was, too, a feeling that participation in a Chamberlain-led government would do little for them. It would not really amount to a power to influence policy and it would muffle Labour's ability to project its own distinctive view on the war effort and war aims. "Constructive opposition" was how the Labour leadership described its chosen stance. This promised Labour political gains from advancing the argument that a successful war effort required socialist measures, while avoiding the odium that in the minds of many of its supporters would attach to working with Chamberlain.

That normal politics were not wholly appropriate to the emergency or, indeed, practicable was, however, recognized in the parties' agreement to observe an "electoral truce". By this arrangement, at least for the time being, they undertook not to contest by-elections against the candidate of the party that held the seat at the start of the war.

For the first eight months of the war, then, and in harmony with the non-urgent character of the Phoney War, the need for coalition government was denied. Not until the crisis of May 1940, which brought Chamberlain down, did British politicians come to terms with the reality that total war and party politics were incompatible.

In the meantime, Chamberlain reorganized his government by bringing in new men. Public opinion would expect some broadening of the government's base and also Chamberlain needed to re-establish his own position in the Conservative Party after the near-rebellion that had occurred on the eve of war. Churchill came in as First Lord of the Admiralty and Eden as Dominions Secretary: two anti-appeasers to give the war cabinet a more pugnacious look. But Chamberlain was loath to cast off his trusted associates; Halifax stayed as Foreign Secretary and Simon as Chancellor of the Exchequer, Hoare became Lord Privy Seal and Hankey came in as Minister Without Portfolio. The war cabinet of nine still looked pretty much like the old guard that had backed the discredited policy of appeasement, an impression confirmed by the continued presence and influence in Downing Street of Chamberlain's advisor Sir Horace Wilson.[1] A number of MPS (eventually about 60), sceptical of the suitability of Chamberlain's administration for the task ahead, formed themselves into the All-Party Action Group, chaired by the Liberal MP Clement Davies. Although intended at first to act as a source of constructive advice and pressure, it became increasingly anti-government in tone. Nor did the reorganized government convince Chamberlain's Conservative critics that the higher direction of the war was in the best hands, the more so as time passed and a policy of "masterly inactivity" seemed to be what the Cabinet had settled for. In fact the Cabinet's decision to assume a war of three years, the first of which would be "preparatory", produced a sharp sense of anti-climax after the drama of the events of early September, and served to sustain the critics' suspicions that Chamberlain had not altogether given up hope of a negotiated agreement with Hitler or Hitler's replacement. He had not wanted war, he had been virtually forced by his own party into declaring it and his bitter and disappointed demeanour made him an uninspiring war leader. Could it be that he was holding back from all-out war because he believed a fresh opportunity for a settlement would emerge?[2] There were many voices pressing Chamberlain to re-open talks. It was to be expected that when Hitler offered peace on 6 October the likes of Cyril Joad, G. D. H. Cole and the Peace Council would urge Chamberlain at least to accept a truce. But the pressure also came in a continuous stream from right-wingers of his own party, such as Lords Brocket, Ponsonby, Londonderry, Buccleuch and Darnley. Only the deep feelings of personal affront that Hitler's perfidy had aroused in Chamberlain prevented him from considering a return to negotiation "as long as that man was in charge of Germany's affairs".[3] The doubts of Chamberlain's Conservative critics about his commitment to the war were encouraged by his negative response to their suggestions for a more vigorous direction of the war effort. He rejected the idea of a smaller non-departmental war cabinet and the widely-canvassed suggestion for the creation of a minister to oversee the war economy. Both ideas were urged on him by, among others, the Watching Committee, an informal body of Conservatives initiated by Lord Salisbury in April 1940. In the government only Churchill and the Secretary for War, Hore-Belisha, disapproved of the minimalist approach of their colleagues. Chamberlain's reaction was to drop Hore-Belisha in his April Cabinet re-shuffle.

Meanwhile, the Labour Party was given ample opportunity to put its policy of "constructive opposition" into practice. As the party of central planning, it was well placed to make the argument for its adoption as the most efficient way of meeting the demands of the war and the requirements of the civilian population. Party spokesmen urged the creation of a Ministry of War Economy staffed by trained economists and led by a minister of Cabinet rank to plan and co-ordinate the war economy, providing, as Herbert Morrison put it: "power of direction, of decision and . . . of drive".[4] But, as has been seen, Chamberlain was resistant to such suggestions even when they had come from more friendly directions, characteristically seeing them as likely to undermine his own authority. By the spring of 1940, then, Chamberlain's position in the Commons was much less secure than it had been in September. Even his supporters had less confidence in him and rumours of fresh alignments under new leadership had begun.[5]

The debate on the fiasco of the Norway expedition provided the opportunity for the various political forces wanting Chamberlain to stand down to get their way. The vote at the end of the debate gave the government a majority of 81 but this, compared with its normal majority of over 200, led Chamberlain to regard it as a no-confidence vote. Failing to persuade the Labour leaders to join him in the coalition government he now belatedly recognized as inevitable, he resigned, thereby opening the way for an all-party coalition headed by Winston Churchill. Chamberlain fell because he complacently took for granted the firmness of his support in parliament. His remoteness, his inflexibility, his irritability and dismissiveness towards those who offered constructive criticism naturally riled his enemies but it also exasperated his friends. Too much goodwill had been lost by April 1940, so that what ought to have been an occasion for a display of solidarity turned out to be an issue of confidence. But it was more than just a question of defective management and political style: Chamberlain fell because, after eight months of war, he was seen, even by many of those who had always supported him, to lack the inspirational qualities of a war leader. Again, the First World War was a reference point: many would have remembered that Lloyd George was the inspiring war leader that Asquith was not. It is a hindsight view of events that sees Churchill's assumption of power at this moment as the inevitable turning of the nation towards the man cast in heroic mould, destined to be the saviour of his country at a time of critical threat.[6] Had he been willing, the unheroic but more flexible Halifax could have succeeded in getting wide support for a coalition headed by himself. In any case, the urgent military situation produced by Hitler's attack in the west came only after Churchill had been invited to form his government. Nevertheless, the readiness with which disparate parliamentary forces accepted Churchill as leader does suggest that he was widely perceived to have the ability and personality needed to improve the higher direction of the war.

Churchill had come in from the cold when he was made First Lord of the Admiralty in September 1939, but he was still something of an outsider even within his own party. He knew he could survive as leader of a coalition only with the goodwill of many members who had disliked or distrusted him in the past. Quite apart, then, from the intrinsic appropriateness of a national government in time of war, of which Churchill was himself persuaded, he really had little choice but to proceed through the conciliation of interests. Chamberlain was still the leader of the Conservative Party and, despite the rebellion of May, retained a sizeable following. This meant he had to be in the new five-strong War Cabinet that Churchill had resolved on. As the Labour leaders objected to Churchill's proposal to offer him the position of Leader of the House, he was made Lord President of the Council instead.[7] The Labour Party had to be accorded a significant share of power and this need was met by the entry of Clement Attlee and Arthur Greenwood into the War Cabinet as Ministers Without Portfolio and the giving of 14 of the other 63 ministerial posts to Labour Members, including Herbert Morrison as Minister of Supply,

Ernest Bevin as Minister of Labour, Hugh Dalton as Minister of Economic Warfare and Albert Alexander as First Lord of the Admiralty. The Liberals, as a small party, came in only at the margins with Archibald Sinclair as Secretary of State for Air. Tory anti-Chamberlainites increased their voice in government (Eden being there already, now as Secretary of State for War) in the persons of Leo Amery (Secretary of State for India) Duff Cooper (Minister of Information) and Lord Lloyd (Colonial Secretary). Here, for the first time since 1915, was a truly national government. It was, however, less sharp a break with the past than the drama of the event suggested, since two-thirds of Chamberlain's Government were retained and parliament itself was still numerically dominated by the Conservatives.

For Labour this was the right moment for a change in its position. Constructive opposition had in fact become an increasingly frustrating stance as the months of the Phoney War went by. Labour's spokesmen had made convincing but fruitless attacks on various aspects of the government's conduct of the war economy: the inadequate performance of the Ministry of Supply, the over-cautiousness of Kingsley Wood's first war budget, the foot-dragging in improving relations with organized labour, the scandal of continuing high unemployment. Towards Labour's suggestions for improvements in these areas, Chamberlain was invariably dismissive or indignant, on one occasion after Questions summoning Attlee and Greenwood in order to harangue them about the "disloyalty" of the Opposition. Labour's stance was a difficult one for another reason: there was growing unease at the grass-roots of the Party about the loss of Party independence that was implied in the electoral truce, in the making of official contacts between Labour front-benchers and government ministers and in the requirement on Party agents and trade union officials to take up places on the local and regional committees of the Ministry of Information. The benefits of the posture adopted in the autumn were less clear by the spring and with the main obstacle, Chamberlain, being removed there was a good case for Labour participation in a coalition government. Attlee presented this case to the Party in terms of national responsibility and political opportunity. Having helped to bring Chamberlain down, Labour must now take its share of responsibility for government by participating in a coalition that had the nation's confidence. The compromises this must entail, however, would be more than outweighed by the enhanced opportunity power-sharing would give Labour to improve the lives of ordinary people. As he put it to the assembled delegates at the annual conference in Bournemouth: "I am quite certain that the world that must emerge from this war must be a world attuned to our ideals . . . There will be heavy sacrifices and we have to see to it that those sacrifices shall not be in vain".[8]

The Party's overwhelming endorsement of the leadership's proposal to accept Churchill's invitation marked a significant point in Labour's history. During the nine years in the wilderness it had strong pacifist and anti-coalitionist tendencies. Now, although the pacifist element was still there (20 Labour members had signed a memorandum in October in favour of a negotiated peace), the Party had nearly half the seats in the war cabinet of a coalition government, and with it a power potential disproportionate to its numbers in parliament.[9] In the words of Kingsley Martin: "from opposition-mindedness to full partnership".[10]

The coalition formed in May 1940 was regarded by its members as a temporary arrangement brought on by necessity and, like most coalitions, it was subject to the strains that arose from the need to subordinate party interest to the common purpose. It saw the war out, nevertheless, at least until victory was won in Europe. All sides recognized that while their visions of the future of Britain might differ, none were achievable without the prior completion of the task of defeating Hitler, and for this a united effort was indispensable.

In its first year the Coalition Government was preoccupied with the country's survival of the desperate crisis that came almost at once with the German western offensive. The fall of France, the retreat at Dunkirk, the Battle of Britain and the Blitz engendered a national solidarity that left little or no role for party politics. Such political debates and arguments as there were were at national level and revolved around the question of how best to organize the nation for war.[11] The urgency of this question intensified as German military successes progressively weakened Britain's position and threatened her very existence as an independent nation. Alongside the purely military dimension of the crisis was the key issue of war production. Conservative and Labour approaches to economic questions traditionally had different emphases. Progress under the aegis of a coalition would naturally involve a conscious effort by both to show pragmatism and a spirit of compromise. This was rather more easily achieved within the government than among Members in the House as a whole. Cabinet wrangling was more often than not a consequence of clashes of personality than of real disagreement. For instance, the outsize egos of Ernest Bevin and Lord Beaverbrook gave the issue of labour supply a contentiousness it might have been spared had it been in the hands of more equable, amenable men. On the whole, Conservative and Labour ministers were able to agree policy and, in the interests of unity, to defend what was agreed against criticism.

For there was no lack of criticism. Indeed, as the coalitions's honeymoon period passed and as the steady stream of bad news from the war fronts and evidence of under-performance in the war economy reached the newspapers, the voices of Select Committee spokesmen and back-bench MPs of all parties became increasingly critical of the government's direction of the war effort. To produce the most effective policies, however, the government had also to meet the political need of satisfying the disparate elements within its ranks. In this situation compromises were inevitable, but it was not for that reason easier to persuade the party rank and file in the House to accept them. In December 1941 the Chancellor, Kingsley Wood, backed by Treasury officials and Sir Andrew Duncan at the Board of Trade, pressed for statutory wage restraint. He was reacting to a series of large wage settlements in the engineering, shipbuilding and agricultural sectors, which he felt likely to set off an inflationary spiral. At Bevin's insistence the proposal was withdrawn as likely to undermine party co-operation. But in the Conservative ranks the feeling was that organized labour was taking unfair advantage of the situation. On the other hand, when in the same month Bevin sought a solution to the labour shortage in the introduction of a National Service Bill, it was the Labour Party's rank and file who cried foul. The Bill provided for the conscription of women to the auxiliary services and the statutory obligation for all men between 18 and 60 to do some form of national service. What aroused the indignation of many Labour MPs was the "inequality of sacrifice" represented in these measures of compulsion, since the government had not proposed comparable control of industrial management. After intense argument within the Parliamentary Party, during which Attlee threatened to resign if he did not get its backing for the Bill, 40 Members voted for an unofficial amendment that called for the immediate "public ownership and control of all industries vital to our war effort". The episode showed that the strain of deferring long-held political aims in the interest of national unity was beginning to show in the Labour Party. Equally perturbing for the coalition leadership, was the reaction of the Conservative Parliamentary Party to the vote. A meeting of the 1922 Committee expressed alarm that the coalition might become a screen behind which "creeping social-ism" would be introduced; it demanded and received an assurance from Sir John Anderson that this would not be allowed to happen. On both sides of the coalition, then, there was some restlessness and dissatisfaction during the difficult passage through "the tunnel". Party leaders found themselves suspected by many of their followers of allowing advantage from the coalition to slip to the other side.

Three times during this period parliamentary criticism of the gov-ernment rose to the point of threat to Churchill's own position. On each occasion military failure was the immediate cause; in strategic questions Churchill's responsibility was more obvious for he invari-ably took a leading role in determining where, when and even how military operations should take place. The first of these crises for Churchill's Government came in May 1941, after the costly military withdrawal from Greece and retreat before Rommel's forces in North Africa, and against a background of continuing German success in sinking British ships in the Atlantic and in inflicting serious bomb damage on British cities. The critics were not well organized and Churchill rose to the occasion by making a spirited defence of his policies. By 447 votes to 3 the government convincingly received the confidence of the House. But a Gallup poll a month later that gave Churchill an 87 per cent approval-rating as prime minister also showed that only 58 per cent of those polled were satisfied with the government's conduct of the war. Almost immediately after the May confidence vote the dramatic German victory in Crete ensured that criticism of the government and prime minister continued in and outside parliament. It was not until early 1942, however, that Churchill had to face the second challenge to his leadership. This time, along-side the usual criticisms of the management of war production, there was condemnation of the strategy that had allowed Japan to inflict a series of humiliating defeats on British forces in the Far East, with the consequent loss of Hong Kong, Malaya and Singapore. The three-day debate on a vote of confidence again resulted in an overwhelming endorsement of Churchill's Government (464 votes to 1). Neverthe-less, Churchill recognized the strength of feeling that had been expressed both in the Commons and in the 1922 Committee of the Conservative Party. There was no individual who commanded enough support to challenge his leadership, but there were rumours and intrigues that were vaguely threatening. One such rumour was of the formation of a centre party of Liberals, disaffected Tories and others looking to Beaverbrook as a replacement war leader for Churchill.

It was in response to this situation that Churchill reconstructed his Cabinet, creating a new Ministry of Production, to appease those who had been pressing for a co-ordinating body for the supply ministries, and bringing in Sir Stafford Cripps as Leader of the House, thereby exploiting the popularity Cripps had won in strengthening Anglo–Soviet relations while ambassador in Moscow from 1940. The reshuffle served to mute the rumblings of discontent for a few months, but they gathered pace again at the end of June when once more a major military reverse occurred: the capture by Rommel's Afrika Corps of the British-held fortress of Tobruk, in Libya, together with the taking prisoner of 30,000 British troops. This was a body blow to the government. A no-confidence motion was got up by a group of back-benchers from all parties led by the Conservative Sir John Wardlaw-Milne who, as Chairman of the Select Committee on National Expenditure, had long been a leading critic of the government's performance on the home front. This, the most serious challenge yet to the government and to Churchill's leadership of it, ended in much the same way as its predecessors with a clear vote of confidence. But this time 25 Members voted against the government and 40 abstained. Many who voted to support the government did so with misgivings. Had the dissidents and critics been united, and had there been an obvious alternative to Churchill, events might have taken a turn like that of May 1940. At the same time as the Tobruk Debate, in a by-election at Maldon in Essex the electors delivered a rebuff to the government by returning the Independent Tom Driberg with a large majority, in preference to the official Conservative candidate. Churchill himself was anxious; he knew that his good-will capital was running out and that his survival would depend on delivering success. It was not long in coming: the triumph of El Alamein dispelled the doubts about his competence, and as military successes continued in North Africa and elsewhere, his position became unassailable. There were no more motions of censure, and rumours about the formation of alternative governments disappeared from the corridors of the palace of Westminster and the columns of the press.

It was no coincidence that the turn of the military tide was when the issue appeared that was to dominate domestic politics for the remaining years of the war: reconstruction. When survival itself was uncertain, detailed discussion of the future of British society was naturally muted. By the end of 1942 a growing expectation that the war would end in victory made people more inclined to give their minds to the shape of things to come. In this, Churchill himself, however, was out of step with most of his fellow-countrymen. For him, anything that was not directly concerned with the winning of the war was a low priority, hardly worth his attention.[12] His view was that reconstruction issues would be contentious and that to address them while the war was still on would divide the coalition, weaken national unity and divert energies from the war effort.

In contrast, Labour had from the start seen the war as an engine of social reform. In *Labour's home policy*, published in April 1940, the war was presented as an opportunity for socialism. Not only would the efficient prosecution of the war entail the adoption of the more efficient methods of central direction and economic control and planning, but significant steps could be taken to "lay the foundations of a juster and more generous life".[13] The Party did not wait for the government to formulate a programme of reconstruction; a Central Committee on Problems of Post-War Reconstruction was set up and began work in July 1941, overseeing subcommittees on various subject areas: international relationships; land and agricultural reorganization; transport; coal and power; scientific research; machinery of central government; machinery of local government; social services reorganization (including committees on social insurance, health, housing and education); social and economic transformation. In addition, regional councils of Labour submitted their own reports on reconstruction. All this activity was distilled into a general statement on the war as the gateway to a socialist society, drafted by Harold Laski under the title *The old world and the new society* and approved by the national executive in February 1942. This document set up the ideological framework for a detailed policy of social reform. By the time the Coalition Government began to take reconstruction seriously in late 1943, therefore, the Labour Party had worked out and adopted policies in the fields of local government, health and social security.

It would be wrong to imply, however, that the pressure on the government to take up reconstruction came solely from the restless ranks of the Labour Party or, indeed, that this was the main source of that development. Three years of war had helped to broaden opinion in favour of social reform, extending even into the Conservative Party at Westminster in the shape of the Post-war Problems Central Committee, chaired by R. A. Butler. This body was never wholly identified with progressive policies but the small group of MPs that later became known as the Tory Reform Committee did give voice to relatively advanced ideas involving a greater role for the State in employment, health and social security. Bombing, evacuation, rationing, conscription and direction of labour had enhanced that role anyway, thereby weakening the hold of *laissez-faire* and libertarian precepts. By 1942 discussion of social reform had become widespread in the many public and private reconstruction committees.

J. M. Keynes's 1940 book *How to pay for the war*, which included a proposal for family allowances, derived from the discussions of one such group meeting in Bloomsbury in the first year of the war. A series of social reform conferences were set up by the warden of All Souls' College Cambridge, W. G. S. Adams. The future Archbishop of Canterbury, William Temple, convened the Responsibility Group and G. D. H. Cole organized a Reconstruction Survey at Nuffield College Oxford. At the London School of Economics the Agenda Group invited all-comers in the search for a coherent social policy. In all this ferment of talk it was not surprising that an entirely new political party was born, the Common Wealth Party, idealistically committed to a libertarian form of socialism in which "economic man" would give way to "co-operative man". But for the average citizen, an awareness of the reconstruction debate came not through participation in committees or party activity but via the popularizations of the *Daily Mirror, Picture Post* and J. B. Priestley's *Postscript* talks on the radio. The basic theme of all this was that there could be no going back to the social conditions of the 1930s; out of the national effort to win the war must come a more egalitarian society, the planning of which must not be put off until the war was over.

It was into this already lively and widespread debate that the Beveridge Report dropped like a bombshell in December 1942. Not that it was intended by its initiators to be a bombshell; rather, the appointment, in June 1941, of a Committee on Social Insurance and Allied Services was partly to investigate and find ways of rationalizing anomalies and inconsistencies in the arrangements for workmen's compensation and national health insurance, partly to sideline the demands of those pressing for the introduction of family allowances, and partly to occupy the energies of the distinguished but interfering and, at 60, still ambitious William Beveridge, who had been taken into the Ministry of Labour as an advisor on manpower and labour questions in July 1940. The Treasury hoped that the Committee would not report until the end of the war, but Beveridge had other ideas. Dominating his civil servant co-members, he not only had the Report ready within 15 months but took the opportunity to go beyond the narrow remit of the Committee to propose far-reaching social reform. He was disarmingly open about his tactics: "It may be possible, through a sense of national unity and readiness to sacrifice personal interests to the common cause, to bring about changes which, when they are made, will be accepted on all hands as advances, but which it might be difficult to make at other times".[14] More remarkable even than his proposals was his initial assumption that they would be accompanied by government action to maintain full employment, introduce family allowances and establish a comprehensive health service. Within this millennial context, Beveridge's plan envisaged subsistence benefits for all. In return for a flat-rate weekly contribution, flat-rate benefits would be made for sickness, unemployment, old age, maternity, industrial injury, funeral costs, orphanhood and widowhood. The reaction in official circles was hostile. At the Treasury there was alarm at the prospective costs of the plan, notwithstanding its suggested limit of the Exchequer's share to £100 million (a product of Keynes's intervention). In the Cabinet this line was maintained by Kingsley Wood, who warned against raising popular expectations, given that the country's post-war financial situation was likely to be difficult. The Minister of Education, Oliver Lyttelton, seconded this, saying that economic stability must be the first post-war priority, since it was the precondition for a successful social insurance scheme. Churchill, too, was negative, averring that as the government existed only "by reason of and for the purposes of war", reconstruction was outside its brief.[15] Labour ministers, however, were more welcoming towards the plan, Morrison, in particular, urging that a start be made on implementing at least part of it. Between Conservative caution and Labour enthusiasm there was room only for uneasy compromise: in the interests of coalition unity the Cabinet agreed to welcome the plan in principle but not to commit itself to introducing legislation during the war. In the Commons, however, the party lines were sharply exposed, Conservatives seeing the proposed compromise as another concession to socialism, Labour members as a betrayal of popular expectations. Such expectations were not imagined: even before its publication, and despite the Treasury's attempts to keep the work of the Social Insurance Committee secret, leaks and rumours about the Report's likely contents filled the Press. When it finally appeared it was a best-seller, 635,000 copies being sold, and its proposals aroused enormous popular interest and public discussion of an overwhelmingly approving nature. Political calculation was therefore bound to enter into the response of the parties. For Labour, the charge of opportunism is unjust, since it had already adopted a comprehensive social security programme that anticipated much of Beveridge's scheme. When Labour ministers pushed for reconstruction decisions in 1943 it was entirely consistent with the Party's original reasons for entering the coalition in May 1940. The Conservatives' commitment to the general principle of social security, while not wholly inconsistent with pre-war thinking in the Party, was more obviously a recognition of the political implications of the popular enthusiasm for Beveridge. Hence Churchill's damage-limiting radio broadcast of March 1943, devoted to outlining his own "Four Year Plan" for economic and social recovery, including "national compulsory insurance for all classes for all purposes from the cradle to the grave".

But Churchill still saw all this as tomorrow's business rather than today's, and therein lay the fundamental difference between the Conservative and Labour attitude to reconstruction, a difference which was to undermine and eventually end the coalition.

The Labour leaders had earned the scorn of their followers when they accepted the Cabinet compromise and had even to endure the embarrassment of a back-bench revolt in which 121 votes were cast for an amendment to the government's motion, demanding immediate legislation. But by the midsummer of 1943, emboldened by opinion poll evidence not only that the Beveridge Plan was hugely popular, but also that Labour was 11 per cent ahead of the Conservatives in the electorate's voting intentions, Labour ministers abandoned caution and struck out with a much more forceful and distinctively Labour line in Cabinet. In June, Attlee, Morrison and Bevin put forward *The need for decisions*, a paper which insisted that to postpone decisions involving financial commitments until the post-war financial position was definitely known would cause only "chaos and confusion". Consistent with Attlee's 1940 view that decisions needed to be taken and implemented in the reconstruction field *before* the end of the war, the paper proposed that the coalition make provisional financial projections and on this basis "accept the necessity of making broad decisions at an early date". Legislation could be prepared, it suggested, in a wide range of areas, including those covered by the Beveridge Report. In the Cabinet discussion of the paper, Conservative ministers yielded nothing to these sentiments, maintaining rather the cautious and prevaricating stance set by the prime minister. Nevertheless, a growing sense that the political cost of allowing so negative an image of the Conservatives to emerge from the Beveridge episode, together with some insistent pressure from the Tory Reform Committee, moved

Churchill reluctantly to board the reconstruction locomotive. Under the slogan "Food, Work and Homes for All" he authorized schemes to be prepared for the transition period between war and peace, and in November appointed Lord Woolton to head a Ministry of Reconstruction, working through a new Cabinet Reconstruction Committee. If this was meant to look as though the government was taking reconstruction seriously, the four Labour members on the Committee (who included the three Cabinet ministers Attlee, Bevin and Morrison) made it a reality. They dominated their less experienced Conservative co-members and kept reconstruction planning from slipping down the government's list of priorities. Here was Beveridge's real impact: he turned what had been until then a matter of brown study and academic debate into the stuff of practical policy-making. With the eyes of the nation upon them the politicians focused their attention on most of the main fields of reconstruction, producing white papers and even in some cases – education, family allowances, distribution of industry – enacting legislation. The impression all this gave of a new consensus at Westminster was, however, belied by the fact that the reforms actually carried through before the end of the war were rather few in number and avoided the most contentious areas of policy. An examination of the way the white papers were produced and how they were received by the rank and file of the parties, moreover, indicates that there was little change in traditional attitudes to social policy. The white papers represented compromises that left neither Conservative nor Labour leaders satisfied and which earned them accusations of pusillanimity or betrayal from their party supporters. The Education Act of 1944 owed its place on the statute book to what the minister who piloted it through Parliament, R. A. Butler, said was the difficulty of finding "agreement between the parties on any matters which involve property or the pocket".[16] Behind the revolutionary-sounding phrase "secondary education for all" which is what the Act was supposed to embody, was in fact a rather unremarkable piece of legislation, largely "codifying existing practice" as Butler himself modestly put it at the time (though re-evaluating it in his 1971 memoirs as a major change, in the direction of making Britain educationally "one nation, not two").[17] The Education Act was not, however, entirely a cynical exercise in political opportunism. It was in some degree a reaction to the traumas of wartime, particularly the evacuation and the serious disruption of educational services. The evacuation highlighted the deficient social conditions in which many urban children were being raised, and for some observers this pointed to a need for educational reform as much as welfare reform. Beveridge had identified "Ignorance" as one of the "five giants" that social reform must attack. A survey made early in 1940 showed that over 25 per cent of the 1.5 million elementary school pupils were receiving no schooling at all, 25 per cent were receiving some home teaching and less than 50 per cent were at school as usual. Although this was the worst period for disruption of education, and matters improved thereafter, most children's education was below peacetime standards in one way or another, whether through having to operate in damaged or doubled-up accommodation, going short of books and equipment, or making do with retired teachers substituting for those called into the services. As early as January 1941, *Picture Post* was calling for an education system that would get more children to stay on at school beyond 14 and that would ensure much greater numbers of children from poor backgrounds reaching university. There was much wartime debate about the aims of education, and a spate of books and reports suggesting ways ahead. The McNair Committee on the Supply of Teachers said in its Report of 1944: "the nation as a whole has woken up to the deficiencies of its public educational system . . . we are witnessing one of the most widespread and insistent of popular demands for its reform".[18] This harks back to the effect of the evacuation on the middle-class conscience but it also hints at the sense many people had by 1944 that the shortage of skilled manpower and the dependence on American know-how testified to the inadequacy of the educational system in enabling Britain to meet the challenge of modern war and, by extension, the challenge of international economic competition in the future. Whether for reasons of individual self-fulfilment or national efficiency, reform of the educational system seemed to have a claim on any government's legislative programme, even if, as it happened, its timing was dictated by political considerations.

In ending the distinction between elementary and secondary schooling, the Act followed a pre-war consensus among professionals and public alike. In future all eleven year-olds in the State-funded system would go to a secondary school through an examination filter which determined aptitudes; the matching categories of schools ("grammar", "modern", "technical") would have "parity of esteem" and none would charge fees. Some on the Labour side argued that only a system that educated all children within a single school would meet the claim that a democratized educational system had arrived; a minority thought this was unrealizable until private education was abolished. But along with the abolition of fees and the promise of the raising of the leaving age to 15, most Labour Members were content that the Party's minimum demands for 20 years were being met. Conservative Members were for their part satisfied by the Act's safeguarding of the right of direct-grant schools to charge fees and the exclusion from its ambit of private education. Educational reform at this stage suited Labour because it seemed a significant step towards a more egalitarian society and it suited the Conservatives because it served to answer the accusation that they were lukewarm about reconstruction, while at the same time deferring action on the much more contentious areas of social policy raised by Beveridge. As the Lord President (Anderson) put it to Butler, he would rather provide money for education than "throw it down the sink with Sir William Beveridge".[19]

In the field of health reform the coalition issued a white paper in February 1944. When Beveridge had called for the creation of a comprehensive national health service as an essential accompaniment to his proposals for social insurance, he consciously articulated a consensus about health policy that had been developing since the beginning of the century. With the wartime establishment of a new centralized state agency, the Emergency Medical Service, a unification of the public and voluntary hospital systems took place that by 1943 was a confirmed part of the consensus as a model for the future. When Woolton introduced the white paper in the Lords, therefore, he characterized it as a natural evolution of the existing system of health provision. It proposed the organization of medical services in regions large enough to allow most of the various hospital and specialist services to be offered within their boundaries. The management of the hospitals would be in the hands of joint authorities (counties and county boroughs combined) that would put out contracts for services to voluntary hospitals. General practitioners would be paid as before by capitation, but consultants and the medical staff of the health centres run by local authorities would be salaried. This outline of the coalition's intentions for health reform might have seemed as likely to reach early legislative form as that for education. But it was not to be. The apparent consensus concealed the fact that for Labour ministers the white paper was no more than a first step, representing minimum objectives, whereas for the Conservatives, it was more like a basis for negotiation with the various interested parties. Labour aimed ultimately at a national health service in which all staff were salaried and in which all hospitals were part of a fully integrated system. When the Health Minister Henry Willinck began a new round of negotiations with the voluntary hospitals, the local authorities and the doctors, it soon became clear that he was bending over backwards to appease these vested interests. This erosion of Labour's minimum position broke the fragile unity of the coalition on health reform. Draft legislation was accepted for presenting to parliament after the war, but Labour ministers recognized that should there be a Labour Government by then, there would be much re-negotiation to be done.

In June 1944, the government published its white paper on employment policy. Given the ideological gap between the two wings of the coalition it might have been presumed that this aspect of economic policy would prove to be beyond agreement. The reality was that the white paper was no more than a gloss on a very limited cross-party consensus on the desirability of tackling the problem of unemployment. It called for the creation of conditions for a "high and stable level of employment" and implied more direct management of the economy than pre-war orthodoxy dictated. But it did not go far in indicating how the latter might achieve the former; it was ambivalent or silent on the vital issues of planning, public ownership and investment. The relatively quiet and approving reception of the white paper in parliament represented less a consensus than an agreement to disagree about future economic policy.

The difficulties in getting far-reaching cross-party agreement on health reform and employment were typical of reconstruction policy in general. What was being revealed, in fact, was that there was no true political consensus in the major areas of reconstruction policy. It was still possible to produce coalition white papers (on land use, and social insurance) and even legislation (on the distribution of industry and family allowances). But the former were vague, ambiguous, and an uncertain guide to future policy; the latter represented the limits of agreement in fields that remained largely contentious. It seemed plain to Labour Members and Labour supporters in the country that the Conservatives were deliberately dragging their feet on reconstruction, that little of substance would be achieved before the end of the war. Labour ministers' reluctance to rock the coalition boat gradually gave way to a more partisan stance. Whereas at the time of the Beveridge Report, they thought that the best chances of making progress towards Labour objectives lay within the coalition, by mid-1944 the outlook had changed. Allied operations in France and Italy were succeeding, the Axis was in retreat, victory seemed certain. Labour ministers could draw closer to their supporters without risking the charge of unpatriotic behaviour. Also the swing to the Left shown in opinion polls and by-elections persuaded them that an early end to the coalition need not be an electoral disaster for the Party, even if the likelihood was still that the Conservatives would win. For their part, the Conservatives" growing assumption that the coalition would not extend beyond the war made them reluctant to work for policy compromises that would probably never take effect. Both sides, then, increasingly took up entrenched positions, effectively stalling the reconstruction process. By the early months of 1945, although the electoral truce was still intact, the coalition, in the words of *The Economist*, was "getting more and more threadbare", the discussions in the Cabinet had become acrimonious, and party political rhetoric had been resumed in the Commons. The coalition ended as the war in Europe ended. It had been a necessity in 1940 and it served its purpose well. Britain's parliamentary democracy was a system which seemed designed for adversarial politics, yet for almost five years its principal actors succeeded in suspending instinctive partisanship for the higher call of defending the nation against mortal threat. But it was never a comfortable experience either for the party leaders or for the rank and file. Its compromises went against the grain of prejudice and habit and left everyone more-or-less dissatisfied. Between ministers and backbenchers the strain was at times almost too much to bear. It was therefore with a mutual sense of relief that normal party politics was resumed in the spring of 1945 and the parties independently took themselves to the electorate.

Notes

1 John Colville, Assistant Private Secretary at No. 10 wrote of Wilson: "Chamberlain did little without his advice . . . being the PM's alter ego, he had come to believe himself as infallible as Chamberlain considered him to be". *The fringes of power*, vol. 1 of *The Downing Street diaries* (London: Sceptre, 1986), p.40.
2 Colville says that Chamberlain thought there would be no real war; Germany would suffer so much from the effects of the blockade that Hitler would be forced out and Goering would offer reasonable peace terms. Ibid., p.50.

3 Harold Nicolson recorded that the appeasement group in the Cabinet were in January 1940 in the USA, holding talks with former German Chancellor Bruning. N. Nicolson (ed.), *Harold Nicolson: diaries and letters 1939-1945* (London: Collins, 1967), p.58.

4 Parliamentary Debates (Commons), 5th series, 2 February 1940, col. 1309.

5 Oliver Harvey wrote at the turn of the year: "The government seem to be losing face in all quarters - even where their stocks, e.g. the City, stood highest, and there is a general feeling that the PM is too old and must go, but also confusion as to who can take his place and how he can be got rid of". J. Harvey (ed.), *The diplomatic diaries of Oliver Harvey . . . 1937-1940* (London: Collins, 1970), p.331.

6 A view encouraged not least by Churchill himself: "I felt as if I were walking with destiny, and that all my past life had been but a preparation for this hour and this trial". W. S. Churchill, *The Second World War*, vol. 1 *The gathering storm* (London: Collins, 1948), p.601.

7 In this capacity Chamberlain presided over the important Lord President's Committee with an efficiency that impressed even Labour ministers. In late July, however, he fell ill, resigned his office at the end of September and died on 9 November 1940.

8 Labour Party Conference Report (1940), pp.123-5.

9 In the 1935 General Election Labour won 154 seats to the Conservatives 387.

10 *New Statesman*, 18 May 1940.

11 Peter Hennessy suggests that in this period of the war Britain was politically united as never before. P. Hennessy, *Never again, Britain 1945-51* (London: Vintage, 1993), p.52.

12 A. Eden, *The Eden memoirs: The reckoning* (London: Cassell, 1965), pp.441-2.

13 Labour Party Conference Report, 1940, pp.191-5.

14 W. Beveridge, *Social insurance and allied services*, Cmd 6404 (HMSO, November 1942).

15 S. Brooke, *Labour's war* (Oxford: Oxford University Press, 1992), pp.171-2.

16 Quoted in K. Jefferys, *The Churchill Coalition and wartime politics 1940-1945* (Manchester: Manchester University Press, 1991), p.129.

17 Ibid., p.128. R. A. Butler, *The art of the possible* (London: Hamish Hamilton, 1971), p.96.

18 Quoted in J. Lawson & H. Silver, *A social history of education in England* (London: Methuen, 1973), p.415.

19 Jefferys, *The Churchill Coalition*, p.129.

Chapter Four

ல

The economy at war

Policies and instruments

Coalition government had come to seem inevitable. So, too, it was thought likely that war would bring increased government control of the nation's economic life: the First World War had shown that while "Business as Usual" might be good for morale, it was unsuitable as a formula for victory. The earlier conflict had also acted as a warning to government of the dangers of unchecked inflation and profits on popular feelings in general and the labour force in particular. This time it would not be necessary to learn by experience that ensuring the supply of the huge armed forces of modern war required nothing less than a centrally-managed economy; practically all civilian activity would be directed to some degree by officials based in Whitehall. Planning for this had in fact been well under way from the 1930s and an impressive weight of enabling legislation was put through parliament in the first days of war.

The transformation from a largely free-market economy to a centrally-directed economy did not come about overnight, however, nor even in the first 12 months of the war. Rather, the transition to a thorough-going economy for total war was an uneven process, as much the product of external events as of the steady implementation of a comprehensive strategy. Those events correspond to two distinct periods in the development of Britain's war economy: from September 1939 to mid-1940, and from mid-1940 to the end of the war.

The first period, the Phoney War, began with an impression, at least, of a government moving quickly to take control of the economy.

Already armed through the Emergency Powers (Defence) Act to issue Statutory Rules and Orders, which it did by the score, it set up new ministries for Supply, Food, Shipping, Economic Warfare, Home Security and Information; all this before the actual declaration of war. But the Phoney War was in fact more characterized by the unhurried pace of the adjustments Chamberlain's Government thought it necessary to make to the economy now that war had finally come. This was deliberate. The calculation was that since Britain was unready for offensive action against Germany, and France was locked into a largely defensive posture, "the long game" was the best strategy. France would hold the Germans, and in the meantime Anglo-French strength would be built up to the point of overwhelming superiority and economic warfare would weaken the enemy's capacity and will to fight. It followed that there was no need to convert the economy at a pace that would cause disruption; the timescale for the strategy, after all, was three years. Such complacent presumption of Hitler's willingness to play the role assigned to him has occasioned much criticism of Chamberlain and his Cabinet. But equally blameworthy is their failure to think through the economic implications of their strategy. As has been shown, the rearmament programme began late, and when war came much remained to be done. If Britain was to field the promised 32 division army before the end of the first year of war and at the same time reach its targets of aeroplane and ship production, a much more rapid and extensive imposition of economic controls was required. Instead of concerning itself with comprehensive planning of the nation's resources, the government focused on the supply of the armed forces. Sir John Simon's first war budget showed concern to limit the growth of government expenditure and control inflation. An export drive was promoted in the belief that a balance of payments surplus might provide the resources needed for the war. The leisurely speed of mobilization was evident in the fact that government expenditure was running only a third higher in the sixth month of the war than in the first.[1] After eight months of war there were still over one million people unemployed. Movement towards husbanding resources and curbing waste was slow and uneven, too. The government did move early on to take over the importation of raw materials, but allocations to industry allowed too many inessential goods to continue to be made. Inessential goods could be imported only under licence, but licences were not difficult to obtain. Shipping space was not rigorously rationed, though all knew that in total war this would be a vital resource.[2] Ration books, ready since 1938, were issued at the end of September but food rationing did not begin until January 1940, and only then because an opinion poll showed that, Press hostility notwithstanding, most people thought it would be the best way of ensuring fair shares of scarce essentials.

The explanation for this sluggish response to the state of war does not lie in official ignorance. Chamberlain, his ministers and his advisers had all lived through the First World War, after all. They knew, therefore, that modern war involved the mobilization of the nation's entire resources. Indeed, in opting for the "long game" they were confirming a belief in the efficacy of a war of attrition, in which victory went to the side that did better at maximizing its resources. Logically, the sooner a start was made to convert fully to an updated version of the total war economy of 1917–18, the more likely it would be that Britain would be that winning side. But Chamberlain's belief that Hitler had been bluffing and had "missed the bus" led him to hold back from this course. He covertly hoped that there would soon be an opportunity to extricate Britain from her situation by diplomatic means, without the necessity for all-out war and the disruption of the economic order this would entail. In any case, he and his colleagues had a horror of upsetting the vested interests of that order. In the words of Angus Calder:

> They were frightened of interfering with private firms. They were terrified of provoking the trade unions. They were scared of the middle-class reaction to "belt-tightening" measures which would help divert workers, factories, raw materials and shipping space from peacetime amenities to war-like manufactures.[3]

He knew that it would involve a greater degree of co-operation with the trade unions, something he was loath to initiate because he believed they would try to use the situation to further their sectional interests. Co-opting prominent industrialists was one thing, bringing the TUC into the corridors of power was another. Should it turn out that his gamble on a short war was mistaken, the official "long game" strategy would smooth the path to the inevitable. As a more charitable historian put it: "He preferred to proceed as if waiting for events in Europe to convince labour, management and public of the need for self-sacrifice".[4]

The events of April–June 1940, as it happened, provided the stimulus for this to be brought about. Hitler's hugely successful western offensives, especially the crushing of France, jolted Britain's leaders out of the complacent belief that they had control of the way the war would be fought. In place of an even matching of forces was a preponderance of German military power, further enhanced by the capture of huge economic resources. The evacuation of the expeditionary force at Dunkirk, the threat of invasion, the fight for control of the English Channel air space, and the start of the bombing of Britain's cities, all served to concentrate minds on the urgency of creating an all-out war economy as a crucial element in what had now become a struggle for survival. Naturally, the willingness of the people to accept the burdens and dangers of this struggle, the so-called "Dunkirk spirit", would have helped any government in this task. As it happened, this crisis also gave Britain the much more vigorous leadership of Winston Churchill. That he led a coalition government, moreover, ensured the support of the whole people for the austerity he now imposed upon them. Unlike Chamberlain, he could make extraordinary demands and know that by and large they would be accepted. The sharpness of the disruption of the strategic plan to which the war economy had been geared produced a period of hyperactive improvisation. Orders and controls descended thick and fast on industry, labour and consumers. Only gradually, over the following years, did a coherent, integrated total war economy take shape. The basic strategy remained unchanged: assuming the crisis would be weathered, Britain and her allies would build up their strength to the point where German power could be successfully challenged. But with no free allies left in Europe, the USA sympathetic but still neutral, the USSR apparently a lost hope and only the distant Dominions as committed sources of succour, the long-term strategy looked unreasonably optimistic. In any case, finding the means for survival came first. For a short time in 1940, therefore, the concept of the "crash programme", to make good a pressing deficiency of supply for some key item of war *matériel*, became operational. Ordnance and aircraft were high priorities in the summer of 1940, and this was recognized in the rapid expansion of factory space and a concentration on the making of only five aircraft types, mainly fighters. Using methods described by Hugh Dalton as "constant banditry and intrigues against all colleagues", the Minister of Aircraft Production, Lord Beaverbrook, presided over a doubling of fighter production between April and September.[5]

Churchill readily recognized that crash programmes were not the solution to the underlying task of rearming Britain for victory. Alongside improvisations like that which produced the nation-saving machines of the Battle of Britain, steps were taken to ensure three things: the equipping of an army of three million that would defend Britain and her empire, and ultimately invade Europe; the building of a modern long-range bomber fleet with which to strike directly at the enemy; and the expansion of the Royal Navy and the Merchant Navy both to keep Britain supplied with the imported raw materials and food she needed, and to choke off those of the enemy.

The institutional heart of the conversion to a full-blown war economy was a revamped Lord President's Committee. A small group consisting mainly of cabinet ministers, chaired by the Lord President of the Council (initially Chamberlain, then from October, Sir John Anderson), it had assigned to it the general supervision of the nation's economic effort. It co-ordinated the work of the other home Cabinet committees with an economic remit (Home Policy, Food Policy) and from January 1941 it oversaw the activities of two other groups, the Production Executive and the Import Executive. The former was chaired by the Minister of Labour and National Service, Ernest Bevin, and its functions included the allocation of labour, raw materials and factory space, and the setting of priorities, when necessary. Sir Andrew Duncan, Minister of Supply, chaired the Import Executive, whose task was "to animate and regulate the whole business of importation in accordance with the policy of the War Cabinet".[6] Over the next 18 months, owing mainly to the skill and effectiveness of Anderson, the Lord President's Committee gained in standing and power, becoming the real powerhouse of wartime economic policy, while other committees gave up part of their functions to it or disappeared entirely.

The picture of "muddling through" giving way to expertise and scientifically-devised planning is completed by the swelling presence and importance of economists and statisticians in the work of the committees and ministerial departments concerned with the war economy. Anderson's committee had working for it the Cabinet's Economic Section, which included some distinguished university economists. The Central Statistical Office, formed at the same time as the Economic Section (January 1941), had also recruited several leading academics in the field, and the Treasury had engaged the services of John Maynard Keynes, an economist of international repute, and of Hugh Henderson and Dennis Robertson, both future professors of economics. From the experts came plans for a total war economy: mobilization of all available labour, drastic curtailment of consumer goods production, complete control of imports, expansion of dollar-earning exports, and measures to ensure fairness in the financial burden that would load the people. A few voices had been raised in favour of instituting a "siege economy" in which the state would direct, feed and house the entire population. But more moderate counsels prevailed. While it is true that the revised Emergency Powers Act of May 1940 placed almost limitless powers in government hands, in practice the conversion to a total war economy proceeded by consent rather than compulsion. Little direct control of industry occurred; ownership remained in private hands and there was no programme to create a state sector. Some basic industries and services, such as the railways and the ports, did come under direction amounting to government control, and the Board of Trade made detailed directives to consumption goods industries, e.g. hosiery, pottery, floor-coverings.[7] For the most part, however, control was indirect. Owners and managers of private firms were left to work out their own ways of adapting to an operational environment in which the government determined prices centrally, allocated raw materials and labour, licensed capital equipment and varied the tax burden.

The general restrictions on civilian production that resulted from the Limitations of Supplies Order of June 1940 and various raw material controls had by early 1941 revealed scope for further diversion of labour and other resources into war production. Many firms were working well below capacity. In the hosiery industry, for instance, the restrictions led to the wasteful development of workers being put onto short time. The concentration of production policy, begun in March 1941, aimed to concentrate the reduced production of the restricted industries in a designated number of factories. This would ensure that every working factory operated at full capacity and the remaining factories were released for war production or storage. By July 1943 concentration had been largely completed, covering 70 branches of industry.[8] In the process, many manufacturers of clothing and household goods had had to conform to the Board of Trade's "Utility" standards. This involved a simplification of design and reduction of product types in order to cut down the amount of raw materials used. In this way it was hoped that the nation's needs might be met from a reduced consumer goods industry.

Of all resources targeted by the concentration of production policy, none was more vital than labour. The acuteness of the problem was all at once apparent in the post-Dunkirk period: not only would the raising of a mass army remove from the workforce millions of men at the most productive stage of their lives, but the equipping of that army would require increased production from a potentially shrinking workforce, once the pool of unemployed had been drained. At the same time, the Axis, starting with a larger population-base than Britain, had through conquest vastly increased its productive capacity. It was widening the gap still further by successfully attacking the merchant ships that brought in imports to beleaguered Britain. All this pointed to the need to make labour the top priority in the organization of the war economy. Over the period to the end of 1942 the government established a system of manpower budgeting and allocation that became its principal planning device. A series of National Service Acts made men aged 18 to 50 liable for military service or essential civilian war service, and women aged 20 to 50 liable for service in the Women's Auxiliary Services or the Civil Defence Services. The Schedule of Reserved Occupations ensured that skilled workers in vital war industries were not called up for the armed forces, and the Essential Works Orders controlled the supply and movement of labour. Employers were prevented from "poaching" the workers of rivals by the requirement that labour might be taken on only through the employment exchanges and the trade unions. The skills shortage was targeted in an expansion of government training centres where skills were taught.

Limited food rationing had begun in January 1940 but increasing pressure on shipping space, together with the switch from production of consumer goods to war goods, led the government progressively to establish a more thorough-going system of rationing, taking in clothing, furniture and furnishing. Basic foodstuffs were rationed by prescribed minimum quantities per week (although bread and potatoes were never rationed); workers in "heavy" industries were allowed supplements; subsidized milk was given to expectant and nursing mothers and children under five. For less essential foods and for clothing a flexible system of "points" rationing was devised. This allowed the consumer to choose between a range of goods carrying a different "points" score.

To support food rationing a drive to raise agricultural production was instituted; its main feature was the conversion of pasture-land to arable, thereby reducing meat production in favour of the more efficient production of cereals and vegetables for human consumption. Farmers were given subsidies to plough up grassland, raise the quality of the reduced pasture, improve drainage and remove unnecessary hedges. Further encouragement came in the form of guaranteed prices and markets, drawing in even the high cost or marginal producers. The organizers of all this were the County Agricultural Executive Committees ("War Ags"), consisting of eight to twelve voluntary members appointed by the Ministry of Agriculture from among local residents, mostly farmers, but including estate agents, seed and feed merchants, dairy-produce retailers, agricultural trade unionists and Women's Land Army representatives. These, together with their small district subcommittees and full-time paid staff, oversaw the production and conversion drive, inspecting farms, giving detailed advice or instructions, allocating machinery, fertilizers, feedstuffs and labour. Under the Defence Regulations they could dispossess tenants who resisted their instructions and send in their own labour to carry out the work, drawing on the pool of the Women's Land Army, conscientious objectors and prisoners of war. Alongside this serious attempt to reduce dependency on imported foodstuffs, and probably still more for purposes of popular morale, the Ministry of Food urged everyone to reduce waste and those who could to grow their own vegetables or keep backyard hens and pigs.

From May 1940 physical planning remained the chief means of managing the war economy: finance was subordinated to strategy. Nevertheless, for several reasons, finance continued to be an important instrument of government policy for the war economy. In the first place, controls had not removed the basic financial incentive from employers and employees. It followed that manipulation of the financial and fiscal regime could help to maximize output and productivity. Secondly, intervention was necessary to maintain the value of the pound abroad and to channel foreign exchange reserves towards essential imported war needs. Lastly, both for the sake of justice and for the sustaining of popular morale, the government needed to use the fiscal system to ensure that the financial burden of the war fell equitably on the nation.

The military reversal of mid-1940 was, as in so much else, the catalyst of change in fiscal policy. It brought Keynes into the Treasury and with him the adoption of his ideas for achieving the above aims and paying for the war without unleashing uncontrollable inflation. Keynes had been arguing from the start of the war against the Treasury's way of assessing revenue on the basis of what the taxpayer could bear. He said it should start at the other end: first work out the national income to ascertain the war-making potential of the economy; then calculate the level of taxation and forced savings needed to allow the government to absorb a greater share of the national income without stimulating inflation.[9] As Keynes explained it, inflation was inherent in a war economy of reduced consumer-goods production and expanded war production. Unless government intervened to stop it, an "inflationary gap" would open up between demand and supply. His solution, properly realised in Kingsley Wood's April 1941 budget, was for the government to absorb the inflation-threatening excess demand through taxation and forced savings.[10] The budget estimated the inflationary gap to be about £500 million. This would be closed by £250 million from additional taxation and £200–300 million from forced savings. Income tax went up to 50 per cent (it had been 9 per cent at the start of the war); personal allowances were reduced; purchase tax was increased to 100 per cent (from 60 per cent). Government bonds were offered at attractive rates, while some other investment outlets were suspended. Banks were pressed to lend their idle balances to the government and made to restrict advances for capital construction.

In the remaining wartime budgets these principles were maintained and refined. In September 1943 Pay As You Earn was introduced to make collection easier and more efficient, and purchase tax was developed into an instrument for reducing or diverting consumption.

Hand in hand with the policy of increased taxation and forced savings went that of cost-of-living subsidies, designed to prevent wage inflation in a full employment economy. Food subsidies, begun in November 1939, became an integral and expanding part of the policy of controlling the cost-of-living index for the rest of the war. Since food represented 60 per cent of the index, the control of food prices was the first priority, but the government held down rents, too, and under the Goods and Services (Price Control) Act of July 1941, checked price rises in a wide range of items such as clothing, household durables, fuel and fares.

Performance

Consideration of the degree of success achieved by the policies and instruments described above might begin with the national income. Like all the other belligerents, Britain could only sustain its huge war production expenditures by increasing the national income. Between 1939 and 1945 national income increased by two-thirds, the most rapid period of growth occurring between 1939 and 1943. Within this growth was a large shift in the distribution of national expenditure. The government sector accounted for 12.5 per cent of total national expenditure in 1938; by 1943 it was 52 per cent. This increase was achieved at the expense of investment in non-war-related activity and of consumption of non-war goods and services. In effect, the war was being paid for by a massive capital investment programme undertaken by the State; the economy became a market where the State financed production and consumption.[11] Gross domestic product grew at an average annual rate of 6.2 per cent, reaching a peak in 1943, 27 per cent higher than in 1939, though falling back by 1944 to below the 1940 level. This compared favourably with the expansion in real output achieved in the First World War: then, the peak year (1917) was only 1 per cent above the pre-war level. Of the principal combatant countries in the Second World War only the United States surpassed Britain's increase in real domestic product.[12]

How efficiently Britain mobilized its enlarged national product is a complex question that continues to generate argument, much of it concerned with the post-war consequences of exaggerated claims made about the wartime performance.[13] A study by Mark Harrison, however, commands general respect for its pioneering attempt to overcome the difficulties of evaluating wartime economic performance comparatively.[14] He concludes that in mobilizing its domestic resources for war Britain did less well than the other main belligerents. The peak percentage on military spending (47 per cent) trailed that of the USSR from 1942 on, of the USA from 1943 on, and that of Germany throughout the war. In terms of labour mobilization alone, however, he concludes that Britain was bettered only by the USSR. Taking 1943 as the point of comparison, Britain had 45.3 per cent of its working population in war-related work, alongside the USSR's 54 per cent, the USA's 35.4 per cent and Germany's 37.6 per cent.[15] Also, only the Soviet Union outdid Britain in exploiting the potential of female labour: in Britain 2.2 million of the 2.8 million increase in gainfully-occupied persons between 1939 and the peak year of 1943 were women.[16] Success in getting women into the workforce was matched by success in deploying them into previously male-dominated sectors. In 1939 only 19 per cent of the insured workforce in engineering was female, 27 per cent in the chemical industry, 34 per cent in the metals industries; by 1943 the proportions had increased to 34 per cent, 52 per cent and 46 per cent, respectively. The pressing need for staff in local and national government was met by the taking on of an additional 500,000 women, raising their proportion in the workforce from 17 to 46 per cent. In addition to the

470,000 women taken into the armed forces, over 80,000 became full-time members of the Women's Land Army. At the peak of female mobilization in 1943 an estimated 7.75 million women were in paid work, and another one million were in the wvs. This growth was achieved, it should be noted, in a singularly unpromising culture medium. Opportunities for women to find steady paid work outside the home were not great in pre-war Britain. They consisted largely of low-skilled, low-paid work for young women without family commitments. Once those commitments appeared, few employers were willing to keep them on. At a time of high unemployment, moreover, there was social pressure on women to make way for men in the job market, a pressure as strong in the home as in the factory. When the wartime labour shortage made women's labour-power essential, therefore, a major change in attitude was required not just of employers, male workers and husbands, but of women themselves, so pervasive was the old mindset that the proper sphere of women was the home and the family. This is reflected in the disproportionate prominence in official propaganda of appeals to women to take up war work, and of publicity about the crucial importance to the war effort of the work being done by women. A Ministry of Labour recruiting advertisement rather heavy-handedly got the message across thus:

> When Marion's boy-friend was called up, she wanted to be in it too. So she asked the employment exchange about war-work . . . In next to no time they had fixed her up at a government Training Centre, learning to make munitions . . . And before long she was in an important war job. At last she felt she was really "doing her bit" . . . Jim was proud of her when he came home on leave. He knows how much equipment counts in modern warfare.

More imaginatively, the government backed the making of Launder and Gilliatt's 1943 feature-film *Millions like us*, in which a not too-idealized picture of women on the factory front was conveyed to potential recruits and unreconstructed male chauvinists alike. But persuasive films and slogans like "Go to It" were of little use to mothers of pre-school children without access to day nurseries, or to married women contemplating the feasibility of managing both a full-time job and shopping for the family. Hence the official afterthoughts of nursery provision in factories on government contracts, and priority shopping-cards for working women with families. The cheerful working housewife in a 1941 publicity film goes from workplace to grocer's shop, with the voice-over saying: "Her things are ready for her. No queuing. No waste of time . . . One of the ways of solving the problems of the Home Front . . . the people on the spot getting together, seeing what has to be done and then doing it." With, it might be added, the facilitating hand of the Ministry of Labour smoothing their path.

Even so, the inducements and appeals did not persuade as many as were needed from the pool of potential workers. The National Service (No. 2) Act of December 1941 makes it plain that even among the young single-woman category too many had been resisting the call. The Act was initially aimed at unmarried women aged 20 to 30, the lower limit being reduced to 19 in 1942 and the upper raised to 40 in 1943. About 200,000 women were formally directed into industry under the Registration of Employment Order or its successor the National Service (No. 2) Act, although many more entered the services or did war work because they expected to be directed to do so. As for married women with family or domestic responsibilities, who were not liable under the Act, few came forward to participate in war work. Most felt that their domestic responsibilities, especially under the trying conditions of shortages and "make do and mend", gave them more than enough to occupy their time, even when there was no objection in principle to the idea of going out to work. A report of the Royal Commission on Equal Pay, published after the war, recorded that nearly 10 million women remained "unavailable" even for part-time work. The limits of women's willingness to come forward were equally exposed in relation to voluntary war service, notwithstanding the remarkable feats performed in this field by, for example, the members of the Women's Voluntary Services (see Ch. 6). As a pamphlet produced in 1944 by the Ministry of Information concluded: "The registrations of women have shown the number available for war work to be largely restricted by domestic responsibilities. The numbers available with no employment and no household duties have been small". While there was general acceptance, approval even, of female conscription, there was no sudden change in the way most women thought about their "natural" role. For many of those formally ineligible the question did not really arise, since the sheer weight of domestic duties left no time for paid work or voluntary service; but even among those for whom it was a possibility, the hold of the traditional role-model appears to have been tenacious. It must be added, however, that despite the real need for female labour, the reactionary attitudes of government, employers and, at least initially, trade unions, on the question of equal pay, obstructed a very obvious way in which more women might have been encouraged into paid work. In the engineering industry, for example, the average wage for women in 1944 was only half that for men. Women in the war industries were typically confined to low-paid, low-status work with few prospects for promotion or access to training and apprenticeship. From the standpoint of the effectiveness of the war economy this prejudice against women workers was counter-productive, since skilled work was desperately needed regardless of the gender of the person doing it.

As Minister of Labour, Ernest Bevin had virtually unlimited power to conscript and direct but he resisted the pressure from some quarters to move swiftly down that road. He understood the workers' dislike of compulsion and resolved to reserve it as a last resort. He was therefore acting exceptionally when, in December 1943, he directed ten per cent of eighteen-year-old conscripts ("Bevin boys") to work in the coal mines, which had been failing to maintain workforce numbers for this essential war work.

Behind the growth in national income and employment lies a remarkable expansion of the war sector of industry, with a corresponding contraction of the consumer sector, and an equally notable growth in agricultural production. Although the planning was short term and the pace rather slow, the Coalition Government nevertheless succeeded in manipulating the economy into fitness for total war. Official statistics published after the war testify to an eight-fold increase in the total output of munitions of all sorts between 1939 and the end of 1943.[17] For example, production of 303 rifles went from 34,416 in 1939 to 909,785 in 1943; machine carbines from 6,404 in 1941 to 1,572,445 in 1942; tank and anti-tank guns from 1,000 in 1939 to 36,324 in 1942; tanks from 969 in 1939 to 8,611 in 1942; aircraft of all types from 7,940 in 1939 to 26,461 in 1944; destroyers from 12 in 1939 to 73 in 1942; submarines from 6 in 1939 to 39 in 1943. Machine-tool production rose from 37,000 in 1939 to 95,800 in 1942 and small-tool production from 17,000 in 1942 to 42,000 in 1943. The achievement represented by such figures is the more remarkable if allowance is made for the constant modifications made in weapons design, the increasing complexity of weapons, and the disruption caused by air-raids and relocation of factories. In addition, the steady drive towards armament in depth for all the armed forces had to accommodate the sudden need to respond to unexpected strategic imperatives, such as the priority for fighter aircraft in the summer of 1940, or for submarine destroyers in 1942. In both cases the demand was met by a switch of resources: production of light bombers and fighters went from 703 in the first quarter of 1940 to 1,901 in the third quarter; the 73 destroyers built in 1942 represented a 92 per cent increase on the previous year.[18] What these figures obscure, however, is unevenness of development in the war industries as a whole and numerous inefficiencies in particular sectors. The dramatic success of the Beaverbrook programme in the aircraft industry was achieved only through the impoverishment of other sectors: labour, skill and materials were channelled towards aircraft production to the point where other important areas of production were set back; in tanks, small-arms and anti-aircraft guns, for example. And even the aircraft industry, the most successful in the war economy, could not keep up the pace it set in 1940; by the end of 1942 targets and delivery dates were not being met. Nor did preferential supplying of other industries necessarily produce satisfactory results. The design and production of tanks was a case in point. Numbers produced look impressive, but British tanks compared unfavourably with those produced by the Germans and the Americans; they were slower, less powerful, less well-armed, and were mechanically faulty. Although some of these problems were overcome in time, by the end of the war the British army had effectively made American Sherman tanks its mainstay.

The policy of reducing consumer goods production reached its projected levels in most branches by the end of 1943. For example, production of shoes for civilian use from 129 million pairs in 1935 to 87.4 million pairs in 1944; blankets from 6.49 million in 1935 to 2.26 million in 1943; women's stockings and socks from 280 million pairs in 1935 to 131.3 million pairs in 1944. To an important degree this reduction followed from the control of raw materials. This was, theoretically, a straightforward problem for Britain: because a high proportion of raw materials were imported, the government's controls over imports and shipping space would serve as control over raw materials. In addition, the fact that the main source of imported raw materials was the USA meant that after March 1941, when Lend–Lease came into effect, practically all imports came under government control. Another way in which raw materials controls came about was through the need to act in concert with partners. By 1942 Britain was constrained by its participation in the Combined Production and Resources Board, formed with the USA, and in the Raw Materials Committee of the Commonwealth Supply Council. Inside Britain raw materials control was rather casual. It was left to the trade associations to allocate imported materials as they became scarce, and, in the case of non-imported materials, the business organizations of the industries that used them. While the expertise of these supernumerary civil servants was an asset, the system did put a unjustified reliance on the willingness of businessmen always to set the national interest in reducing consumption above the trade's interest in increasing it. The civil servants of the Raw Materials Department of the Ministry of Supply had not the technical expertise to enable them to query the recommendations of the trade and business associations. In practice the sheer scarcity of materials, together with the labour shortage and labour controls, acted to prevent business from exploiting its position. By a combination of circumstance and design, therefore, raw materials control worked sufficiently well to enable the production priorities to be achieved.

Food production was an equally successful feature of the war economy. Before the war Britain relied on imports from abroad for 70 per cent of its calorific needs. This was reduced to 60 per cent during the course of the war, thereby saving valuable shipping space for war goods. The planned contraction of livestock numbers (excluding cattle for milk production) went ahead: pig numbers went down by 58 per cent, sheep and lambs by 24 per cent, poultry by 45 per cent. Arable increased from 11.9 million acres in 1939 to 17.9 million acres in 1944, and output rose by 81 per cent for wheat, 92 per cent for potatoes, 30 per cent for vegetables and 27 per cent for fodder. Yield per acre was increased for nearly all crops, with cereals doing especially well: wheat rose from 17.7 cwt per acre in 1936–8 to 19.7 in 1942–5, oats from 15.7 to 16.7 cwt and barley from 16.4 to 18.5 cwt. These remarkable gains in output and yield were mainly a result of the greater use by farmers of fertilizers and machinery. The financial inducements of government grants and guaranteed prices, together with the activities of the War Agricultural Committees, brought about an acceleration of the process of agricultural modernization, through mechanization and the application of science to methods of production and farm management.[19]

None of this reduced the need for import controls. Whether home-produced or imported, food supplies would never be enough to make rationing dispensable. If anything, full employment and rising earnings increased demand. As has often been said, the best testimony to the success of the rationing system was the health of the people. For the population as a whole, the level of health was rather higher during the war than before it. In terms of the war economy, rationing achieved its goal of reducing total food imports to release shipping space for war materials, while at the same time ensuring for the average citizen a diet sufficient and varied enough to maintain good health and working efficiency. Basic and monotonous it may have been, but an under-nourished workforce was not a problem the government had to face, thanks to the combined effects of its policies of simultaneously expanding home production, controlling prices, and rationing the reduced amounts of essential foods.

To the extent, moreover, that the economic strategy depended on national solidarity, rationing and price controls were generally seen as fair. The wartime Social Survey in 1942 found that only one person in seven was dissatisfied with rationing, and among housewives the figure was one in ten.[20]

That the mobilization of resources and expansion of output may be counted as achievements, none would deny. The productivity of labour, however, is an aspect of Britain's wartime performance that has elicited critical comment. Statistics for output per worker show that although it was 15 per cent higher in 1941 than in 1939, this was in fact the best year of the war; thereafter, productivity declined to a point in 1945 only 4 per cent better than the last year of peace. Even this is probably an overestimate, since official figures assume fewer hours were worked on average than was actually the case. This assumption artificially inflates output per hour.[21] A similar distortion arises from the failure of the statistics to take full account of the effort contributed by several categories of worker: the one million men and women over the retirement age; the 900,000 part-time women workers; full-time workers who did part-time munitions work in their spare time; the one million voluntary workers; the 224,000 involuntary workers (POWs); refugee and immigrant (mainly Irish) labour. Further, the average performance figures conceal the fact that in some industries, notably coal and shipbuilding, productivity declined in the war years. It has been pointed out, moreover, that other countries' productivity record was much better than Britain's. In the Soviet Union output per labour unit of time has been estimated to have increased 28 per cent by 1943; in the United States labour productivity rose by 25 per cent between 1939 and 1944; in Germany it rose by 10–12 per cent during the war.[22]

Post-war explanations for what must be counted a relatively disappointing record of industrial productivity have in recent years focused on poor management, unco-operative trade unions, and government failure to invest in industrial restructuring.[23] However, while the apportioning of blame for what happened may be in some respects justified, there were a number of factors conducive to poor performance for which no group or institution could reasonably be held responsible. Disruption, delay and dislocation were inherent in the state of all-out war. Of greatest significance were the qualitative changes to the workforce. Dilution of skilled labour continued throughout the war, and while there were doubtless instances where the skill barrier was artificial, and where the introduction of unskilled labour therefore actually improved productivity, it was more often the case that untrained workers could not match the productivity of their skilled or semi-skilled colleagues. The Schedule of Reserved Occupations husbanded skilled labour, but in the context of greatly expanded output needs there was nevertheless a real shortage of skilled labour. This was a problem that a more vigorous exploitation of training facilities might have mitigated, but there was no escaping the reality that the productivity of the wartime workforce was held back by its changed composition.[24]

A brake on productivity inevitably followed from the vulnerability of industry to air attack. To the obvious effects of direct damage from bombs must be added the diversion of effort involved in maintaining air-raid precautions, repairing damage and relocating plant. The bombing of Coventry in November 1940, for example, destroyed or seriously damaged 70 per cent of its 180 largest factories and all major areas of industrial activity were disrupted. By the time the raids of April 1941 came many firms had dispersed their activities to safer locations away from Coventry.[25]

In any industry productivity was at the mercy of its supply of raw materials or spare parts. The general disruption of war could stop this supply or erode its quality. But it was also inherent in the situation of official controls in which managers had to work to secure their supplies. Temporary shortages of raw materials occurred from time to time despite the elaborate machinery established to give smooth, prioritized allocation. Production delays were the result, with knock-on effect on production and delivery of key items in the manufacturing chain. For example, in January 1941 the Austin Company in Birmingham was forced to cancel subcontract work making aircraft components such as wings, tails and rudders, because of shortages of machinable items.[26]

Frequent modification of design specifications was another check on productivity. Military requirements changed, and research and development constantly produced possible improvements to products.

The Coventry works of the Rover Company was practically halted for several months early in 1941, both because of the failure of the Gloster Company to fulfil its contract to supply essential material for production of the Albermarle, and because of constant changes in the Air Ministry's specification for the aircraft.[27] It could be argued, as Mass Observation did in 1942, that these changing requirements grew out of the basic failings in the government's planning for war production. It was always more or less incoherent and improvised in character; this was even how the government presented the war effort, as Mass Observation pointed out:

> Production propaganda has been overwhelmingly *ad hoc*. The emphasis first on planes and then on tanks has added a special *ad hoc*ness. Production has to be based on steady rhythms, routines, methods, moods. It does not lend itself to catchphrases and sudden spurts. Industrial work requires steady continuous effort. In the nature of things, it must be firmly based on understanding, background information, and appreciation of the process in which one is engaged. No serious attempt has been made to approach the industrial problems of war production in this way.[28]

Some industries were at the point on their growth curve at which further productivity improvements were unlikely. The introduction between the wars of mechanical picks and cutting machinery had made great productivity gains for coal mining, for example, but by the start of the war the possibilities of further mechanization were used up and the inherent tendency of ageing mines to become less productive asserted itself. The best productivity performance tended to be in the newer industries, where technological and organizational change was more easily brought about.[29]

Such change naturally required enterprising and flexible managers: yet another area in which there was unfortunately a shortage of supply. It was all too easy for employers, faced with the difficulties brought by air-raids, government controls and shortages of skilled workers and raw materials, resignedly to retreat into inertia. Inefficient organization of the shop floor too often held back output and productivity. At the machine-tool manufacturer Herbert's of Coventry, for example, production blockages were allowed to persist well into 1941 before the management thought fit to investigate the reasons. Improvement resulted from the investigation, but since managers believed labour shortages were the real problem, and this was something they had no control over, they remained largely negative towards finding compensating efficiencies.[30] Corelli Barnett, in a broad critique of the way one of the more successful industries was organized, set management's failings against a general muddle:

> The wartime British aircraft industry, again true of an older industrial tradition, had no clear operational doctrine as such, no coherent professional philosophy: its way of doing things was the cumulative outcome of countless *ad hoc* answers by "practical men" to the problems posed by rushed pre-war expansion and then by the urgent demands of war.[31]

On the other hand, employers did have a genuine problem: major reorganization of production methods would invariably cause a stoppage in the work, and while in the longer term this might make a factory more efficient, the short-term pressure was for volume production rather than output per worker. From the managers' point of view there were stoppages enough from changes in specifications and interruption to the flow of supplies for them readily to invite another. In any case, changes required co-operation from the workforce and this could not be taken for granted, especially in those industries where labour relations had been disputatious before the war.

The generally unhappy story of labour–employer relations during the war clashes uncomfortably with the broad picture of a nation more or less united and committed to a common goal. This picture is not a piece of retrospective sentimentality: the nation *did* rise to the challenge of resisting fascist aggression, accepting the dangers and hardships this entailed. And yet, in the workplace little changed, it seemed. The sense of corporate solidarity within a wider, united community was rarely to be found. As Mass Observation remarked: "everything suggests extensive industrial inefficiency" and "psychological friction and disunity of outlook".[32] On the employers' side there was a general reluctance to alter a system in which workers were seen as units of production motivated only by the wages they got, and management were seen as the facilitators of company profits and shareholders' dividends. Largely impervious to Ministry of Labour suggestions for improving factory welfare and morale, most employers went no further than to conform to the minimum statutory requirements in these areas. To do more, it was thought, would impair profitability after the war. In any case, while the war lasted profits were easily made; government contracts on a "cost plus" basis removed much of the competition and all of the financial risks.

There was no incentive, therefore, to promote efficiency through welfare, consultation, and the like. The cash nexus was delivering comfortable profits, so why tinker with it?

In representing the workers' interests the trade unions were no less unwilling to modify traditional attitudes. Their whole approach was defensive. Every proposal for change in working practices was treated as a potential threat to hard-won rights, even when their source was no less a figure than that personification of workers' rights, Ernest Bevin. The rank and file, like their representatives, were acutely conscious that the employers were doing well: profits were healthy and there were plenty of rumours circulating about profiteering and avoidance of excess profits tax. Wartime wage rates were an improvement on pre-war for the most part, but war work had its strains, too, and it was easy enough to feel that capital was as exacting as ever in its claims upon the individual. As Mass Observation put it: "Cutting right across industrial morale today is the feeling of the worker that his or her work for the war effort is still for an employer who is making profits out of it".[33] Depressingly for the war economy, then, industrial relations seemed petrified in the grievance-laden, dispute-ridden mould of the pre-war years, despite the assertions of patriotic commitment made by all involved, and despite the general context of national solidarity. Reporting on the situation among industries in the North of England, Mass Observation was devastatingly blunt:

> The most striking feature of the industrial situation here is the survival of strictly peacetime procedure in conflict between employers and men . . . One looked and listened in vain for any sign of unity binding all parties in the fight against Germany. From the men, one got the fight against management. From the management, one experienced hours of vituperation against the men. Both sides claimed to be concerned only with improving the situation to increase the strength of the struggle against Fascism, but nevertheless, the real war which is being fought here today is still pre-war, private and economic.[34]

But in this war labour relations were not simply left to the bosses and unions to manage. From the start the Coalition Government recognized that there would be a labour shortage and that the bargaining power of civilian labour would increase. It followed that if war output was to be maximized and the war economy develop smoothly, labour and labour-relations must be subjected to State regulation.

That this must proceed with the consent and co-operation of the trade unions went without saying. Churchill's invitation to Ernest Bevin to take charge of the Ministry of Labour was as practical as it was symbolic. Bevin was the leading trade unionist of his time and there was no-one more likely than he to succeed in persuading organized labour to accept the constraints on traditional labour rights that all-out war would inevitably bring.

One of Bevin's first actions was to set up a Joint Consultative Committee of representatives from unions and employers. At its first meeting he suggested the formation of national machinery for wages arbitration. The Committee approved the idea, and the National Arbitration Tribunal was accordingly established in July 1940 within the framework of the Conditions of Employment and National Arbitration Order (Statutory Rules and Orders No. 1305). This retained all the existing negotiating machinery for dealing with disputes over wages and conditions of employment, but added the National Tribunal for situations where agreement could not be reached, or where there were no adequate arrangements for reaching agreement. The order made strikes and lock-outs illegal, and the Tribunal's ruling, or that of any other existing arbitration body, was binding on both sides. In the four years that followed the order, although the effect was not dramatic, there was an increase in the use of arbitration in the settlement of disputes. But industrial disputes did not go away; after a significant fall in 1940 the number of strikes rose, and the number of days lost through strikes increased from 1,077,000 in 1941 to a peak of 3,696,000 in 1944. Absenteeism, too, was a persistent feature of the industrial scene, adding its own drag on productivity, especially in the coal, steel, shipbuilding and aircraft industries. It should be noted here that absenteeism was arguably more a product of the strain of working abnormally long hours than of indolence or lack of public spirit. The emotional toll on people living lives of extended danger, disruption of relationships and sheer physical fatigue makes nonsense of the attempt to draw a line between voluntary and involuntary absenteeism. What is astonishing is that however calculated, the rate did not increase in the last three years of the war, when the cumulative effect of multiple strains and anxieties might have been expected to show.

This generally negative picture of wartime labour relations masks the fact that much of the conflict was concentrated in one industry: coal mining. It accounted for 46.6 per cent of the strikes, 55.7 per cent of the working days lost and 58.5 per cent of the workers involved. In coal, as elsewhere, the main cause was to do with pay. Miners' wages rose more quickly than average after the start of the war, but they continued to earn less than other workers in munitions and other heavy industries. The coal industry's reputation for poor industrial relations was carried into the war years and in 1942 serious unrest over pay and an alarming shortfall in coal output caused the government to set up a Ministry of Fuel and Power to regulate and supervise the industry. At the same time it appointed a board of investigation under Lord Greene with a brief to study and report on wage levels and procedures for settling wages and conditions in the coal industry. On the advice of the "Greene Committee" a substantial pay award was made to the miners and a national minimum wage established. New negotiating machinery was set up that brought the coal industry under the National Conciliation Scheme. This produced further improvements in miners' pay during the course of the war. Unrest among miners nevertheless persisted because the awards failed to take account of the claims of particular groups within the workforce, such as the piece-workers in the low-pay areas of South Wales, Scotland and the North East in January 1944, or the craftsmen in Scotland in March 1945.[35] Right to the end of the war labour–employer relations in the coal industry continued to be blighted by mutual distrust and resentment, despite the efforts of the government, Bevin in particular, to manoeuvre the parties towards the co-operation required for the national effort. Some criticized Bevin for being unwilling to use his powers to enforce the compliance of unofficial strikers. True, Bevin was always loath to resort to compulsion if there was a chance of succeeding by other means. But even he had no time for the Trotskyist agitators he believed to be at work in the unrest of 1944 and 1945. He acted on his belief by introducing Defence Regulation 1AA, which made it a punishable offence to "instigate or incite" a stoppage of essential work. In the event the new regulation was never used. There undoubtedly were a tiny number of Trotskyists (members of the Revolutionary Communist Party) active in some of the strikes of the last 12 months of the war, but Bevin's common sense in the end prevailed, in his recognition that political motivation was absent from the actions of most strikers. It was perhaps his sense of frustration at being unable fully to master the problem of strikes that had led him to cast around for this scarcely credible way of accounting for them.

One aspect of labour relations that many expected to generate conflict was the dilution of skilled labour, that is, the upgrading of semi-skilled workers to skilled work and the employment of more unskilled workers. The expectation was largely born of memories of the First World War, when the policy had indeed caused significant unrest. There had been friction not only between employers and workers but between workers and trade union leaders who had negotiated dilution terms with employers. This time, however, the apprehensions turned out to have been needless. Even before the war began, and without the prodding of government, the key actors, the Amalgamated Engineering Union and the Engineering and Allied Employers' National Federation had worked out an agreement on the terms under which there could be a temporary relaxation of the existing arrangements relating to skilled work. They agreed that semi-skilled workers might be employed "where it can be shown that skilled men are not available and production is prejudiced". At the local level a joint committee representing both sides would by agreement implement the policy, keeping a register of the changes, so that pre-agreement practices could be restored as soon as skilled labour again became available. In September 1939 this agreement, which, unlike the First World War precedents, covered the whole engineering industry, was renewed for the duration of the war. Only the gentlest of urgings was needed from Bevin to get the parties to work out together an agreement to facilitate female participation in the dilution process. This was achieved in May 1940. While it is true that in practice it was difficult, especially in some industries such as shipbuilding, to overcome the prejudice of both employers and male workers towards the introduction of women in any numbers, the policy of dilution as a whole was successful: "who does what" disputes fell from 29.4 per cent of all disputes in 1938 to 13.3 per cent over the 1940–44 period.[36] The role of the government, moreover, was unobtrusive and non-coercive. It was able to leave the negotiating to the representatives of those who would be most affected by the policy, limiting itself to giving it a helpful steer, as when, in February 1942, it put through the Pre-War Trade Practices Bill. This laid upon employers the obligation to restore, and retain for 18 months after the war, trade practices that had been relaxed during the war. It was this as much anything that speeded the progress of the policy of getting more women into industry. The shabbiness of an arrangement, however, that would first exploit then stand down women workers when their services were no longer needed, seemed to have occurred to neither the government nor the trade unions.

Entirely in keeping with Bevin's preference for voluntarism combined with compulsion as the route to increased output and productivity, was the creation of joint production committees. These originated in initiatives made in engineering, coalmining and other industries. Some of the initiatives were the response of Communist shop stewards to the German invasion of the USSR and the subsequent offer made by Britain to send supplies to the beleaguered Russians, but the earliest (in the aircraft industry) pre-dated the war. They sought ways of preventing strikes and achieving higher output. Some employers were at first reluctant to respond, since a joint production committee would be sure to reduce the area of management's prerogative. But with government pressure on industry to become more efficient this attitude changed. Symbolically, the Engineering Employers' Federation approached the already converted leaders of the Amalgamated Engineering Union with a proposal to act upon the principle of consultation to increase production.[37] And so, although they never became compulsory, joint production committees came into being in a majority of larger enterprises. In small and medium-sized firms the widespread refusal of management to participate in the scheme disadvantaged the workers in those enterprises, since these were where standards of safety and welfare were typically minimal. They were in place in all 40 Royal Ordnance factories by mid-1942 and there were nearly 4,500 in the engineering and allied industries by the end of 1943. Yard committees existed in nearly all the shipyards, joint site-committees on most of the larger government building sites, and there were 1,100 pit production committees in the coal industry. Of the last, the Minister of Fuel and Power conceded that only a quarter were working to any effect. And while a quantitative evaluation of their contribution to output and productivity is impossible, it can be said that their effect was at the very least positive. The actions that followed the decisions of joint production committees, whether concerned with workers' welfare or streamlining the process of production, always went with the grain of national policy and to the extent that they promoted mutual knowledge and understanding of the positions of managers and workers, they reduced industrial conflict and thereby losses to the war effort through stoppages.

Less than perfect labour relations, it may be concluded, played a part in the relatively disappointing wartime record of industrial productivity. To accord to them the prime position, however, would be to underestimate the parts taken by the disruptions to the material resources for production, the deficiencies of management, and the general unreadiness for a productive surge that was the legacy of the Depression. It would ignore, moreover, what was probably the most important factor of all: the level of capital expenditure. The capital-to-labour ratio declined by 13.1 per cent during the war.[38] In the USA, whose wartime productivity was more than twice that of Britain, there were massive capital inputs, notably in the form of special-purpose machine-tools.[39] Such capital investment that was made in Britain was geared to the government priority of expanding the capacity to produce munitions; the emphasis was on volume rather than on output per worker. In any case, the situation of government by coalition was a constraint: productivity touched issues of economic policy, upon which Labour and the Conservatives were not agreed. This fact limited the policy to that which both sides were willing to accept, thereby ruling out any attempt at a major restructuring of economic policy, however conducive that might have been to greater efficiency.

Even while the war was on, the performance of the economy drew different conclusions from observers on the Left and Right. To the former, the planning and controls that the coalition introduced in the pursuit of efficiency implied that a logical next step was the nationalization of essential industries. The case seemed to be strengthened by the persistence of waste, inefficiency and profiteering. Public opinion, moreover, seemed generally to lean towards this viewpoint. Mass Observation found in 1942 that 28 per cent of "the upper and middle-class" thought that profits were "too high"; that most respondents in all classes thought efficiency would be improved if essential industries were taken into public control; and that 86 per cent favoured conscription of private assets and wealth. Predictably, on the Right the problems of war production pointed to very different solutions: the removal of the excess profits tax and bureaucratic regulation, an end to restrictive labour practices, curbs on wage increases and on the incremental expansion of social welfare. There was clearly no common ground between these two positions. Inevitably, therefore, the government followed an equidistant line, retaining the planning, the controls and the tax on profits, but leaving essential industries in private hands, and limiting its conscription of private assets and wealth. If it was nothing else, the war economy was an exercise in "the art of the possible".

Commentators have been on the whole kinder to Britain's war-time leaders in evaluating the outcome of their financial policies. The weapons of taxation, forced savings, rationing and the stabilization of the cost of living brought rigorous austerity, but were the means by which financial disaster was averted. Receipts from direct taxation quadrupled and those from indirect taxation tripled; forced savings increased seven-fold; the cost of living index, after a sharp increase between 1939 and 1941, stabilized thereafter; real personal consumption was reduced to 79 per cent of the pre-war level.[40] The extent to which Britain battled to pay its way is reflected in the proportion of government expenditure borne out of current revenue. It was 37.6 per cent in 1940–41 but had actually increased to 54.2 per cent by 1944–5.[41] This still left nearly 46 per cent to be met by other means. Initial government hopes that increased expenditure could be met by an export drive soon proved illusory: export earnings began to decline at once and by 1943 were half the level of 1938. Meanwhile the cost of imports had risen by one-third. Nor was the forced savings policy equal to the need: the deficit was £10 billion by the end of the war. In the first year the gap was managed by running down gold and hard currency reserves and selling overseas assets. Another recourse was the accumulation of external debt. Fortunately, much of this was held in the form of sterling balances, that is, the credits of Sterling Area countries held in blocked accounts in London, accumulating through exports to Britain. Of Britain's £3.4 billion external liabilities in 1945 £2.7 billion was accounted for in this way.

These policies together would still have been insufficient to finance the protracted war in which Britain was engaged; it took the economic and financial collaboration of the United States to save the situation. In March 1941 the Lend–Lease Act allowed Britain to have what goods it needed without having to find the money at once. From this point Britain effectively had free access to the products of the United States' war economy. In total, Lend–Lease aid to the British Empire was £5.5 billion, amounting to 17 per cent of its munitions needs. Britain also received aid from the Empire; Canada alone supplied three billion Canadian dollars-worth of Mutual Aid (written off as a gift at the end of the war). The significance of the American intervention is clear: Lend–Lease was the life-line desperately needed and sought in 1941. Without it Britain would have been unable to carry on the struggle.

Notes

1 S. Pollard, *The development of the British economy*, 2nd edn (London: Edward Arnold, 1969), p.157.
2 Ibid., p.157.
3 A. Calder, *The people's war* (London: Jonathan Cape, 1969), p.69.
4 K. Middlemas, *Britain in search of balance 1940-61*, vol. 1 of *Power, competition and the State* (Stanford: Hoover Institution Press, 1986), p.18.
5 Central statistical office, *Fighting with figures* (London: HMSO, 1995), p.170.
6 Announcement in *The Times*, 2 January 1941.
7 A major crisis in the coal industry led to government control under the new Ministry of Fuel and Power in June 1942.
8 G. Allen, "The concentration of production policy", in *Lessons of the British war economy*, D. N. Chester (ed.) (Cambridge: Cambridge University Press, 1951), pp.167–81.
9 Pollard, *Development of the British economy*, pp.324–5.
10 R. Stone, "The use and development of National Income and Expenditure estimates", in Chester, *Lessons of the British war economy*, pp.87–8.
11 A. Milward, *War, economy and society 1939-1945* (London: Allen Lane, 1977), p.60.
12 M. Harrison, "Resource mobilization for World War II: the U.S.A., U.K., U.S.S.R., and Germany, 1938-1945, *The Economic History Review* (May 1988), p.185.
13 See especially C. Barnett, *The audit of war* (London: Macmillan, 1986).
14 Harrison, "Resource mobilization for World War II", p.185.
15 Ibid., p.186.
16 CSO, *Fighting with figures*, p.38.
17 Ibid., pp.148–79.
18 Ibid., pp.151, 170.
19 Pollard, *Development of the British economy*, pp.314–17.
20 Calder, *The people's war*, p.405.
21 CSO, *Fighting with figures*, p.56.
22 Milward, *War, economy and society*, p.230.
23 See especially Barnett, *Audit of war*.
24 Altogether, 23,383 men and women in equal numbers completed training in government training centres and emergency training establishments between July 1940 and September 1949 (excluding coal-mining training centres). CSO, *Fighting with figures*, p.63.
25 D. Thoms, *War, industry and society: the Midlands 1939-1945* (London: Routledge, 1989), p.108.
26 Ibid., p.54.

27 Ibid., p.52.
28 Mass Observation, *People in production* (Harmondsworth: Penguin Books, 1942), p.59.
29 Milward, *War, economy and society*, p.230.
30 Thoms, *War, industry and society*, p.59.
31 Barnett, *Audit of war*, p.153.
32 Mass Observation, *People in production*, p.72.
33 Ibid., p.256.
34 Ibid., pp.24-5.
35 C. Wrigley, *A history of British industrial relations 1939-1979* (Cheltenham: Edward Elgar, 1996), pp.30-31.
36 Ibid., p.28.
37 Ibid., p.36.
38 CSO, *Fighting with figures*, p.25.
39 Milward, *War, economy and society*, p.187.
40 CSO, *Fighting with figures*, p.221; Pollard, *Development of the British economy*, p.327.
41 CSO, *Fighting with figures*, p.221.

Chapter Five

❧

Aliens, dissenters and outlaws

In the disastrous circumstances of June 1940 the pugnacious posture adopted by Britain's leaders was clear enough. But what did the people feel? For reasons of nationality, religion, ideology, and perhaps other less worthy motives, a number of Britain's inhabitants were not roused into enthusiastic support for the leadership's unabashed defiance any more than they had welcomed the declaration of war nine months earlier. How large that number was, was unknown even to the government, and this was itself a source of anxiety: was the less than wholly-united society of the 1930s basically unchanged, or was the state of war having the predicted effect of healing divisions and drawing the nation together against the external threat?

One group, at least in theory, posed a potential threat to the nation's security. Not all Britain's inhabitants were British citizens; some were citizens of countries with which Britain was now at war.

"This is no ordinary war, but a struggle between nations for life and death. It raises passions between nations of the most terrible kind. It effaces the old landmarks and frontiers of our civilisation."[1] The words were said in November 1914 on the occasion of the resignation, after a press campaign against him, of the First Sea Lord, Prince Louis of Battenberg. The writer was Winston Churchill, then First Lord of the Admiralty. Now, 26 years on, as Prime Minister, Churchill presided over a re-run of a flight from civilization that resulted in the imprisonment of thousands of refugees from fascism, who had naïvely supposed that their oppression was over when they reached Britain's shores. To be sure, there was no intention to treat every person of German or Italian origin as an enemy, and no-one disputed the need to identify and detain those who did pose a potential threat to national security. But subtleties were lost in a short-lived but nonetheless deplorable wave of popular emotion in the anxious weeks of spring and summer 1940.

The first internments had been made at the start of the war. There were about 80,000 German or Austrian nationals living in Britain, three-quarters of them refugees. The authorities combed out those they believed to be Nazi sympathizers and interned them in a converted Essex holiday camp. In October the remainder began to pass before tribunals that classified them according to one of three types: Class A for those thought dangerous, and therefore to be interned; Class B for those allowed to remain free, but whose movements would be restricted; Class C for those (mostly refugees) who were judged harmless, and who would not be restricted. By the spring of 1940 the tribunals had completed the job: only about 600 "enemy aliens" were classified for internment, and 64,200 of the 73,800 cases considered were given "C" classification.[2] So far, the "frontiers of civilization" were still clearly discernible. Germany's dramatically successful invasion and occupation of Norway in April–May 1940 changed the whole atmosphere, however. The use of parachute troops, reports of assistance given to them by an advance guard of resident German exiles and pro-German Norwegians, and the establishment of a collaborationist "quisling" regime, fuelled the alarming feeling that Britain was equally vulnerable to "assisted" invasion. Pressure from the military authorities led the Minister for Home Security, Sir John Anderson, to agree on 12 May to the internment of all adult male enemy aliens living in the coastal areas. He had hoped to avoid this, but most of the Cabinet were for it and for the extension of the round-up to all Class B enemy aliens a week later. By this time the Press and many MPs were calling for a comprehensive round-up. Beaverbrook's *Daily Express* and Rothermere's *Sunday Dispatch* and *Daily Mail* had led the anti-alien campaign from early in the year and now seized on the report of the returned British Ambassador to the Netherlands, Sir Nevile Bland, which spoke of the need to forestall a repeat of the Germans' success in Norway and the Netherlands, by interning at once all Germans and Austrians living in Britain. Anderson authorized the chief constables to intern any Class C aliens about whom they were suspicious. Italy's entry into the war on 10 June, and the fall of France a week later, removed any residual reluctance to abandon the "alien but reliable" category of persons; by

August there were very few Class C aliens still at liberty in Britain. In an atmosphere bordering on panic, therefore, a sensible plan, drawn up with proper regard to the needs of national security, was set aside, to be replaced by a policy that effectively lumped all aliens together as enemies or potential enemies. All over the country long-standing residents, some of them respected and popular in their communities, some of them known for their anti-fascist views, were arrested. Thus was the Italian owner of a pet-shop in Tooting, south London, who had lived there since 1898, taken off in a police-car for internment.[3] Nor were refugees from fascist persecution, many of them with great talents and distinguished records in their fields, spared the round-up. They included the scholars Niklaus Pevsner, Ernst Gombrich and Hilda Himmelweit, the scientists Rudolf Peierls, Klaus Fuchs, Hermann Bondi and Otto Fritsch, the writer Arthur Koestler, the musician Rudolf Bing and the psychologist Hans Eysenck.

That all distinction between aliens who were a danger and those who were not disappeared in this panic was bad enough; what made internment a matter of national shame was the manner in which it was carried out. There had been no advance provision of suitable accommodation, so the rapid round-up resulted in thousands of people regardless of age, sex or state of health, being herded together in makeshift accommodation scarcely fit for human beings. In Bury, hundreds of Italians were put up in an abandoned cotton mill that was dirty, verminous, lacked proper sanitation, and whose roof was holed. In Sutton Park in Warwickshire, internees slept in tents without mattresses or groundsheets. Deficiencies in feeding, medical provision and sanitation were made less tolerable by the separation of spouses, petty postal censorship and the denial of access to radio, newspapers and books. While steps were taken to create a more humane regime in five large permanent camps on the Isle of Man, some 7,000 of the 27,000 internees were deported to camps in Canada and Australia. For 650 of these misery was the prelude to death by drowning: the ship that was carrying over 1,000 of them to Canada, the *Arandora Star*, was torpedoed and sunk off NW Ireland. Among those drowned were the pet-shop owner from Tooting; an Italian merchant, who had lived since adulthood in Edinburgh, who was a known anti-fascist and whose sons were serving in the British Forces; P. M. Salerni, an Italian aircraft engineer, who likewise had lived many years in England, and who had married an Englishwoman; and three celebrated London chefs, Zavattoni of the Savoy, and Zangiacomi and Maggi of the Ritz.[4] Other deportees reached their

Dominion destinations stripped of their valuables by the soldiers who had guarded them on the journey. Many of these, too, were opponents of or refugees from fascism.

The hysteria that had given rise to this episode had run its course by mid-July. As the reports of the mishandling of the round-up began to mount, the Cabinet acted by transferring responsibility for the internment camps from the War Office to the Home Office, calling a halt to further internments and ordering an enquiry into the selection methods used for the *Arandora Star* contingent. By the time the Commons debated internment at the end of August, although the criticisms of the government's handling of the matter were sharp, it was clear that amends were being made.[5] Anderson's contribution in admitting that "most regrettable and deplorable things" had happened took some of the sting out of the outraged comments of Members. The demand of the Conservative MP Major Cazalet that "this bespattered page of our history" be "cleared up and rewritten", was met by the promise of a review of every case.[6] Release of enemy alien internees began almost at once. It was nonetheless a slow process, involving a long wait for many wholly blameless and harmless people. If officials boasted that by February 1941 10,000 had been released, that still meant seven times this number had spent the winter as prisoners. Some attempt was made to render the wait more tolerable by ameliorating the regime in the new camps on the Isle of Man, although much of the humanization came from the internees themselves: courses of study at a camp university and a camp technical school; art exhibitions that included the work of Kurt Schwitters; chamber concerts given by three young Viennese musicians, messrs Brainin, Nissel and Schidlof. The fortuitous coming together of the latter produced, to the inestimable enrichment of the world, the future Amadeus String Quartet. But such happy outcomes were unusual; for most internees the time they spent behind barbed wire was a disruptive and spiritually impoverishing interlude, and it was small comfort to them to know that in the end the only aliens held were those who manifestly posed a threat to national security. No financial compensation was made to them, and on release they had to make their way as best they could in the already difficult austerity conditions of wartime Britain. While most reintegrated themselves into society, participating in the war effort in one way or another, a small number of late refugees actually saw out the war in internment, since they had nowhere else to go and no source of income.

Indiscriminate internment amounted to self-inflicted injury, since among those imprisoned were many people of whose talents Britain was greatly in need in its hour of crisis. It was this that drove the former Cambridge science don C. P. Snow, in 1940 working as a civil servant recruiting scientific experts for the war effort, to lobby for the release of 15 refugee scientists who had been rounded up and held, mostly in Brixton prison. This he achieved, but he tried in vain to persuade the government to exploit the scientists' specialisms. The Ministry of Aircraft Production banned work on radar developments not only to these recent refugees but to naturalized British citizens, and anyone else whose parents were not born in Britain. After weeks of futile effort, during which it seemed that all the brain-power he had assembled would go to waste, Snow succeeded, through his contacts Professors Blackett, Thomson and Cockroft, in getting government approval for refugee scientists to work in the experimental field of atom-bomb research, then taking place at several British universities, under the auspices of the Maud Committee.[7] Considered as too great a security risk to work on radar, they gave their talents instead to the work that ultimately produced the atom bomb.

On balance, the internment episode reflected more credit than shame upon British society. What began as a dangerous and near-hysterical lurch towards the police state ended in a re-assertion of tolerance and calmness. May 1940 was, after all, a time of national peril and justifiable anxiety. That British traditions of tolerance and justice were being broken was recognized, but accepted as an urgent, if temporary, necessity. As the leader-writer of *The Spectator* put it: "the internment plan will fall hardly on thousands of completely innocent men and women. It must be so. No risks can be taken now. And most of those interned will soon be able to dispel suspicion and regain their liberty".[8] The assurance was made good. In the end that journal's optimistic caution more truly represented national consensus than the rabid, racialist patriotism of the *Daily Mail*. Two confirmations of this came with the Gallup poll of July, which showed that only 43 per cent of the people wanted all aliens to be interned; and the unhindered publication in November of Francis Lafitte's Penguin Special *The internment of aliens*, which pulled no punches in its criticism of official behaviour. Whether or not it was the intolerable incongruity of a situation in which the upholders of liberty and democracy against totalitarianism were themselves adopting police-state methods, British officials were soon able to take comfort from their American counterparts' equally uncharacteristic departure from civilized behaviour, in their post-Pearl Harbor round-up of Japanese–Americans. Evidently, dangerous times required decisive action by those responsible for national security; judging the extent of what was needed was difficult.

Altogether less anguish was generated by the detention of British nationals deemed, because of their political affiliations, to be unreliable. As with the aliens, there was no move at the start of the war to carry out an undiscriminating round-up; in the same way, it was only when the threat of invasion loomed that the authorities took no chances and arrested Sir Oswald Mosley and as many members of his British Union of Fascists as they could catch. Under an extension to Defence Regulation 18B, which empowered the Home Secretary to imprison anybody he thought likely to endanger public safety, other individuals known for their fascist or pro-German sympathies were also detained. These included the Conservative MP Maule Ramsay, founder of the Right Club, and Admiral Sir Barry Domville, a former chairman of an Anglo–German friendship association known as The Link. The big fish were held in Brixton prison and the rest mainly in a special camp for British detainees on the Isle of Man. In all, about 1,800 were detained without trial, but after August 1940 each case was reviewed, and by mid-1941 three-quarters had been freed. Selective releases continued beyond this time, even extending to Mosley, who from November 1943 was allowed to return to his home in Oxfordshire, provided he remained within a 7-mile radius of it and reported regularly to the police. Mosley's release was not a popular move, according to a Gallup poll, and there were widespread demonstrations, with Press backing, in favour of his re-internment. But the Home Secretary Morrison had acted on the medical advice that Mosley was seriously ill. He stuck to his decision; humanitarian grounds were sufficient, but he was doubtless aware of the propaganda value to Britain of so bold a libertarian act. It was one in the eye for Lord Haw-Haw. The popular outrage proved to be no more than a passing squall.

In the heated imagination of Goebbels' Propaganda Ministry, Britain's Celtic fringe was fertile ground for potential allies or trouble-makers. As the Easter Rising of 1916 had shown, Ireland was a source of weakness for Britain when she was engaged with a Continental enemy. Constitutional developments between the wars had only partially removed this weakness: although the Irish Free State had come into existence, and declared its neutrality in the war that began in

1939, the six counties of Ulster remained within the Union. This kept alive the IRA, an organization of militant nationalists dedicated to achieving the union of all Ireland. In the nine months before the outbreak of war the IRA had been conducting a campaign of violence in England: incendiary devices in Coventry department stores, bombs in the London Underground, tear-gas bombs in London cinemas, attacks on letter boxes and post offices. This was accompanied by demands for the withdrawal from Ireland of all British institutions and representatives, and the incorporation of Ulster into the Irish Free State. Although the Irish Prime Minister, Eamonn De Valera, acted strongly against the IRA, interning such members as it was possible to apprehend, the outrages continued after the outbreak of war. It was clearly a possibility that Germany would be encouraged by this to consider Ireland as an invasion route into Britain. The government trod carefully round Irish nationalist sensitivities by making voluntary in Ulster the military service that was compulsory in the rest of the United Kingdom, but at the same time it built up a military presence of four divisions in the province. In the event, Ireland was not the heel of Achilles it was feared to be. The government of the Free State remained steadfastly neutral; 60,000 Irish citizens came to Britain to ease the labour shortage; many others volunteered for the armed forces, Anglo–Irish economic intercourse increased, and the IRA campaign petered out amid internal squabbles.

Government anxiety about the reliability of Wales and Scotland, fed by the pre-war growth in those regions of nationalist parties opposed to war, and exploited by German propaganda in 1940, appeared to be justified by the performance in April of that year of the Scottish National Party in a by-election in Argyll. Its candidate William Power stood against the official government candidate, Labour and Liberal not standing, and received 37 per cent of the vote. The Secretary of State for Scotland, Tom Johnston, confided to colleagues in July 1943 his fears that Scottish nationalism was taking hold. In February 1944 the SNP nominee Douglas Young just missed taking the Kirkcaldy Burghs seat with 41 per cent of the vote. And in the Motherwell election of April 1945 Robert McIntyre took the seat for the SNP. But in reality, most Scots and even more Welsh did not take the nationalists seriously. How readily this majority would have reconciled themselves to an indigenous "quisling" regime in the event of a successful German occupation, is hard to say, but so long as the latter remained no more than a threat, there was nothing to suggest that the Union was vulnerable. Much of the fuel for pre-war Scottish and Welsh nationalism had been provided by unemployment, locally far worse in Wales and Scotland than in England. The war changed this, bringing a boom time to the devastated industrial centres of the Welsh valleys and Clydeside, restoring jobs and raising living standards. Although few could be deceived into thinking the change was permanent, the advent of better material prosperity nevertheless blunted the appeal of the nationalist parties. They constituted a challenge that could be lived with; indeed, that they were free to continue their activities unhindered, was in itself a vindication of the oft-repeated claim of Britain's propaganda that this was a war fought for freedom, tolerance and democracy. When it became clear that the German-operated radio stations *Free Wales* and *Radio Caledonia* were more a source of amusement than excitement in those regions, the government knew it had little to fear: the nationalist "fifth-column" was an illusion.

For two years, until the German attack on the Soviet Union in June 1941, the British Communist Party's official stance was opposition to the war. Even though it was a small party, with just one MP, this stance was potentially threatening to the war effort, since the Party's support was concentrated in areas of industrial importance: the valleys of South Wales, Clydeside, the Midlands. Communists were prominent in the leadership of the trade unions in the coalmining, shipbuilding and aircraft industries of these areas. In truth, the official line was problematical for many of the membership and even for some of the leaders: Stalin's pact with Hitler in August 1939 had thrown the Party into disarray. Membership fell from 17,000 to 12,000 and some left-wing associates like Harold Laski, John Strachey and Victor Gollancz severed relations with the Party.[9] For the natural opponents of fascism to be cast in the role of bystanders while others fought it with arms went against the grain, even when it was rationalized as a tactic that promised power for communism in the political confusion that would follow military defeat. While the official line, therefore, continued to be that the war was an "imperialist" war in which both sides were competing for world domination, the Communist Party worked to show that it was not defeatist: an end to the war did not mean giving in to Hitler. What was needed was the sweeping from power of the old ruling elite and the setting up of a government of the people. This in turn would cause the German people to overthrow Hitler and open the way to a "People's Peace". A front organization, the People's Convention, was created to advance this project by drawing together the various groups and individuals who for one reason or another were dissatisfied with the limited vision offered by the government's war aims. When the Convention met in January 1941 at the Royal Hotel in London, 2,000 delegates attended, representing trade union branches, dissident Labour Party branches, co-operative societies, youth organizations, tenants associations, shelter committees and many other groups. On the platform were leading figures from the churches, the theatre and literature as well as the Communist Party itself. The speeches were variants on the grand theme of the need for changes to the system that had brought Britain to the verge of defeat and that still seemed unequal to the task of extricating it from its enfeebled and threatened condition. In the meantime the Communist Party spearheaded campaigns for the improvement of Air Raid Precautions (especially the provision of more and better shelters), improvement of conditions in the services, an end to profiteering, and restoration of living standards and democratic rights. What the Party was doing, in effect, was offering itself as an alternative government, an opportunity having been created by the Labour Party leadership's entry into coalition.

There is evidence that the Party's stock was rising in the country at this time. Membership had risen to about 20,000 by spring 1940 and the weekly sales of its newspaper the *Daily Worker* increased by 54,000 to 362,000 in the year ending in January 1940. Within ten months a Scottish edition had been created and was recording small but rising sales. Considering the blow to the Party's credibility dealt by the Nazi–Soviet Pact, the leadership could be quietly content with the way it had apparently retrieved the situation.

For the government, the role played by the Communist Party occasioned anxiety rather than alarm. The Joint Intelligence Committee had in May 1940 warned that Communists ought to be seen as potential "fifth columnists", and the Ministry of Information was receiving intelligence reports in the same vein from the regions through the dangerous spring and summer months of 1940. But at Home Security and at Information the ministers refused to be pushed into panic measures. Even at the height of the fifth column scare, when the *Daily Mail* was leading an insistent Press campaign behind the slogan "Intern the lot", British Communists were not included in the round-up. The extension to Defence Regulation 18B, which was used to detain Mosley and his associates, left the Communists at liberty. The worst that happened to them was that the Party's principal organ the *Daily Worker* was finally suppressed under Defence Regulation 2D in January 1941, after a period of seven months under warning that this was being considered by the Home Secretary, on the grounds of "systematic publication of matter calculated to foment opposition to the prosecution of the war to a successful issue".[10] Although Anderson naturally deplored the general posture of the Communists, he was unconvinced that they were a real threat to security and, in any case, he thought a crackdown would be literally counter-productive: the industries most needed for the war effort were precisely those in which organized labour was dominated by Communist officials. There was no evidence, moreover, that this domination was being used to disrupt war production. Anderson correctly concluded that the Party's position was an uncomfortable one and that its carping about ARP, servicemen's rights and the like, was only an attempt to recover some credibility with its supporters and to make up the loss of members that resulted from Stalin's deal with Hitler.

The Communists probably owed their relatively favoured treatment, at least in part, however, to the Foreign Office. During the Phoney War Anglo–French strategists considered the option of attacking Hitler through his Soviet props. Two ideas were put forward by the French. The first involved sending an expedition to bolster the Finns' resistance to Russia in the "Winter War"; the other was for bombing raids on Baku, Batum and Grozhnyi in the Caucasus region, an important source of Soviet-produced oil for Germany. Britain vetoed both proposals. The reason derived from a conviction in the Foreign Office that the Nazi-Soviet pact would not last; the intrinsic conflict of both ideology and interests would eventually be uncontainable and hostilities would follow.[11] In the meantime, Britain's best plan was to avoid any policy options that would unnecessarily antagonize Stalin, to do nothing to consolidate his arrangement with Hitler. It followed from this policy that a tolerant attitude towards Britain's Communists might be wise: whereas in Germany the Communist Party was outlawed and its members were in prison, in Britain they were free, a fact symbolized by their one MP Willie Gallacher's continued presence in the Commons. Although there was some Press agitation against them, the government resisted the pressure. Britain could rightly claim that, unlike Germany, it did not discriminate against its Communist citizens. This put food for thought on Stalin's table.

The wisdom of the policy was borne out when, as predicted, Hitler ruptured his pact with Stalin in June 1941. And with the German invasion of the USSR, the worries about Communist "fifth-columnists" disappeared; from that point on the Communist Party was unambiguously behind the war effort. Its motives were, of course, more to do with saving the Soviet Union than with sustaining the capitalist order in Britain, but when being pro-Russian had the endorsement of the leaders of that order, as it had after June 1941, the loyalty of the Communists was not to be impugned. Pragmatism prevailed and there was no more talk of harassment or suppression.

It was to be expected that the reintroduction of military conscription would re-create the problem of conscientious objection, possibly on a larger scale than in the First World War, in view of the growth of active pacifism in the interwar years. For its part, the government was determined that conscientious objectors would be treated in a humane and civilized manner, with none of the atmosphere of persecution with which the earlier conflict was infected. At the second reading of the Military Training Bill, six months before war broke out, Chamberlain set the tone: "I want to make it clear here that in the view of the government, where scruples are conscientiously held we desire that they should be respected and that there should be no persecution of those who hold them". The fact that pacifism in the 1920s and 1930s was to be found right across the political spectrum was recognized in a widening of the grounds of objection, to include political beliefs. Even so, when war came, it was perturbing for the authorities that as many as 2 per cent of those called to register objected on grounds of conscience. But by the spring of 1940 the rate began to fall; in March it was down to 1.6 per cent, in July to 0.5 per cent, and then continuing to fall to its lowest point of 0.2 per cent in December 1944.[12] As in 1916, local tribunals were set up to consider the cases of objectors. But there the similarity ended, for this time their remit was limited to this task, being quite divorced from military recruitment. Instead of being organized by the War Ministry, the tribunals came under the Ministry of Labour and National Service. There was, moreover, no War Ministry voice in the tribunals; they consisted of a chairman, who was always a county court judge, and four other members, one of whom was appointed after consultation with trade unions. These entirely civilian bodies were typically made up of middle-aged to elderly people from professional and academic life appointed by the Ministry, having regard to "the necessity of selecting impartial persons".

Under the National Service Act a man who objected to doing military service or combatant duties had to apply to be placed on the register of conscientious objectors. The local tribunal would then hear his case, coming to one of four decisions: registration without conditions (i.e. exemption); registration on condition that he undertook civilian work under civilian control; conscription for non-combatant duties in the armed forces; rejection of the application. If he was dissatisfied with the decision of the local tribunal, he could apply to the Appellate Tribunal, whose decision was final. Of the 59,192 people who appeared before tribunals (of whom 1,074 were women), 3,577 were registered unconditionally, 28,720 were registered for civilian work, 14,691 were registered for non-combatant duties, 12,204 were removed from the register and conscripted. In its operation, this system succeeded in avoiding the bitter feelings engendered by its forerunner in 1916–18. There was just one period of unpleasantness, in the spring and summer of 1940, at the height of the "fifth column" scare, and this was not of the tribunals' doing. Local councils found themselves under popular pressure to dismiss conscientious objectors and to refuse employment to those whose grounds had been accepted by the tribunals. The minutes of the debates on the question held in council chambers provide an ugly echo of the wave of intolerance that briefly disturbed the spirit of "live and let live" normally prevailing in British society. Attitudes worthy of Nazism's most fanatical ideologues found their spokesmen in elected councillors across the country: "it is time we took some steps to get rid of these leprous sores", "I have no time for CO's. They are like worms and should be trampled upon", "send them to the pits", "They should be shot at dawn", "They have a yellow streak". Plainly, for some, conscientious objection had more to do with cowardice and selfishness than with religious or moral scruples.[13] Conscientious objectors were dismissed from the employ of 19 out of 63 County Councils and 32 out of 95 County and City Boroughs, and a further 6 of the former and 14 of the latter dismissed them for the duration of the war. Protests from the Ministry of Labour and National Service and from chairmen of local and Appellate Tribunals, failed to deflect the resolve of those councils which were prepared in this way to undermine the spirit of the law that recognized the right of conscientious objection. Such councils were nevertheless a minority and, in any case, by the end of 1941 many of them had changed their stance, probably because public opinion generally had swung round. In a war where the home front was as dangerous as anywhere, pacifists, too, were demonstrating courage and self-sacrifice in the work of the rescue services. Over the war period as a whole, official and popular attitudes towards conscientious objectors were characterized far more by tolerance and understanding than by the hysteria briefly glimpsed in 1940. As things turned out, resistance to the war was a small, manageable problem for the government. Only about 3 per cent of objectors went to prison for their principles, compared with 30 per cent in the First World War. After the fall of France the Peace Pledge Union's support began to fall away and leading figures in the movement such as Bertrand Russell, Maude Royden, C. M. Joad and A. A. Milne announced their support for the war against the evil of Hitler and Nazism. The government was able, in these circumstances, to take a relaxed view of the danger of war resistance and to highlight its own virtue in its treatment of resisters. Thus the high profile exemptions granted to creative artists like the composer Benjamin Britten, the pianist Clifford Curzon and the painter Victor Pasmore, which demonstrated the authorities' sensitivity to the claim that creativity was a precious resource that must be nurtured, even in the midst of war. Again, the contrast with the barbarous way in which pacifists were treated by the enemy was striking, and provided grist to the mill of those whose task it was to show that this was indeed a war between freedom and tyranny, good and evil.

Whatever attitude conscripts had towards the idea of military service, once in uniform they usually accepted their situation and saw it through. Nevertheless, about one per cent went absent without leave, 80,000 from the army alone and at the end of the war, there were about 20,000 deserters unapprehended. The life of a deserter could rarely be an easy or comfortable one and it must be presumed that the majority of those who took this step did so because the stresses of their lives had become intolerable. For RAF bomber crews, for example, the casualty rate was about 35 per cent; small wonder that from time to time endurance gave way to primitive self-preservation, and bombers destined for the Ruhr "lost their way" and crash-landed in neutral Sweden, where their crews might see out the war without ever again being shot at. More typically, refugees from the military life disappeared into the general population, usually in large cities. In London they swelled the numbers of homeless men made up of deserters of many nationalities, American, Canadian, Australian, alongside the British. Since they had no papers and no ration books, they often stole to survive.[14] Larceny and burglary constituted the bulk of the 59 per cent increase in the numbers of indictable offences in England and Wales between 1939 and 1945 and this was one of the reasons why. Desertion was a blemish on the face of the People's War, as officially depicted; yet it was never enough to impair significantly the performance of the fighting forces or to merit drastic counter-measures.

As a new category of crime, although not recognized as such by the law, looting was virtually created by the bombing. To many of those who ended up in court, picking up something from or near a wrecked and abandoned building seemed more akin to salvaging than to stealing, in the topical spirit, even, of "make do and mend". Casual or impulsive looting of this kind, although not officially condonable, was at least understandable, especially where children were involved. But at the other end of the looting continuum were the activities of organized gangs, who swooped on fresh sites before the emergency services arrived. Numerous cases also arose of heavy-rescue and demolition squads, and even civil defence workers, taking advantage of their official work to help themselves to objects of value. During the London Blitz looting was on such a scale that the police set up a special squad to counter it. Extra patrol cars were laid on and plain-clothes officers infiltrated the rescue services to catch or deter looters. Birmingham's heavy raids in the late spring of 1941 were accompanied by serious looting, according to reports prepared for the Ministry of Home Security.[15] Whether all this amounted to a threatened breakdown of civic morality is hard to say; much of the evidence about looting is anecdotal or impressionistic. Even the Ministry of Home Security's study on Birmingham was carried out, mainly by interview, 12 months after the raids. Looting was the sort of activity that lent itself to rumour and exaggeration in the telling. Who did not know of the notorious robbing of the dead and unconscious of their valuables, following the destruction of London's Café de Paris in March 1941? Who would admit to not having seen, or heard about at first hand, an incident of the kind after a local raid? The government itself had no real idea whether the problem was serious or nugatory. Nor were local authorities better judges; at Portsmouth, for example, in January 1941, the authority requested troops to stand guard through the town against looters (thereby angering army officers, who thought it entirely unnecessary, and local citizens who felt insulted).[16] Perhaps the best measure of the seriousness of the problem is the attitude of the courts. Looting from bombed premises was in theory punishable by death or penal servitude for life, but at no time were such draconian sentences imposed. What happened, as more and more cases came up, was a tendency away from the leniency of probation orders towards deterrent sentences of five years in prison.[17]

Rumour and supposition were similarly inseparable from two other wartime activities that incurred public condemnation: profiteering and black-marketeering. Stories of fortunes made by manufacturers from government contracts in the First World War were an unshakeable part of popular memory; predictably, they were wheeled out again when once more the whole of industry went into war production mode. The government's imposition of an Excess Profit Tax was a recognition that it was bad for the national effort if, at a time of sacrifice and austerity, a few were seen to be doing well out of the war. However, the problem was that the quickest way of getting manufacturers to supply urgently needed goods was to offer them "cost plus" contracts. For routine items already in production a maximum price could be set, or cost plus a fixed profit. Where the item was wholly or partly new, however, the only way of getting agreement was on the basis of cost plus a fixed percentage, and this opened the door to profiteering. Manufacturers could artificially inflate their costs and they could absorb excess profits into bogus expenses and salaries without actually breaking the letter of the law. It was all very cynical and opportunist. And yet, on the whole, the big firms supplying the great bulk of war needs kept to the spirit of their contracts. Rumours and accusations persisted but profiteering was more mythical than real and was largely confined to small, maverick producers of goods and services.

The black market was a product of the interruptions to international trade, and the policies of Limitation of Supplies for producers and rationing for consumers. When it instituted these policies the government had two aims. The first was the prevention of price inflation in a situation where demand exceeded supply; the second was encouragement of national solidarity and effort by making sure everyone got a fair share of a reduced cake. It knew it was striking the right chord when it introduced rationing of basic foods and consumer goods in January 1940, because soundings of public opinion in the first months of the war had revealed overwhelming support for such a measure.[18] What those with money could thereafter no longer obtain on the open market, however, they could buy on the black market, where there were plenty of willing suppliers. At least, this is how it seems, for as with looting and profiteering, hard facts are difficult to come by and all is permeated with anecdote and hearsay. Every diarist recorded, and every family could subsequently recall, first-hand experience of at least "under the counter" episodes (the "grey market"), if not direct contact with the big-time operators.

Thus did Warwickshire housewife Clara Milburn, failing to see her greengrocer's notice declaring the unavailability of bananas, oranges and onions, ask for, and get (at a price), the oranges she wanted.[19]

For peacetime criminals the war simply provided new opportunities. As the police commander whose division covered most of London's docks observed: "Carcasses of meat and crates of tinned fruit disappeared . . . But such petty thefts have always been a fact of life in the docks, and the war didn't particularly change any habits".[20] Opportunities also came the way of people with no criminal past. Retailers found loop-holes in the coupons system to secure extra goods, which they could then sell on the black market. Food producers could easily hold back part of their product for the higher price it would get on the black market. Particular temptation lay before the many small farmers of Northern Ireland; the border with the Irish Republic was easily crossed and a vigorous two-way black market traffic developed. There could be few families who did not at some time have cause to be grateful for the existence of the black (or grey) market: the extra eggs to make a cake worthy to celebrate the home-leave of a serving soldier-son, the extra few gallons of petrol for a birthday expedition to the coast or hills, the length of cloth that would become a silver wedding evening gown. Understandable and innocent, perhaps, but the government took a stern view: far from providing a necessary service, the black market threatened the whole economic strategy for waging war, and undermined the very principle of equality of sacrifice. The Minister of Food, Lord Woolton, appeared in a publicity film to excoriate the immorality of the black-marketeers and to issue a warning of retribution. He set up a staff at the Ministry to keep a look-out for large-scale black-market activity and appointed nearly 900 inspectors to enforce adherence to the food regulations. The Board of Trade likewise waged war on those who were running a black market in clothing and consumer goods. It could not be otherwise. Although the vast majority of the population abided by the regulations most of the time, should an attitude of "everyone for himself" ever have taken hold, especially in the early part of the war, the defiant posture struck by Churchill's Government would surely have come to grief.

As much could be said of all the hostile, reluctant, or indifferent elements in the population. Taken together, they had the potential to sink the project of 1940. As it happened, things did not fall apart; the centre held and, perhaps more impressively, the crisis model lasted out the war.

Notes

1 *The Times*, 1 November 1914.
2 P. Graham & L. Graham, *Collar the lot!* (London: Quartet, 1980), pp.45-6.
3 A. Calder, *The myth of the Blitz* (London: Jonathan Cape, 1991), p.114.
4 Ibid., p.114.
5 The cause of distinguished exiles was taken up by nationally-known figures such as H.G. Wells, Professor Gilbert Murray and Augustus John. M. Panter-Downes, *London war notes 1939-1945* (London: Longman, 1972) p.89.
6 364 HC Debates, cols. 1532-38.
7 L. Mosley, *Backs to the wall: London under fire 1939-1945* (London: Weidenfeld & Nicholson, 1971), pp.62-3.
8 *The Spectator*, 17 May 1940.
9 A. J. P. Taylor, *English history 1914-1945* (Oxford: Oxford University Press, 1965), p.458.
10 Calder, *The myth of the Blitz*, p.83.
11 L. Woodward, *British foreign policy in the Second World War* (London: HMSO, 1962), pp.16-17.
12 Ministry of Labour and National Service, PRO Lab. 6, piece 405.
13 Quoted in R. Barker, *Conscience, government and war* (London: Routledge & Kegan Paul, 1982), p.61.
14 P. Ziegler, *London at war 1939-1945* (New York: Alfred A. Knopf, 1995), p.230.
15 T. Harrisson, *Living through the Blitz* (London: Collins, 1976), p.250.
16 Ibid., pp.185-6.
17 Ziegler, *London at war*, p.149.
18 Attlee went to see the prime minister on 7 November 1939 to report that he was getting an enormous number of telegrams demanding the imposition of rationing. J. Colville, *The fringes of power*, vol. I of *Downing Street diaries* (London: Hodder & Stoughton, 1986), pp.54-5.
19 C. Milburn, *Mrs. Milburn's diaries* (London: Fontana, 1980) p.100.
20 Ziegler, *London at war*, p.227.

Chapter Six

❧

Defending the land and the people

Bombing and invasion represented the extremes of official predictions about the course a war against Germany would take: at the very least the enemy would launch a mass bombing assault, at worst he would invade. He would be hoping to subdue Britain by the former, making the latter a simple matter of occupation. A third possibility was a naval blockade designed to starve Britain into submission. As it turned out, none of these materialized quickly, or in the anticipated order.

By the time Hitler had decided on invasion, and the necessary ships and barges were being assembled in the Channel ports, measures had been taken to consolidate the pre-war preparations to meet this threat. These measures assigned roles for all the armed services and for the civilian population as a whole. It should be added that there was a point, just before Dunkirk, when Churchill had felt it necessary to ask his chiefs of staff about the prospects of Britain being able to continue the war alone. "Not for long" was their view. The final retreat from France made them gloomier still. Churchill, however, took great comfort from a crucial fact, demonstrated at Dunkirk: Britain still controlled the air, and as long as that remained true, no invasion could succeed.

For the Royal Navy the anti-invasion role it took on in the summer of 1940 consisted largely of constant patrolling of the coastal waters from Harwich to Portland. It used a rotating 200–300 out of over 1,000 light vessels, backed by flotillas of destroyers ready to engage enemy vessels and break up any attempted landing. Its other task was the laying of minefields in western coastal waters to enable naval vessels to be concentrated in the more vulnerable waters of the east and south coasts.

Most of the army that the conscription process had been building up since May 1939 for action overseas faced the prospect in July 1940 of fighting on home soil. Its size after Dunkirk was sufficient to make it necessary for the invading enemy to mount an invasion force of at least 100,000 men.[1] Such a force would be impossible to conceal and would therefore face air and naval attack. The British army was nonetheless being trained and stationed for counter-invasion duty. General Ironside, Commander in Chief Home Forces, had begun building fixed defences of anti-tank ditches and pill-boxes several miles back from the coasts. General Brooke, who succeeded him in July 1940, favoured a more forward defence, but one which avoided manning every yard of coast. Only the most vulnerable beaches, creeks and harbours were manned, reducing thereby the number of possible landing places available to an invading force. The bulk of the troops were formed into mobile reserves (Churchill called them "Leopard" brigade-groups) that could be directed quickly to any point where the enemy succeeded in making a lodgement. In this way the Army avoided the "Maginôt syndrome", the commitment of defence forces to static positions that gave little flexibility and diluted counter-attack strength. However, the soundness of the strategy could not conceal the fact that the arming and training of the new recruits took time and expertise. An invasion in 1940 would have faced a half-armed, half-trained army. Further, equipment losses at Dunkirk had been serious; all the Expeditionary Force's heavy equipment, including over 600 tanks, had been left behind. The army had little more than rifles, and not enough even of them. By July the tank total stood at 800. Shortages of artillery and rifles had to be made good by the importation of obsolescent First World War stocks from the United States. Visiting the "invasion sectors", Churchill noted the paucity of Bren-gun carriers and tanks in the exercises the commanders put on for him.[2] He remained cheerful and optimistic nonetheless, because at heart he never believed the Germans would attempt to invade, and if they did, they would fail. The basis for this confidence was his thinking about air power. He was certain that the RAF had the capacity to protect the Royal Navy from German bombers and thereby guarantee the maintenance of Britain's supremacy in the coastal waters. In short, invasion required control of the air, and this Germany did not have. It followed that the first stage of the German plan must be to engage and defeat Britain's air force. This was the contest for which the Royal Air Force was preparing itself in June and July.

In the campaigns against Poland, Norway, the Low Countries and France, Goering's Luftwaffe had acquired a formidable reputation. The numbers, range and quality of its aircraft and the skill of its airmen made it seem invincible. Whatever it was set to do it could achieve, it seemed. Then came Dunkirk. For the first time the Luftwaffe was checked: it was unable to prevent the evacuation. The agency of its failure was the RAF. Day after day during the evacuation Fighter Command maintained patrols and engaged superior numbers of German fighters and bombers. Every available plane was deployed, even from the Metropolitan Air Force, the last reserve. Pilots sometimes flew four sorties a day. The German losses were unprecedentedly large; at the conclusion it was clear that a decisive air defeat had been inflicted on the Luftwaffe. Most public attention in Britain focused on the rescue armada, especially the motley collection of ferries, fishing-boats and pleasure-steamers – the "little ships". But Churchill took pains to draw attention to the significance of the RAF's victory over the Luftwaffe. In his speech to parliament on 4 June, after describing the success of the RAF, he went on: "When we consider how much greater would be our advantage in defending the air above this island against overseas attack, I must say that I find in these facts a sure basis upon which practical and reassuring thoughts may rest".[3] Churchill spoke thus while accepting the general belief that the Luftwaffe had a large numerical superiority. In fact, the strength of the air forces, as became known much later, did show a 2 to 1 German advantage in numbers of front-line aircraft of all types, but roughly equal numbers of fighter aircraft, in the short term the most important type. Britain's production of fighters doubled from 703 to 1,409 in the second quarter of 1940 and increased to 1,901 in the third quarter, as a result of the unconventional but effective methods used by Beaverbrook at the Ministry of Aircraft Production. This made good the fighter losses suffered in France, but the pilots were not so easily replaced: a worryingly high proportion of the pilot force in July was inexperienced.

On 14 May the Minister of War, Anthony Eden, broadcast an appeal for men aged 16 to 65, who were not in the armed forces, to offer their services for local defence. His idea was that here was a potential counter-force to invaders parachuted into Britain behind the coastal defences. Within a week 20,000 men had enrolled as Local Defence Volunteers. By June, renamed, at Churchill's suggestion, the

Home Guard, they numbered 1.5 million and had begun drilling and training. Half of the recruits were veterans of the First World War and so already had valuable, if rusty, military skills. Units served a geographical area but additional units were set up by factories, offices, and institutions like the General Post Office, railway companies and parliament itself. To begin with they lacked uniforms, equipment and even rifles and ammunition, but gradually these deficiencies were put right. The role of the Home Guard was essentially to supplement the regular forces in dealing with invaders. As Churchill combatively put it: "defending our Island whatever the cost may be". Watching from dusk to dawn for airborne landings was the major initial task. There was also the equally routine job of guarding vulnerable points by manning roadblocks and checking drivers' identity cards. More exciting were the staged exercises and the street-warfare training many units received at privately-run Home Guard schools like that at Osterley Park, set up and run by a Spanish Civil War commander, Tom Wintringham and financed initially by *Picture Post.* All this looked a bit desperate: what chance had middle-aged amateurs against the awe-inspiring Wehrmacht, fresh from its triumphs in France? But in 1940 the Home Guard filled a psychological need. In deciding that Britain would fight on alone, Churchill simultaneously led the people and expressed their will. Once the die was cast, so to speak, everyone needed to feel they were taking part in the business in hand; the Home Guard was an outlet for such feelings. In time, moreover, its amateurish appearance disappeared; by 1942 the average age had decreased, it was equipped with machine-guns and grenades, and its training, often alongside Regular Army units, included learning how to fire anti-tank and anti-aircraft guns.

For the rest of the civilian population the allotted role was to co-operate with a simple set of instructions designed to impede invaders. People were to be on the look-out for parachutists or the appearance of any kind of stranger. They were to keep maps hidden, unattended vehicles immobilized, garages and outbuildings locked. If invasion did occur (the signal would be the ringing of church bells, silent since the start of the war), everyone was to "stay put": after the fall of France the problem for defence forces of refugee-clogged roads was well-known. A Ministry of Information film of July 1940, *Miss Grant goes to the door*, depicted two middle-aged sisters using a revolver taken from a dead parachutist to confront a disguised German officer who appeared at their village home. The implication seemed to be that ordinary citizens might "have a go", but on the whole the official message was that they should act as extra eyes and ears for the defence forces, but leave the engagement of the enemy to them.

While the human defences of the country were being organized to repel invasion, the face of the land itself changed. Around the coasts, designated "Defence Areas", beaches and estuaries were given over to rolls of barbed wire and lines of concrete tank-traps. Pill-boxes and gun mountings appeared wherever it was thought invasion routes might lie. Flat, open spaces such as sports grounds and lowland pastures, which might serve as landing grounds for enemy planes or gliders, were scattered with obstructions ranging from scrapped motor vehicles to old bedsteads. To delay or confuse the enemy (and unintentionally the native traveller), signposts were taken away.

In the event, only one aspect of all this anti-invasion preparation was put to the test. As Churchill had expected, it was the RAF that would be called on to enter the lists and whose performance would determine the nation's fate. After four weeks of indecision, a breathing space put to good use by his adversaries, Hitler issued on 7 July his first directive to prepare an invasion. It had three requirements: the RAF must be effectively nullified, the minefields in the crossing zone must be swept clear, and the Royal Navy must be held back from the Channel. This done, the German army would land 260,000 men in three days on the coast between Brighton and Folkestone, and complete the subjection of Britain within a month. Hitler, then, came to the same conclusion as Churchill: the precondition for invasion was control of the air.

Despite the setback at Dunkirk, the head of the Luftwaffe, Hermann Goering was confident of being able to achieve this objective. Knowing that the Luftwaffe was larger and was more battle-experienced than the RAF, he assured Hitler that he could destroy the air defences of southern England in four days of concentrated attack. The operation required both fighters and bombers, the former to engage Fighter Command in the air, the latter to destroy its airfields and operations rooms. Three-quarters of the Luftwaffe's fighters were of the Messerschmidt 109E type, fast, manoeuvrable, and armed with four machine-guns. Its weakness was that its range was only 100–125 miles and its endurance 90 minutes. The remainder of the fighters were of the Messerschmidt ME110 type, which had much greater range but whose poor manoeuvrability made it unsuitable for combat against British Hurricanes and Spitfires. For bombing Goering was relying on the light Junkers 87 Stuka, which was slow, weakly-armed and had a low ceiling, and the medium Heinkel 111 and Dornier 217, which were also weakly-armed, and therefore needed heavy fighter escort for daylight operations.

Britain's needs, being of a defensive nature, centred on fighters. Two-thirds of these were Hurricanes, one-third Spitfires. Both types had an armament of eight guns; the Spitfire had the edge in speed and manoeuvrability. Together they were a match for the ME109s in most situations. They also had the immeasurable advantage of the radar early-warning system, backed by the Observer Corps. The coastal radar stations could pick up the approach of enemy aircraft, simultaneously alerting observers in the 1,000 manned posts and the Operations Room of the Fighter Group covering southern England. As the attackers appeared, their numbers, composition, speed, height and direction would be gauged by the observers and telephoned to the Operations Room. There the information would be plotted on large tables by discs, moved to reflect the changing situation. Finally, Controllers watching these tables would send orders to aircraft in the Fighter Stations or already in the air. With this system the RAF could neutralize the advantage of surprise that normally lies with the attacker and avoid the waste of resources that constant patrolling would entail. It appears that although the Germans knew the radio masts on Britain's coasts were something to do with her defence system, they did not realize how important they were, and therefore made no plans systematically to destroy them.

What is usually described as the preliminary phase of the Battle of Britain began on 10 July with an attempt by the Luftwaffe to establish air supremacy in the Dover Straits. It involved attacking convoys and skirmishing with British fighters in order to ascertain their tactics and capabilities. But by the beginning of August the Germans had lost twice as many aircraft as the British and so, on the 13 July, Goering proceeded to the next planned phase, the attack on Fighter Command's bases. This was designed to destroy Fighter Command on the ground or, by provoking it into a major battle, destroy it in the air. The height of this phase was 15 August, when the Luftwaffe flew 1,800 sorties, its largest ever number in one day. They included a flight of 100 bombers, escorted by 40 ME110s, sent to attack Tyneside. German intelligence had erroneously calculated that the attacks of the previous two days had reduced RAF Fighter Command to 300 machines and that eight of its main bases were out of action. Believing the North of England to be undefended, the Luftwaffe was taken completely by surprise when, as its aircraft crossed the coast, they were met by seven squadrons of Hurricanes and Spitfires. Thirty German aircraft were downed without loss, and the raiders turned back to their Norwegian base, mission unaccomplished. Meanwhile, over southern England the main battle ended with a clear defeat for the Luftwaffe: 75 losses against the RAF's 34. Attacks on shipping continued, mainly with Junkers 87s but they were so badly mauled that they were thereafter taken off front-line operations. Some bomb damage was done in the south London suburbs, and Croydon airport was temporarily put out of action. But when bad weather brought a lull on 19 August it was clear that the attackers were getting the worst of it: at this stage German losses were 290 to Britain's 114. On 24 August the battle entered its most critical phase. It began well for the Luftwaffe with crippling blows against No. 11 Fighter Group, which covered London and southeast England. Five of its forward airfields and all but one of its seven sector stations were extensively damaged. It is generally recognized that had the Luftwaffe continued its heavy attacks against adjacent sectors and inflicted similar damage, the whole communications and control system of Fighter Command might have collapsed, with consequent loss of control over London's air approaches. During this phase (to 6 September), moreover, Fighter Command was at its most depleted. It lost 103 pilots killed and 128 seriously wounded, nearly a quarter of its total strength. Replacing such losses with trained men was beyond the capabilities of the training centres. And although total aircraft losses were fewer than those of the enemy, the losses of fighter planes were beginning to outstrip production.

It was fortunate, therefore, that at this point the German leadership faltered in its tactical thinking: the attacks on the airfields and control centres were reduced and those on the radar stations abandoned. Instead, resources were switched to the bombing of London and other cities. This diffusion of effort, which was to have an important effect on the outcome of the battle, originated in a mistake. On the night of 24 August some German bombers, directed to attack aircraft factories and an oil refinery close to London, mistook their targets and instead bombed the City and East End, causing considerable damage. Churchill ordered the RAF to retaliate by bombing Berlin, which it did over several nights. The damage to Berlin was less than that to the Nazi leaders' pride, for they had assured the German people that Berlin would never be bombed. They were perhaps also worried about the effects of the attacks on civilian morale. And so reprisal attacks were ordered on British cities. For Fighter Command this was a welcome respite, during which its weaknesses were made good. The air battles continued, culminating in a major confrontation on 15 September in which Fighter Command threw every plane it had at the enormous armada Goering had assembled for the *coup de grâce*. It was a decisive day. At its end, the Luftwaffe had lost 60 aircraft, the RAF 26. A further two weeks of smaller air battles confirmed this pattern of losses. It was clear that the contest for air supremacy had gone Britain's way; the invasion threat was lifted; the war was not over.

From this time onwards, the word "invasion" never held the menace it had for the British people in 1940. The apparatus created to counter it remained in place, but increasingly it looked redundant. Instead, "invasion" became associated with the entirely benign arrival of large numbers of American servicemen in the build-up for Overlord, finally taking on the offensive connotation of that operation itself. Without the Battle of Britain there would have been no build-up, no Overlord; such was its pivotal importance in the course of the war. By failing to subdue Britain in 1940 and instead embroiling himself in the ill-fated attack on Russia, Hitler made possible the resurgence of Allied power in the West, with Britain as the springboard of its attack on his empire.

At the height of the battle Churchill had lauded the bravery and stamina of the fighter-pilots with the words: "Never in the field of human conflict was so much owed by so many to so few", and over the years since, the resonance of that Homerian line has preserved a popular image of the destiny of nations resting on the shoulders of this small group of gallant young men, modern counterparts of the 300 Spartans in the Pass of Thermopylae. It is a distorted image, and one that Churchill himself attempted to correct when he later came to write his account of the war. Then, he acknowledged the work of the many on whom "the few" had depended. It takes nothing away from the credit of the pilots to say that they were only as good as the aircraft, the information and the orders allowed them to be. Air Chief Marshall Dowding, who was responsible for air defence, devised a strategy, the basic soundness of which was vindicated by the outcome, notwithstanding the tactical differences that emerged between his Fighter Group Commanders, Park and Leigh-Mallory. Keeping the aircraft armed and serviced was itself a major undertaking; the ground crews rose to this challenge, often working under the pressure of time and bombing. Then there were the people who operated the system of intelligence and communications in the radar stations and observer posts, in the telephone service, in the operation rooms of the Fighter Groups; they, too, maintained their services through periods of intense and exhausting activity. The performance of the workers in the aircraft factories matched that of the men who flew the planes; Beaverbrook's success in maintaining the supplies of fighters, despite the fearful rate of loss in battle, was attributable as much to their Stakhanovite efforts as to his ingenuity in ensuring the sector's short-term priority in national production. Another major contribution to the maintenance of fighter strength came from the Civilian Repair Organization. This was the umbrella title for an *ad hoc* arrangement that drew on the skills of hundreds of small firms, formed into repair units at designated centres. At its peak the organization was returning nearly 200 damaged fighters per week to operational service.

Every battle is lost as well as won. In explaining the outcome of this particular battle, historians, including Churchill himself, have placed German errors alongside British merits. One of these has already been alluded to: the failure of German intelligence to discover the importance of the coastal radar network and the consequent failure to destroy it. Without the advance warning of enemy movements that this system afforded, the "narrow margin" would not have existed. The other major error was the decision at the end of August to switch the attack from the fighter stations to London. This enabled Fighter Command to recover from the previous month's battering and to continue the battle in the air.

At the risk of spoiling an heroic story, some commentators have suggested that the Germans were not wholly serious about invasion and did not make an all-out effort to achieve it.[4] They cite the pessimistic attitude towards the project of Admiral Raeder and the Naval Staff, the lack of enthusiasm of Goering and the Luftwaffe command, and the sceptical and half-involved stance of Hitler himself. And yet, in the end, a great deal of German blood and treasure was spent on the scheme. Once the battle for the air was begun, Hitler was serious enough. It would have suited him to complete his conquest in the west by adding Britain's scalp to his collection. His failure meant a loss of face that was hard to take; he would seek compensation in Russia, and in the meantime subject Britain to the test of mass-bombing.

The mass-bombing of pre-war imaginings had not materialized as feared, at the very outset of the war, and its eerie absence encouraged complacency. However, the slow start was misleading, the complacency unapt. Over the course of the war, bombing came to be a very significant part of the experience of millions of civilians in many parts of Britain. It was an ever-present menace, though of varying intensity, from the late summer of 1940 until the closing months of war. A first phase may be identified in the bombing that rather erratically formed part of the Battle of Britain. Goering's principal target was the RAF, but his air force also made raids upon other selected targets. The abortive assault on Tyneside on 15 August has already been mentioned. Merseyside was the next target: for four nights from 28 August bombs fell on the area, igniting large parts of Liverpool's centre. Most of the early bombs, however, were dropped in the London area, the worst damage being suffered by Croydon, the City and the East End. In June there were about 100 civilians killed; in July 300; in August 1,150.

The next phase began on the night of 7 September with a devastating raid on the dockland area. For 76 consecutive nights after this (2 November excepted), with an average of 200 aircraft, the Luftwaffe bombed London. Almost 10,000 people were killed in the onslaught and huge and indiscriminate damage was caused to buildings and utilities. Most of the population was forced to spend the nights in shelters, and the work of the capital was disrupted. The raids slackened off towards the end of the year, partly because of poorer weather conditions, partly because the attack was extended to provincial cities. On 14 November a massive raid was made on Coventry, an important centre for the making of armaments and aircraft. Over eleven hours from dusk to dawn, 400–500 bombers, operating in relays, released 503 tons of high explosives onto the city, killing 554 and seriously wounding 865, razing 100 acres of the centre, destroying 1,000 houses and damaging another 32,000, and severely damaging 21 important factories. The effect was even more striking than the earlier attacks on London. Coventry was a medium-sized town, in the heart of England, well away from the coasts. Here was the holocaust vision made real, confirmation of the prophecy that "the bomber will always get through" and of the consequences for urban communities. In fact, the ease with which the enemy was apparently able to strike owed a lot to the ideal conditions of a clear, moonlit night, the element of surprise, and an unusually successful marker raid that found and lit up the target for the bomber fleet. Bombers nevertheless got through elsewhere; nearly all the main industrial centres came under heavy attack during the following months, and few large towns anywhere escaped entirely. The big blitzes were on coastal cities (not by chance: they were easier to locate than inland cities), Southampton, Plymouth, Bristol, Merseyside, Clydeside, Hull. Of inland cities, Manchester and Birmingham suffered most. This phase culminated with a renewal of the heavy raids on London; that on 10 May destroyed the Chamber of the House of Commons and knocked out all but one of the main railway stations. At this point about 43,000 people had been killed by bombs.

A lull of nearly a year followed. The Luftwaffe was heavily committed on the Eastern Front and therefore had little spare capacity to keep up the attack on Britain. There was an occasional small raid and some sneak attacks by fighter bombers on eastern and southern coastal towns.

The lull was broken by the attacks beginning in April 1942 on Exeter, Bath, Norwich, York and Canterbury – the so-called "Baedeker" raids. These small-scale attacks, which lasted until early June, were Hitler's response to Britain's bombing of the historic Hanseatic ports of Lübeck and Rostock. And like their German counterparts, the British cities suffered disproportionately because they were assumed not to be targets, and therefore had weak defences and minimal post-raid services.

"Tip and run" raids on a variety of targets continued until January 1944, when a new phase of bombing opened, the "Little Blitz". This lasted until March and consisted of attacks on Bristol, South Wales and Hull, but especially on London, which suffered 13 major attacks.

The final phase was experienced by London and the Home Counties only and it took a novel form. Reports of secret long-range weapons being prepared in Germany were dramatically confirmed when pilotless planes carrying high explosives began crashing into the capital on 15 June. By the time the launch sites in France were overrun by Allied troops in late August these V1s or "flying bombs" had killed 5,475 people, seriously injured 16,000 and caused major blast damage to property.

Finally, in early September the relatively slow and attackable V1s were succeeded by the unstoppable and even more destructive V2s, or "rocket bombs". Fortunately, the launch sites of this futuristic weapon were also overrun, but not before 1,724 people had been killed and over 6,000 seriously injured.

It is not to discount the suffering of the civilian population from bombing to record that the actual human cost was much lower than pre-war planners anticipated. Instead of the predicted 1.75 million deaths and 3.5 million injured there were 60,000 deaths and 300,000 injured. Horrific though it was, 14 November 1940 in Coventry was atypical; few in Britain experienced its like. Instead, the average urban dweller was required to adjust to a level of danger and disruption that was endurable and, with luck, survivable.

What the citizen did not know, and which for obvious reasons he could not be told, was that the bombing would have been a great deal more accurate had it not been for the timely interventions of applied science. The Germans had developed a radio directional beam that could guide their bombers to their targets even at night or in fog. Intelligence Research at the Air Ministry uncovered this potentially devastating secret and the scientists quickly came up with a solution that involved radio stations in Britain "bending" the beam, so that the attackers were directed away from the cities, unknowingly to unload their bombs onto open country. This greatly reduced the effect of the attacks made in the summer of 1940, only one-fifth of the bombs falling in the target areas. But the Germans then switched to an improved device, known as the X-Gerät, which resisted bending or jamming. With this, very accurate raids, such as that on Coventry, were made during the first part of the winter of 1940, until British scientists again perfected a way of jamming the device early in 1941. At the same time there was a breakthrough in designing small radar sets that could be installed in fighter-planes, and improvements were achieved in radio ground-to-air control. During March and April the Luftwaffe's losses were becoming disproportionate to the damage it was causing. There can be no doubt that this aspect of what Churchill called the "Wizard War" made a significant contribution to the protection of Britain's cities and people from the worst that the enemy could deliver.

The contingency had at least been anticipated, and preparations to meet it had been going on for more than two years. But the immensity of the task of providing adequate protection for 48 million people meant that there were gaps in the provision that even the bombless months of the Phoney War did not suffice to fill.[5] But first came the execution of that part of the plan that sought to remove to safety vulnerable sections of the population. It began on 1 September and in three days evacuated 1.5 million people, mainly schoolchildren with their teachers, and infants with their mothers, from the designated danger areas to the reception areas. It was a remarkable feat of organization on the part of the local authorities that carried it out. Inevitably, though, the broad picture is marred by particular mishaps and organizational failures. Not one evacuee was hurt in the operation, but for some it was an unhappy experience, beyond the obvious aspect of family break-up that it often entailed.[6] In terms of its main objective, the evacuation was only a qualified success; its voluntary nature had always made the exact size of the take-up uncertain, but it was disappointing that at its end there were still large numbers of children in the areas thought most likely to be bombed. It is true that probably another two million people privately moved out of the danger zones, taking up temporary residence in the countryside. But much of the value of the September operation had been lost by the end of the year because nearly half the schoolchildren and almost all the mothers and infants had returned; the pull of home was all the stronger when it seemed that bombing was not going to happen after all. When the Blitz finally did come, in the autumn and winter of the following year, there was a second evacuation, joining up with the evacuation of children from the coastal areas that began in May. The government set up a scheme for "assisted private evacuation": free travel vouchers and billeting certificates were given to people who could make their own accommodation arrangements in the countryside. Assistance was also extended to people who wished to leave cities not in the original, now out-of-date, designated danger areas. But the story repeated itself: the drift back to the cities began and even speeded up this time, despite the bombing rather than because of its absence.[7] Although many children spent the rest of the war in the reception areas, in the end the evacuation scheme, conceived as part of ARP, involved only a minority of those eligible.

Another sort of evacuation went ahead according to plan: under "Yellow Move" 25,000 civil servants, together with their records, moved out of the capital and set up their offices for the rest of the war in spa towns and seaside resorts.

But most people were still living in areas threatened by bombing. In these areas military measures were stepped up at the start of the war: barrage balloons and anti-aircraft batteries. Local authorities had Post Office pillar boxes coated with gas-detector paint, requisitioned taxis for use by the Auxiliary Fire Services and private cars and vans for the ambulance service, and laid in supplies of papier mâché coffins for the burial of the thousands of dead expected. Citizens saw the advice and instructions of the ARP leaflets incorporated into the routine of everyday life. The blackout was total: no street lighting, traffic lights reduced to small shielded crosses of colour, no lights in trains and very little on motor vehicles. This was strictly enforced at first, but by the end of the year it was relaxed a little, allowing dim or "glimmer" street lighting at crossroads and other places, and masked headlights on vehicles. Railway carriages were allowed a faint bluish lighting. Shop windows could be illuminated at a low level but had to revert to darkness during alerts, a condition that also applied to pedestrians using dimmed hand-torches. Air Raid Precautions as they affected ordinary people were almost entirely the responsibility of the 250 local authorities, acting under Home Office guidelines. Each appointed an ARP controller whose task it was to implement the policy, working with the chief medical officer, the local authority surveyor and chief warden, and co-ordinating their work with that of the police and fire brigade. About half of the country's ARP controllers were the chief paid officers of their authority (Town Clerks or their equivalents); the remainder were elected members, often mayors. Once the bombing began, these men were immensely powerful figures, on whose competence the security and welfare of whole communities depended. And yet, they owed their positions mainly to seniority or prior status and received little in the way of training for the task they had taken on. Under their control were over 1.5 million civilians who made up the "fourth arm" – wardens, firemen, rescue-men, ambulance drivers, medical staff, telephonists and messengers. Four-fifths of these were voluntary part-timers. Nearly a quarter were women. Local control centres were set up and it was from these that the ARP controllers and their officers worked when an air-raid occurred; in large cities and in the counties there were sub-control centres, each in charge of its own area and responsible to the controller. Wardens' posts, fire stations, first-aid depots and rescue stations were distributed evenly over the area. When a raid took place the system was activated by the spot report of the warden to the control centre (there were normally six wardens to a post, and a post to every 500 people). The warden's judgement of the situation was critical; on it depended the sending of the right services to the right places. When the help came, the warden directed it to where it was needed. If it was delayed, he began the work of rescue himself. Wardens, 90 per cent of whom were part-time volunteers, were thick on the ground because of their multi-functional role during raids. In the Phoney War they were often resented as unnecessary, officious busybodies, most of all in their enforcement of the blackout. But once the action started they came to acquire almost heroic status. The system took account of the likelihood, borne out by events, that there would be great variations in the intensity of attack between one area and another. If one area's resources were insufficient for the needs of a night, the controller could ask for outside reinforcements. His request went to Regional Control, which was linked to all the control centres and could order additional services in from other areas to the hard-pressed area.

The local authorities were also responsible for post-raid services. After an attack, rest centres and emergency feeding arrangements needed to be in operation, rehousing and billeting undertaken, repairs carried out to gas, water and electricity mains and sewage pipes, damaged houses made habitable. And the citizens needed to be kept informed about what was being done and what they needed to do.

Much of the planning of civil defence was naturally the product of informed guesswork rather than actual experience. It would be surprising if the reality of mass-bombing had not revealed gaps and deficiencies in these preparations. The Blitz was among other things, then, a learning experience for everyone involved; some made better students than others.

In the protection of civilians from air-raids, no aspect was more important or more controversial than the provision of air-raid shelters. Official policy had from the start emphasized dispersal: big, deep shelters, it was thought, would encourage a "shelter mentality", that is, people would retreat from all activity and simply live in them. So provision concentrated on the family-sized Anderson shelters. Many city-centre houses did not have the garden that the Anderson shelter required, however. Just before the outbreak of war, therefore, and rather late in the day, local authorities were encouraged to start building public shelters. When in June 1940 Sir John Anderson was able to announce that the shelter programme was completed, providing for 20 million people, it was because of the building of thousands of brick and concrete surface shelters on street pavements and wasteland. His satisfaction was misplaced, for once the bombing started, the inadequacy of these communal shelters was quickly revealed: they were unable to withstand the blast of a near-miss, let alone protect against a direct hit. It turned out that many had been built without cement because of a shortage and a misleading government circular to local authorities which suggested using lime to "stretch" the cement content in the mortar and concrete. Consequently, people stopped using them and looked for alternatives. In London the obvious places were the deep stations of the Underground railway. During the Big Blitz thousands of inhabitants of the East End, who otherwise had only the unsafe street shelters, regularly slept there, showing a preference for the deepest stations – Oxford Circus, Piccadilly Circus and Hampstead. Those from West Ham might feel more bitter than most about official neglect; an argument between the government and the local council had left them without even street shelters. The council had refused to build shelters when instructed to do so in 1937–9, insisting that the war was unnecessary and would not happen. Pressed by the government, they replied that they would build them only if the government paid for them. The matter was still unresolved when the Blitz began,[8] at which point, the council panicked and demanded the immediate evacuation of the Silvertown district. On the occupation of the Underground stations and evacuation of Silvertown, the government wisely gave in to popular feeling. At the same time, it reviewed its policy on shelter provision, especially its prejudice against deep shelters. Anderson was replaced, amid some talk of scape-goating, and his successor Herbert Morrison ordered an immediate start on the construction of deep shelters for 70,000 people. He also made interim arrangements for regularizing the use of the Underground stations as shelters: the installation of bunk beds and sanitation, and a system of registration by which ticket-holders were assured of regular places. Disused stations such as Museum, City Road and South Kentish Town were specially opened up as shelters, and the Aldwych branch line was actually closed altogether and the section turned into a vast shelter.

None of this was of help to the people of Coventry, where much of the housing in the centre was too crowded for garden Andersons, and where there were no deep shelters or the alternative of the Underground.[9] The same deficiency added to the sufferings of the inhabitants of Southampton and Portsmouth. Only after the series of widely-spaced attacks on the latter did the city council begin to consider deep shelter provision, and even then, it rejected a plan for a comprehensive system under the city and settled for one to bore tunnels into Portsdown Hill, three miles out.[10] Purpose-built deep shelters were therefore unavailable in time for the Big Blitz (London's were put to good use in the Little Blitz and V-weapon raids of 1944). Councils did come to recognize the need, but only when it had been demonstrated locally; the London Blitz hardly counted as part of their learning experience. Nightly testimony to their lack of foresight was given in the "trekking" of the inhabitants to the relative safety of the surrounding countryside. This sad spectacle was a feature of 1940–41 in Coventry, Southampton, Plymouth, Portsmouth, Liverpool and elsewhere.

Morrison meanwhile took steps to improve and augment existing shelters. The cementless street shelters were demolished at government expense, and a new indoor family shelter, the "Morrison", was made available, free for most families.

Though to a lesser extent than over shelter provision, there was official failure to anticipate need in another area of Civil Defence: fire prevention and fire control. The neglect is more surprising when put alongside the extensive preparations made to deal with high explosives and (in the end, needlessly) with poison gas. Fire services were organized on a local basis. At the start of the war there were 1,666 local authorities with this responsibility. Many of the brigades were very small and lacked up-to-date equipment. The main preparation for war was in the field of manpower: the 6,000 regular peacetime firemen were augmented by 60,000 full-time auxiliaries and hundreds of thousands of part-time auxiliaries. This more than met the human resources required; what the experience of the Big Blitz revealed, however, was major organizational weakness, which impeded their efficient use. Typically, during heavy or repeated raids a local service was unable to deal with all the fires in its area. In these circumstances the solution was to request help from the fire service of neighbouring areas. In many instances the necessary assistance was forthcoming and sufficient. The system was flexible enough to allow, for example, reinforcements to arrive from Nottingham to fight Southampton's fires, and brigades from Rugby and Plymouth to appear in the London Blitz. But there were difficulties. Fire chiefs naturally tended to husband the resource of their regulars and send the less experienced part-timers. Some brigades charged for their help and offered it only to those areas with whom advance arrangements had been made. At the "incident", confusion could arise from differences between brigades in their routines and command structure. Assistance from distant brigades was sometimes made useless when the couplings of their equipment turned out to be incompatible with those of their hosts. By the end of the Big Blitz it was clear that nothing less than a unified fire service was needed. Morrison announced the creation of the National Fire Service in May 1941, to remain in being for the duration of the war. Within six months a more streamlined and efficient fire service was in place, though ironically, the need for it was never as great as it had been during the blitz of 1940 to 1941.

Some of the urgency of fire-fighting in that phase of the war might have been mitigated had there been adequate attention to fire-watching. The hazards of incendiary bombs were well known; a single canister embedded in the roof of an unattended building could initiate a major conflagration. And yet, there was no requirement on the public to participate in fire-watching as a preventive measure. The exception to this was the Firewatchers Order of September 1940, which required owners of large factories, warehouses and yards to provide night-time fire-watching. Many such premises were saved because of this simple safeguard. The massive fires in the East End of London during September and October of 1940 were in part a product of the failure of the government to give the Order a more general application. Moreover, the destructive fires in Coventry on 14 November and in Manchester on 22–23 December showed that the authorities in those cities had learnt nothing from London's prior experience. Nor had London itself. On 29 September, the City, left largely deserted for the weekend, was ravaged by fires set off by incendiary bombs. In the middle of it all was St Paul's Cathedral, largely unscathed, for significantly, it had its team of fire-watchers, who acted quickly to deal with the incendiaries that poured onto it. But most other buildings were unwatched. From Fleet Street to the Tower of London whole areas were reduced to smoking rubble; many treasured ancient buildings and churches were gone forever. The following day at an angry Cabinet meeting Churchill ordered that steps must be taken to ensure that such a disaster never happened again. Morrison announced the introduction of compulsory fire-watching, to extend to all men aged between 16 and 60; soon the increase in the number of incendiaries being dropped caused the Order to be extended to women. The tone of his radio broadcast on the Order implied that the people had been neglecting their civic duty, but as the Press, the *Daily Mail* in particular, had been urging the government to improve fire-watching organization for months beforehand, this sounded like officialdom seeking to appease its guilty conscience. The benefits of improved fire-watching were felt even in the few months that remained of the Big Blitz; by the time of the Baedeker raids and the Little Blitz it was part of civil defence routine. Few of the six million members of the Fire Guard, as it was called from August 1941, found the 48 hours duty a month anything other than an irksome chore. The service lacked status and funding, and seemed futile for most of the time. But it certainly limited the damage to property and the toll on fire-service lives. In Canterbury, for example, fire-watchers saved the cathedral despite the 6,000 incendiaries that were dropped on it, and in London 75 per cent of the fires in the Little Blitz were extinguished by fire-watchers without help from the fire-service.[11]

The "post-raid services" aspect of ARP planning was largely the product of intelligent guesswork. Here, too, the actuality produced surprises. Instead of problems of gas decontamination and mass burials, the authorities were faced with accommodating, feeding, and otherwise meeting the welfare needs of large numbers of bombed-out families. How well they coped with these scarce-foreseen tasks varied greatly from place to place. The detailed reports made by Mass Observation provide a vivid record of those differences. In Coventry, Mass Observers noted that after quickly getting the streets cleared of rubble, the civic authorities relapsed into a sort of hopeless inertia. Ten days after the raid there was little or no public transport, only two Rest Centres were operating, the utility services were confused, and there was almost no information. "The whole tempo would have been altered in Coventry if the authorities had expended 5 per cent of their energy in considering the problems of those who had not been wounded but only had their windows broken and their ears bombarded by twelve hours of row." Mass Observation's suggestions included mobile canteens, loudspeaker vans to give information, special reserves of voluntary workers, and rest centres on the safer periphery. The Council's lack of leadership and energy contrasted with the vigour and enterprise of the factories in getting back to full production, mostly within five days.

In Southampton there was a similar failure of civic leadership. The senior elected figure, the Mayor, left his key post at 3pm every day to get to his safe house in the countryside; the Town Clerk stayed at his post but was indecisive. Problems of evacuation, rest centres, food relief, transport, utilities and the like, mounted amid a general confusion, made worse by the absence of information. In consequence, large numbers of inhabitants took to trekking to and from the surrounding villages. The chaotic, unorganized nature of this led a group of RAF officers virtually to take over the main evacuation depot at Central Hall, after which there were improvements. Morrison sent the Inspector-General of ARP to investigate the Southampton situation, and as a result of his report the Regional Commissioner was asked to intervene.

Not all of Mass Observation's reports were as critical of the authorities as those on Coventry and Southampton. Nevertheless, their observers witnessed "the same sad things happening again and again" whether in Portsmouth, Bristol, Clydebank, Hull or elsewhere, and the organization condemned the inadequacy of the local and national measures supposedly providing for human welfare.[12] Writing

in 1950, the eminent sociologist Richard Titmuss endorsed Mass
Observation's view:

> The same thing for each of some thirty cities ... the same
> meagre provision of clothing, blankets and washing facilities, first-
> aid, lavatories, furniture and information and salvage services,
> the same inadequacy of unsupported public assistance officials
> and of casually organized volunteers, the same weak liaison with
> the police and civil defence controls ... All these faults were
> constantly in evidence during the winter of 1940–1 as one city
> after another was bombed.[13]

And not just then: right through the war the authorities underestim-
ated the need and learnt little from their own or others' experience.
Neither callous indifference nor lack of imagination can explain this
failure. The answer probably lies in the pride of individuals, the
governed as much as the governors. In the first place, the elected
leaders of city councils and, by extension, their paid officers, embodied traditions of local pride which they jealously guarded. Learning
from others was not part of this tradition. "What Manchester (or
Liverpool, or Birmingham) does today, London does tomorrow" was
more the attitude. To admit failure to cope with an emergency was
unthinkable: not only was it defeatist, but it would hand over to
outsiders what properly belonged "in the family". Leaders would call
upon the services of other authorities but nowhere did they resign
their powers to them. As it happened, the Minister of Home Security, Herbert Morrison, was himself steeped in this tradition; he was
therefore the last person to override a locally-elected authority. There
was the network of Regional Commissioners, set up to deal with
major breakdowns of authority, but the government was as reluctant
to use them as local authorities were to accept their powers. In
parallel with the pride of the local leaders was that of the citizens.
For the most part they took their leaders to be as much victims of
the external situation as themselves. Everyone was, so to speak, in
the same boat; grumbling was acceptable but to go beyond that
would be rocking the boat, when what was needed was unity. Besides, standing on one's own feet was deemed virtuous, depending
on charity shameful. A tendency on the one side, then, to insist that
everything was under control and on the other to "carry on" and
make light of adversity, combined to limit the possibilities of managing that adversity in the most effective way.

The record of central government in adapting ARP to the actual circumstances of bombing is scarcely more impressive than that of the local authorities. Its best work was on the purely technical side; the national shelter policy, the creation of the National Fire Service and the organization of fire-watching, have already been cited as prompt responses to revealed needs. On the "welfare" side of Civil Defence, however, the departments of government most involved, Health, Home Security and Food, showed little ability to translate experience into improvements of policy. There were some notable exceptions to this. For example, the establishment of a Directorate of Emergency Works, which sent mobile squads of men, some specially seconded from the army, to tackle the repair of damaged houses in London. Or the scheme devised by the Food Minister, Lord Woolton, creating mobile feeding convoys, known as "Queen's Messengers", which operated countrywide, first going into action in Coventry. But they were on the whole backward in analyzing their own performance, partly from a sense of self-satisfaction, partly from a spiky defensiveness about departmental independence, partly from the inadequacy of the procedures for collecting the information on which the analysis was based. It was at the Ministry of Health that this deficiency had most impact, since it was the ministry ultimately responsible for a large part of post-raid services: the casualties (killed, injured, psychologically damaged); emergency repairs to homes; restoration of water and sewerage services. Ministry of Health inspectors did not begin making detailed local surveys until early 1941. Their reports identified many serious deficiencies in local post-raid services, but no action followed this, other than the sending of a copy to the relevant local council. Things were better in Scotland. There, the Scottish Department of Health created "flying squads" to help locally, improved its inspection service, and actively developed co-operation between authorities.[14] In July 1941 Whitehall belatedly began to take seriously the lessons to be learned from the Big Blitz. Food, Health, Home Security and Transport got together to produce for the War Cabinet a special report entitled *Preparations for heavy air attacks next winter*. This correctly identified the areas that most needed improvement: joint-planning between the relevant ministries; co-operation between local authorities; information flows at all levels. In short, everyone needed to speak to and learn from one another. Some steps were subsequently taken towards this laudable ideal, but local and departmental particularism remained an obstacle. In all this generally lamentable story there was one aspect which showed government, central and local, learning and changing. Major problems had beset the health and welfare authorities of the reception areas as a result of the influx of evacuees from the cities. Treasury spending limits had given the local authorities a reason – and an excuse – for failing to provide for this extra burden. In December 1940 the Treasury relaxed its controls; more money might be spent on hostels, group homes, welfare centres and social clubs, and on a wide range of emergency services. Within six months major improvements were in place: 90 emergency maternity homes, 230 residential nurseries for under-fives (many of them Blitz orphans), 660 hostels housing 10,000 children whose families had broken up through illness, death or war service. The staffing of this emergency provision was largely voluntary, but the need was, albeit belatedly, tackled with something like the dispatch its urgency demanded. On the whole, though, government, local or national, muddled through the problems caused by bombing, failing to comprehend the need for bold, even radical, action to meet them. It was as well for Britain's urban populations that there was no repeat of the intense and prolonged bombing of 1940–41.

Any examination of how Britain dealt with the impact of bombing reveals the importance of self-help; the authorities may have provided the framework, but much of the action was that of volunteers, especially in the area of post-raid services. And where there was no framework, they created that, too. In Southampton, a month after the first of its five big raids, there were just two feeding centres in the town; one of these was St Michael's Church Hall, operated by Christian Scientists, offering tea-and-sandwich comfort to bombed-out inhabitants neglected by their representatives. The Misses Kelly, voluntary helpers at Portsmouth's beleaguered Citizens' Advice Bureau, were dealing with hundreds of enquiries a day in the informationless void that that city was in the early spring of 1941.[15] In Islington "Mrs B", a beetroot-seller, took charge of the ineffective rest centre in Ritchie Street and organized the bedding and feeding of its 300 homeless inmates.[16] Every city had examples like these of vigorous response to need by individuals or small groups. At a more organized but still largely voluntary level, were the Women's Voluntary Services, without whose contribution it is hard to imagine the post-raid services functioning at all. Typically, the afore-mentioned initiative of Woolton for mobile feeding convoys depended for its success on the wvs, who provided most of the personnel. Founded in 1938, they had uniforms (green and maroon) though no system of ranks, and they deployed a million volunteers in the welfare of human beings caught in the miseries of war. They filled the gaps left by the regular services: setting up field kitchens amid the wreckage of bombed streets; staffing the British Restaurants (non profit-making providers of cheap meals, set up by the local authorities) and mobile canteens for the homeless, for rescue workers and clearance gangs and building-repair workers; running clothing depots and mobile laundries, rest centres for the bombed-out, and nurseries for the children of working mothers. Their presence permeated the home front in this people's war. The whole voluntary effort in which they, alongside the many other voluntary organizations, participated, was testimony to the strength of British society under the testing conditions of total war and a sign that elite concern about popular morale was misplaced.

It is an understandable thing that the success of the government and people of Britain in defying the force that had subdued most of Europe became a matter of national pride. It remains an unassailably heroic story. But it cannot be doubted that, whatever the ultimate outcome might have been, Britain's survival in 1940–41, almost unique in Europe, depended on the accident of geography. Without the "moat" of the English Channel, German armed might would surely have extended over Britain. Britain's defence posture was, of course, consistent with her geographical position and was arguably sufficient to its needs. But the British people might nonetheless count themselves fortunate that they were spared the moral dilemmas of collaboration and resistance that faced other nations. The resourcefulness and resilience on which they justifiably prided themselves had never to be put to the test of face-to-face contact with the Wehrmacht, the ss and the Gestapo.

Within eight months of the ending of the Big Blitz, although victory still seemed an age away, Britain's whole outlook had changed. Instead of the predominantly defensive posture that she had perforce to adopt since Dunkirk, she had gone over decisively to the offensive. No longer alone in the fight, Britain could begin to think more seriously about taking the war to the enemy. One of the visible signs of this change was the build-up of attacking forces inside Britain itself, including the forces of Britain's allies. There had been small numbers of foreign troops in Britain since 1940 – Free French, Poles, Canadians and others. But in early 1942 United States forces began to arrive, the start of a process that eventually brought about three million American service personnel to Britain: combat soldiers, airmen, drivers, cooks, construction workers. The ultimate aim of this process was the formation of an immense force that would overcome Nazi rule in Europe, using Britain as its launching platform. Most of these friendly invaders had to wait two years or more before leaving in the great venture of Operation Overlord. But others joined their British partners in the successful combined operation against Axis forces in North Africa late in 1942. American airmen, meanwhile, went into active service alongside their counterparts in the Royal Air Force, mounting from their East Anglian and Midland bases massive bombing raids on German industrial centres. The presence of so many foreign fighting men in Britain was a heartening demonstration for the British people that the invasion of Britain now meant only this, that the years of dangerous isolation were past, and that victory was possible, after all.

Notes

1 At this point, 20 per cent of Britain's males aged 21 to 40 were in the Army.
2 W.S. Churchill, *Their finest hour*, vol. 2 of *The Second World War* (London: Cassell, 1949), pp.232–3.
3 Ibid., p.103.
4 See for example, P. Calvocoressi, G. Wint, J. Pritchard, *Total war* (London: Penguin, 1989), p.151; G. Wright, *The ordeal of total war* (New York: Harper Row, 1968), p.29.
5 See Chapter 2.
6 See Chapter 8.
7 For London there was a third evacuation when the V1 attacks began in June 1944.
8 L. Mosley, *Backs to the wall: London under fire 1939–45* (London: Weidenfeld & Nicolson, 1971), p.128.
9 In Bristol, residents took matters into their own hands by invading seven underground tunnels and turning them into unofficial shelters.
10 T. Harrisson, *Living through the Blitz* (London: Collins, 1976), pp.136, 198.
11 N. Longmate, *How we lived then* (London: Hutchinson, 1971), p.137.
12 Harrisson, *Living through the Blitz*, pp.292–3.
13 R. Titmuss, *Problems of social policy* (London: HMSO, 1950), p.309.
14 Ibid., p.303.
15 Ibid., pp.162, 192.
16 Titmuss, *Problems of social policy*, p.263.

Chapter Seven

✣

Morale

Among the legacies of the First World War was the belief, widely held - especially in Germany - that Britain and her Allies had triumphed because of the collapse of civilian morale in Germany and Austria–Hungary. The implication was that in modern war the prowess of the armed forces was in itself insufficient for victory: if the "home front" did not hold firm then all was lost. And not just the war. Where morale crumbled, social unrest followed and governments fell: the two revolutions in Russia in 1917 and those in Germany and Austria–Hungary in 1918 were an alarming reminder to governments everywhere in 1939 of the political consequences of failure to sustain the spirit and commitment of the people.

While the civilian "stab in the back" could be seen as a self-justifying myth, assiduously promoted by the German military, there remained within it the basic truth that in wars of nations the fighting spirit of the people was important. In a short war, perhaps, advance build-up of war *matériel* and the momentum of the offensive might make a significant role for the civilian unnecessary. But what the First World War had demonstrated was that in a longer conflict the servicing of the needs of mass armies demanded a sustained willingness on the part of the civilian population to endure hardship, sacrifice, anxiety and danger. Total war meant the summoning into the armed forces of a large proportion of the country's able-bodied adult males. Almost every family was thereby torn apart. Those members who remained at home were burdened with fear for the safety of those dispatched to the fighting, fear which the increased lethality of modern war would often turn into grief and despair. Total war also meant shortages of everything, even the basic needs, even food enough to sustain normal health and fitness. At the very least it meant a life robbed of many of the rights, opportunities and pleasures of peacetime.

In the 20 years following the armistice of 1918 the art of war had developed in ways portending for civilians an increased risk of violent death. The most significant development was in the capacity of aircraft to reach and bomb distant targets. Terror bombing, that is, bombing aimed at breaking the spirit of the enemy's civilian population, had had a limited trial-run in the final year of the First World War; as the Second World War began, it was widely accepted that this aspect of modern warfare would be much more significant in scale and intensity. The home front would be as dangerous as the battle front; civilians would, in effect, be in the front line from the start. It was a prospect that the government viewed with apprehension. Would the people be able to endure it? Worse, would there be mass panic and overwhelming popular pressure for peace at any price? The official view was on the whole pessimistic. Like the appeasement policy before it, the unwarlike strategy of the Phoney War period reflected the unwillingness of Chamberlain's Government to bring closer the moment when this doomsday scenario would be enacted.

Nevertheless, steps were taken which suggest that official pessimism was not absolute, that it was worthwhile attempting to prevent alarm and despondency from taking hold of the populace, that even in modern war it was possible to imagine that the people would tolerate its conditions, and work for and believe in ultimate victory. The driving impulse behind the government's pre-war programme for civil defence and Air Raid Precautions had been fear of the consequences for public order of failing to have it ready for the eventuality of war. Mitigating the strains of modern war on civilians, through properly thought out and resourced arrangements of a practical nature, made sense when public calm and resolve was sought.

But that desirable state of affairs depended also on how people perceived their condition and prospects. An excess of bad news, the circulation of alarmist or defeatist rumours, or simply insufficient information about what was happening could act negatively upon public morale. It was to ensure that the most positive presentation of war news was received by the public that a Ministry of Information was created at the outbreak of the war. Its basic brief was to sustain the morale of the people since this was the means by which its other objectives, defined by the War Cabinet in July 1941, were to be achieved: "to stimulate the war effort and to maintain a steady flow of facts and opinions calculated to further the policy of the government in the prosecution of the war".[1]

One of the Ministry's first tasks was to urge people to co-operate with the implementation of the elaborate plans for the evacuation of schoolchildren, infants and mothers from the major cities to the countryside. The idea was that minimizing the number of casualties from the expected air bombardment would help preserve public morale. For millions of civilians this was their first experience of the government's concern for their mental wellbeing. The initial response to this entirely voluntary scheme testified to the fact that the popular view on what bombing would be like was close to official wisdom. In any case, those who could, had been privately removing themselves to safer parts from midsummer onwards. Hotels, boarding houses and cottages to let in Scotland, Wales and the West Country were fully occupied well before the official evacuation began, confirming the government in its opinion that a mass flight from the towns would happen anyway, and that they had been right to put in hand a scheme to ensure that it happened in a calm and orderly way. Apprehensions of mass panic, however, turned out to be unjustified. Had the war begun in the way many had forecast, with immediate heavy strikes by enemy bombers against the principal cities, Churchill's talk of three or four million people pouring out of London under pressure of continuous air attack might have become a reality. As it was, no such pressure was experienced; the evacuation was allowed to proceed without the additional fear and disruption actual bombings would have brought. The whimsically code-named "Operation Pied Piper" succeeded in moving one and a half million people from the "evacuation areas" to the "reception areas" in the space of four days. This was fewer than had been planned for; there was great regional variation, in proportion to the energy with which local authorities promoted the scheme. Less than half the school-age population of the evacuation areas in the event made the move. And paradoxically, the morale of those who stayed appears to have been higher than those who went, the consequence of the failure of the expected Luftwaffe bombardment to materialize. In the absence of the altogether more serious problems that bombing would have brought, attention focused on the lesser difficulties experienced by many of those involved in the evacuation. Whether mothers went with their children or not, families were broken up. Disorientation and homesickness commonly afflicted even children lucky enough to be billeted with welcoming and caring families. There were many cases where the social distance between guests and hosts made for an unhappy experience on both sides. Most of the visitors were from areas characterized by poor housing and poverty; houses in the reception areas with space for guests tended to belong to the comfortably off. Differences in urban and rural life styles were also a source of conflict. Harold Nicolson believed that the ill feeling was "not between rich and poor but between the urban poor and the rural poor", but this reads like a class defence.[2] The conclusion American historian Travis Cosby made in his detailed study of the evacuation was that, whereas the wealthy and middle-class inhabitants of the reception areas avoided evacuation duty, working-class householders welcomed evacuees, "or at least tolerated them in a benign fashion".[3] Within a few weeks the pain of the mismatch was evident, both in the wave of complaints from hosts – mainly about the verminous conditions, dirty habits and slovenly ways of their guests – and in the accelerating tendency of parents to bring their children back home, once it seemed clear that it had all been a false alarm. Evacuation, although in most respects an organizational success, had become less a palliative for the rigours of modern war on the home front than a cause of discontent and social strain. Much of this was self-regulating; the return to the cities continued, so that by the end of the year 40 per cent of the school-children and 90 per cent of the mothers and infants had returned home. Nevertheless, if social solidarity was to be a factor in winning the war the glimpse of class war revealed in the evacuation of 1939 was not a wholly encouraging episode.

The hang-fire of the Phoney War made redundant another aspect of the government's anti-panic policy. During the Munich crisis 38 million gas masks had been issued; when war was declared, everyone was enjoined to carry their mask at all times. The sense of security it was supposed to impart was not sought, however, since the Luftwaffe failed to appear, and by November most adults, at least, regarded it as dispensable and left it at home.

Although it was a relief to the government that war had not immediately brought about the mass emergency it had thought probable, the state of popular morale continued to be a source of official anxiety. Ministry of Information soundings of the people's mood found boredom and apathy to be widespread. There was bewilderment about the anti-climax following the tension of the final negotiations to avert war. Why had Britain not followed up its stand for Poland with military action against her attacker? Was the government not serious about waging war, and looking rather for a diplomatic get-out? Was the whole ARP operation mistaken and unnecessary?

Scepticism, complacency, false optimism – these were dangerous attitudes which, in the view of the Ministry, might easily degenerate into defeatism: when the real test came, public morale would be unequal to it.[4]

But the government's own actions, or lack of them, make the generally negative public attitude understandable, if not justifiable. Chamberlain made no effort to set out the country's war aims, and the leisurely pace of the process of controlling resources and mobilizing the economy for war gave the wrong signals to the average patriotic citizen looking for a lead. Moreover, the Ministry of Information, charged with the task of sustaining public morale, was for most of this period a troubled institution whose own morale was poor. Its chief officers were aware that nothing could be worse for morale than denying the public adequate information about what was going on; that, within the limits of security needs, as much as possible of war aims, military strategy and the ends and means of home-front policies ought to be made clear to the people. The problem was that the sources of much of this information, the defence departments, were unwilling to part with it, taking an exaggerated view on what information might be of military value to the enemy. They treated the new ministry as an untrustworthy upstart and were no more co-operative towards the Press and Censorship Board, which for seven months from October 1939 took over from the Ministry responsibility for news and censorship. In consequence, little "real" news reached the media at all and people started turning instead to German versions of the news, especially to that of William Joyce (Lord Haw-Haw), who nightly plugged the news gap via the transmitters of Radio Hamburg, with predictably depressing effect on the public mood.[5] Other disruptions to the Ministry's activities arose from several organizational changes, frequent changes of personnel (including no less than three Ministers between October and May), and a steady reduction of its powers. Despite this unsettled backcloth, accompanied by criticisms of the amateurishness of its communications to the public, the aloofness of its house style, the absurdities and inconsistencies of its censorship (largely the fault of the service departments, it must be said), the Ministry of Information was at least able to establish a reasonably reliable system for gauging the state of public morale. It did this by tapping into a variety of information sources: the reports of its own Regional Information Officers, the surveys carried out for it by the independent Mass Observation organization, police duty-room reports, which came via the Home Office, the Postal Censorship on mail leaving the country, and the reports of the BBC's Listener Research Department. From this amalgam the government came to know that it was on the whole failing to convince the people that there really was a war and that its direction was in safe hands. When the news of the defeat in Norway came through in April, its impact on an already apathetic public was disproportionately large. In the view of the Home Intelligence Division public morale was brought to its lowest point in the eight months of the war. Not that defeatism was rife. Public opinion polls showed that although Chamberlain's approval rating had fallen from its 70 per cent high in November, it was still standing at 50 per cent just before his resignation in May. And there was a heartening response to Eden's broadcast appeal for recruits to serve in the Local Defence Volunteers: within 24 hours 250,000 recruits had come forward. People might distrust the authorities and express dread of what the future held, yet in response to a poll taken at the point where the Low Countries were being overrun, only 3 per cent thought that Britain might lose the war. This optimism was apparently undented by the retreat of the British Expeditionary Force from Dunkirk and the fall of France. No doubt such irrationality came in part from a psychological need to avoid contemplating the prospect of defeat, but partly also from a stubborn belief that, as ever before, Britain would prevail against her foreign enemies. Had the ruling elites as much blind faith in Britain's destiny there would have been more good cheer in high places. For, as Harold Nicolson noted in his diary, there was near-panic in "Service circles" at the threat of invasion that followed France's collapse.[6] As we have seen, the government's moves to intern enemy aliens, tighten censorship and to prosecute those who spread alarm and despondency were a reaction to alarm signals from army chiefs rather than to actual signs of popular faint-heartedness. Nicolson's own department was as guilty as any of underestimating the spirit of the people: on 22 May 1940 it set up a Home Morale Emergency Committee to suggest measures to "counter the danger of a break in morale" and, after the fall of France (and disbelieving its own soundings), undertook a programme to stamp out rumour (the "Silent Column" campaign), to reassure the people of the resources and resolution of the armed forces and Empire, and to rally them behind the strategy of "repel the invader". Much of the propaganda put out during the perilous summer of 1940 reflected the mixed feelings of those in power about the capacity of the civilian population to rise to the demands of the crisis. In *Britain at bay*, made by the GPO Film Unit for the Ministry of Information, with J. B. Priestley providing the commentary, the audience is plied with reassuring facts: the strength and expansion of Britain's armed forces, the support of her Empire and Dominions, the gearing up of her industrial might for war, her historic success in repelling would-be invaders, and the present determination of her people to defend their stand. The "To-Arms" bugle-call may have provided an apt musical motif for the film, but it scarcely shuts out the sound of whistling in the dark.

Nicolson later rather shamefacedly repented his glumness and admitted to feelings of anger and pride over Dunkirk ("How infectious courage is!"), although he remained convinced that defeat was coming.[7] Government lack of faith in the people's spirit was still in evidence in the second week of June, when the Cabinet decided that no news of the evacuation of Narvik should be made public. But by August the Silent Column campaign had been abandoned, an official recognition that the government had over-reacted and had not trusted the public enough.

Priestley was also the BBC's choice when it cast round for a morale-raising speaker who would command the ear of the ordinary citizen. The Corporation rightly judged that his down-to-earth, Yorkshire-accented voice would be more effective for the job than the public school, received-pronunciation tones of the majority of its speakers. Using the *Postscript to the news* spot after the nine o'clock evening news for his weekly fifteen-minute talk, Priestley had on average an audience of 31 per cent of the adult population. At a time when it was most needed, here was a voice of the people that could effortlessly reach the minds of the people by speaking of their courage, humour and quiet determination. These, he said, were qualities that the Nazis lacked and which in the end would defeat them. More whistling in the dark, perhaps, but nevertheless striking a sympathetic chord with the public and helping to create for the British people an image of itself which, idealized though it doubtless was, served as a model to be aimed for in the testing times that lay ahead. The "Dunkirk spirit", that amalgam of reality and myth, was first evoked, of course, by Winston Churchill in his uncompromising "we will fight on the beaches" speech to the Commons on 4 June. Churchill's role in sustaining popular morale – and indeed, elite morale – at this low point in Britain's fortunes, was itself uniquely important. As Vere Hodgson reflected in her diary: "We have never been so near defeat as we were in June, nor so near invasion on our actual soil. It was just touch and go – and he saved us".[8] His stature was far more than the product of press lionization. In his speeches, bearing and actions at this time he personified defiance and resolution, and this readily communicated itself to all who saw or heard him.[9]

In September 1940 the dread of the unknown that might lie ahead gave way to coping with the more concrete reality of the next phase of the war: bombing. The arrival at last of the long-expected and much-feared assault on the civilian population revived the anxiety of government departments that the people would be unable to endure it. By May 1941, when the "Big Blitz" slackened off, the speculation was over: they did endure it, morale intact. It was a severe test, which on more than one occasion caused official qualms to re-surface, but at its end it was plain that, in the words of a September 1940 propaganda film, Britain could "take it", that the doom scenario of moral and social collapse was wrong.

As the London blitz began, the government showed the extent of its secret fears: a second evacuation was put into operation; a network of psychiatric clinics near London was prepared to deal with bombing neuroses or shell-shock; members of the 4th Battalion Grenadier Guards at Wanstead were put on stand-by to help the police keep order in the East End; the BBC was instructed to report on bombed towns in a future-orientated way, emphasizing planning, rebuilding, improvements; the existence of time-bombs was kept secret; when Bond Street and Burlington arcade were hit, it was not reported; the evidently unsuccessful night-fighters were withdrawn and the no more successful, but more reassuring, anti-aircraft barrage was stepped up. It is true that reports came in of bitterness and class resentment in the East End over the inadequacy of air defence and shelter provision, and what looked like official indifference towards the Luftwaffe's concentration on that side of the capital, but this faded when the Underground stations were allowed to be used as night shelters and when the bombing spread to include the more affluent districts. Mass Observation, surveying in Coventry after the hugely destructive air-raid of 14 November, reported signs of "hysteria, terror, neurosis . . . suppressed panic"; but within a week the city had resumed normal work and production.[10] Plymouth was bombed six times between November and the following April, an experience which decided many of its inhabitants to "trek" nightly into the surrounding countryside. But the Home Secretary Herbert Morrison's assumption that this signified the collapse of Plymouth's morale was mistaken: the "trekkers" returned to the city every morning to get to work and, as in Coventry, normal life and production was re-established. In terms of the practical response of the authorities to air-raids, however, performance was sometimes pitifully inadequate. Although the London blitz furnished plenty of instruction, those responsible in the regions for ARP and post-raid services showed repeatedly that they could not or would not learn from the experience of others. The same mistakes of organization occurred in Coventry, Plymouth, Southampton and the rest: slowness of response; absence of clear instructions to the public as to what they should do; insufficient shelter provision; failure to tackle with vigour the repair of the public utilities and the provision of emergency accommodation and feeding. In short, a general hopelessness and lack of leadership is not too harsh a judgement on many civic authorities in 1940–41. And yet, by any measure, public morale held up: no hysteria, no mass panic, no defeatism. Home Intelligence surprised itself by discovering that in the early raids on bombed towns, morale was high and that there was "even a feeling of growing exhilaration".[11] Its intelligence reports on the heavier bombing of the autumn and winter concluded that the general picture of morale was good. The number of patients attending London hospitals with neurotic illnesses declined, and there were so few patients for the special psychiatric clinics that most were closed. The waiting Grenadier Guards were stood down.[12] So confounded was the government by civilian reactions to bombing that instead of feeling it had to conceal the reality of what happened, for example, in Coventry, it was able to have the king and queen visit the city so that their warm reception by its valiant citizens might be recorded for the newsreels to show nationwide as evidence of the indestructibility of the people's spirit and, by implication, as an inspiration for all who had yet to experience bombing. In this way, a process begun a month earlier in the making of the film *Britain can take it* was continued and complemented, that is, the creation for propaganda purposes of an image of the British people under fire that was compounded of both wish and reality. Made for the MOI by the Crown Film Unit with Humphrey Jennings as director and the American columnist for *Colliers Weekly Magazine*, Quentin Reynolds, providing the script and commentary, this five-minute film sought to encapsulate the "spirit of the Blitz" by showing Londoners calmly adjusting to the disruption and danger of the bombing, getting to work, doing ARP duty, sleeping in shelters. In admiring tones, Reynolds assures his audience that "there is no panic, no fear, no despair in London Town . . . London can take it". Many more films were to follow – documentaries, newsreels and feature films – that took up and elaborated the stereotype of British civilians braving the bombing with calm resolution, instinctive comradeliness and undimmed cheerfulness. But this was no mere propaganda construct: its basis was essentially true. The majority of civilians really did make the best of their situation, adjusting to the changes, carrying on with what they had been doing as far as possible. Mass Observation and Home Intelligence reports provide overwhelming evidence to support the claim that has often been made that the emergency brought out the best in most people, that neighbourliness and disregard of class distinctions came more readily in this situation of shared danger and anxiety. It could be said that to some extent people were trying to live up to an image of themselves set by the propaganda stereotype and that there was a sense of pride involved for the citizens of, say, Liverpool to show that they could match the "performance" of Londoners. No amount of attention paid to the counter-indications of looting, absenteeism, black-marketeering and panics can conceal the fact that, although ubiquitous, this behaviour attached to but a small minority of the population. The Ministry of Information studied reports of defeatism, anti-war feeling, scapegoating, looting, criticism of local authorities' air-raid and post-raid services, depression, hysteria and trekking. It concluded that none of these attitudes or behaviours was significant or lasting; the people appeared to be infinitely resilient. As its report of October 1941 put it: "There is at present no evidence to suggest that it is possible to defeat the people of Britain by any means other than extermination".[13]

Writing many years later, Tom Harrisson summed up Mass Observation's more subjective impressions of public morale in equally unequivocal words: "The Blitz . . . failed over any period of more than days appreciably to diminish the human will, or at least the capacity to endure".[14] Outsiders, with no reason to be partisan, confirmed the home-produced findings. While it is true that in March 1941, at a time of heavy air-raids, Ed Murrow thought that morale was "near-rock-bottom", this was an untypical report: the overall picture he and his fellow-American correspondents (Reynolds, Farson, Sevareid et al.) presented to their audiences was one of a people, bloody but unbowed, "carrying on" and "taking it", in the catch phrases of the day.[15] To the extent that confidence in the government is an indicator of morale, the opinion poll soundings tell a similar story: in August 1940 Churchill's approval rating, according to Gallup, was 88 per cent and was still at 87 per cent the following June. Satisfaction with the government's conduct of the war was not as high but stayed above 50 per cent during this same period, despite the absence of good news from the battle-fronts.

At the height of the Blitz a Gallup poll showed that 80 per cent still believed Britain would win the war, albeit after a long struggle. This did not stop the Ministry of Information from seeing its main task as convincing the people that in the end Britain would be victorious. Because there were as yet no grounds for optimism, it thought the government ought to create incentive by making a firm pledge of post-war social reform. There was no Home Intelligence evidence, however, to show that the people would not fight without such a pledge. Besides, Churchill was against using post-war social reform as a morale-raiser, and forbade the MOI to use the idea.

With the arrival of Brendan Bracken as Minister in June 1941, the Ministry of Information reviewed its aims and methods, concluding that morale propaganda as such was unsuccessful and generally discredited, and that while the Ministry ought still to be aiming to sustain morale, this was best achieved through explanation and education directed at both the government and the public. Bracken believed his department should act on the premise that the public were happy to make sacrifices if the need was clearly explained and the burden fell equitably. The people did not need to be chivvied into calmness and courage.[16] Hitherto the Ministry had taken wrong or unnecessary measures because it had misunderstood and distrusted the public, questioned its courage and confused its grumbling with defeatism.[17] Taking a new brief in June 1941 to co-ordinate the publicity of all government departments, with the object of making it consistent, cohesive, and efficient, the MOI played an important part in persuading the government that victory depended on an openly-acknowledged partnership between government and people.[18] As the start of the long haul through "the tunnel" began, those in authority at the local or national level were rather more knowledgeable about the mettle of the people than they had been a year before, and also more experienced in the ways of exploiting it.

At the same time, the nature of the problem changed. With the removal of the menace of invasion and the petering out of the Big Blitz, panic and defeatism were no longer seen as threats. In their place came apathy and war weariness. The sense of crisis was gone but there was a long wait for good news from the military fronts; not until the victory of the 8th Army over Axis forces at El Alamein was there anything much to cheer about. Some comfort could be taken from the ending of Britain's isolation through the entry of the USSR and the USA into the war, but neither of those events made an immediate difference to the progress of the Axis. A succession of reversals had a depressing effect on the national mood: the scrambled retreat from Greece in April 1941, followed by defeat in Crete a month later; the sinking by the Japanese of the battleships *The Prince of Wales* and *The Repulse* in December, followed by their capture of Hong Kong, Malaya, Singapore and Burma; in North Africa, the fall of Tobruk and the Army's retreat into Egypt in June 1942. And all along, although this was not common knowledge in the way the high profile episodes listed above were, the steady attrition of shipping losses inflicted by the U-boats. These events were, as we have seen, at a time when dissatisfaction with the government was at its greatest and when challenges were made to Churchill's leadership. Things never seemed quite so bad after El Alamein. At last the war news began to include unambiguous successes: Operation Torch and the clearing of North Africa; Stalingrad and Russian advances; Allied landings and advances in Italy, followed by the Italian surrender; American landings in the Solomon Islands and New Guinea. There could be no doubt about the war's outcome: light was at last visible at the end of the tunnel. It was a long tunnel, nevertheless. The certain prospect of ultimate victory was the bedrock of the people's morale, but it did not ensure their stamina, their commitment, their ability to defer gratification through the long months and years it was taking to get to those "broad sunlit uplands" Churchill had spoken of. Of all the tasks of government in this period, none was more difficult to tackle than that of persuading the civilian population not to become complacent, to slacken its effort, or to withdraw its willingness to comply with the austere regime the war demanded. Relieved of the mental burden of imminent catastrophe, people naturally sought for themselves an easing of the frustrating constraints of wartime life. This is not to belittle the continuing stress and anxiety that many thousands experienced through the dangers to which their loved ones in the fighting services, merchant marine and rescue services were exposed. It is merely to note the very real difference made to the state of mind of the nation by the ending of the emergency of 1940–41. For the government, the alarm signals of war weariness were to be seen in the opinion polls and Home Intelligence reports. The national unity of the 1940 emergency was giving way to revived class feeling and apprehensions about a return after the war to the bad old days of high unemployment and low living standards. Disaffection was also read into the strikes, absenteeism and flagging productivity increasingly besetting the industrial sector, and in the incidence of anti-social behaviour such as looting, black-marketeering and profiteering. A judicious mixture of pressure and persuasion was believed to be appropriate treatment for the malaise in industry (see Ch. 4) and a policy of zero tolerance the remedy for the "anti-socials" (see Ch. 5). Other ways, too, were devised to keep the mental state of the nation healthy, notably censorship, propaganda and welfare.

At the outbreak of war it was clear that the government intended to use the mass communications media as instruments of war on the home front, not just for dissemination of information, but also for fostering and maintaining the popular will to win. For the former function it avoided the crudity of direct controls, using instead the more subtle technique of getting the media to exercise self-censorship, while at the same time imposing tight government control over the sources of information. This meant that news editors were very dependent for their material on what the service ministries and the MOI chose to release and on the already censored offerings of the commercial news agencies. Any other material they might come by had to be used with caution; the government's Defence Notices provided guidelines on sensitive material, and wise editors submitted to the Censorship Division of the MOI items they were uncertain about. Under Defence Regulation 3 it was an offence to "obtain, record, communicate or publish information which might be of military value to an enemy". Concern to keep the enemy in ignorance had led the government in the early months of the war, as we have seen, to starve the media, and thereby the public, of news. The generally resentful reaction of the media to this apparent indication of official distrust eventually led to a better working relationship. Official sources became more communicative, and nervousness about the reliability of the media abated despite, or perhaps because of, the decision which for 18 months from January 1941 kept the Communist *Daily Worker* and *The Week* from appearing. A fairly close watch was kept on the BBC, but the Corporation's fears that the government would take it over proved altogether false; certainly Churchill, in May 1940, talked about taking it into government control, but by the time Bracken became head of MOI in July 1941 the idea was not being pressed. Bracken himself thought the only point in taking such a step would be to tackle deteriorating public morale, and as morale was by this time evidently steady, there was no need. McLaine describes the BBC's wartime relationship with the MOI as one of "protective custody", with the Corporation enjoying a large measure of independence and the Ministry shielding it from the occasional demands for it to be taken over.[19] The government secured the co-operation of the film industry with much the same mixture of voluntarism and regulation used with the other media, with the added devices of dispensing the scarce supply of film stock, labour and studio space, and awarding contracts for films to favoured companies, that is, to those who showed themselves to be amenable to the government's view of the role of cinema in the war effort. From the start of the war the newsreel companies were working closely with the head of the Films Division of the MOI, Sir Joseph Ball, and important commissions were quickly forthcoming. An agreement was also secured between the government and the Cinematograph Exhibitors' Association under which cinemas would set aside about ten minutes of each programme for films the government wished to be shown, although it must be added that had the Association refused this, Defence Regulation 55 could have been used to enforce it.

In all its dealings with the media the government never seriously departed from the principle of freedom of expression: censorship applied to facts not to opinion. Defence Regulations existed to ensure that the enemy did not gain advantage from the unwise or inadvertent communication of militarily valuable information, such as the presence and size of certain army regiments in particular locations, the name of a torpedoed naval vessel, or the destruction of a particular armaments factory.[20] But there was bound to be an area between fact and opinion where the line was hard to draw; even practised editors found themselves in trouble with the authorities. Ministers, too, irritated by media criticism, occasionally strayed across the line. Churchill himself reacted to the *Sunday Pictorial's* attack on ineffectual ministers in October 1941 by demanding the paper's suppression. On this occasion the Home Secretary, Morrison, persuaded the Cabinet to veto the idea. "The democratic principle of freedom for expression of opinion" he said, "means taking the risk that harmful opinions may be propagated".[21] The suppression of the *Daily Worker* and *The Week* appeared a more clear-cut issue: the charge on that occasion was that they had published material "calculated to ferment opposition to the war", and were thereby in breach of Defence Regulation 2D. Their reappearance in September 1942 ran no such risk; on the contrary, with USSR as protagonist in the Allied cause, they were only too keen to do their bit.

Preventing the media from helping the enemy was hardly the major problem the government had imagined. More worthy of its attention was the potential the media had for maintaining the commitment and effort of the people. For the most part the professionals were more than willing to co-operate in this endeavour. Although the Press was the least biddable of the media, its general tone was constructive and there were many occasions when it was prepared to collaborate with government departments. *Picture Post*, for example, worked with the MOI to produce issues on special topics that the Ministry wanted the magazine's five million readers to know about. There was nothing, of course, to stop the Press promoting its own morale-sustaining themes. Many newspapers and magazines, *Picture Post* among them, took up the recommendations of the Beveridge Report as at once a war aim worth fighting for, and the perfect antidote to war weariness. Some in government would have preferred the Press not to have made so much of this particular topic, but did come rather grudgingly to recognize its incentive value. Much the same price had to be paid for the collaborations the government made with the film industry. The newsreel companies were normally obliging, their product invariably in tune with whatever campaign theme the MOI was currently promoting. The freer spirits of the documentary and feature film industries, however, were less willing to become mere executants of official policies. Alongside films whose official propaganda provenance is plain, therefore, the output of the war years includes films whose message for the British people reached beyond victory to the sort of society that might emerge from it.

Writing in October 1941, Ian Dalrymple, the head of the Crown Film Unit, which used the talents of many of the members of the pre-war documentary film movement, gave a succinct statement of its propaganda philosophy:

> When we make propaganda we tell, quite quietly, what we believe to be the truth . . . We say in film to our own people "This is what the boys in the services, or the girls in the factories, or the men and women in Civil Defence, or patient citizens themselves are like, and what they are doing. They are playing their part in

151

the spirit in which you see them in this film. Be of good heart and go and do likewise".[22]

Numerous short documentaries were made that focused on particular service or civilian groups, reminding the public at large of everyone's dependence on everyone else. Jack Holmes's *Merchant seamen* (1940), Humphrey Jennings's *Heart of Britain* (1941) and Paul Rotha's *Nightshift* (1942) fall into this category. Serving a similar inspirational purpose were a number of feature-length documentaries such as *Target for tonight* (1941) on the RAF, *Fires were started* (1941) on the Auxiliary Fire Service (AFS) and *Western approaches* (1944) on the Merchant Navy, in which dramatized episodes of the war were reconstructed, using their real-life participants. Something of the realism of documentaries found its way, largely via inspired emulation, into feature films made by the commercial studios, for example, Noel Coward's *In which we serve* (1942), which was about the Royal Navy, and Carol Reed's *The way ahead* (1944), which paid tribute to the ordinary army serviceman. Many other feature films were made that took up the theme of the British people, in and out of uniform, working like a team for victory. At Michael Balcon's Ealing Studios this was the thrust of three films released in 1942–3: *The bells go down* (about the AFS), *San Demetrio London* (Merchant Mariners get their damaged tanker safely to port), *The foreman went to France* (Englishman, Scotsman and Welshman prevent vital machinery falling into German hands. Was this, one wonders, a conscious borrowing from Shakespeare's *Henry V*, also a rescue story in which the British nationalities team up for a French trip, and which itself appeared on celluloid in 1944?). Meanwhile American William Wyler directed *Mrs Miniver* (1942), in which Britain's class system was obligingly shown not to be dysfunctional, after all.

Cinema audiences (which meant 70 per cent of the adult population, according to the Wartime Social Survey) were therefore well dosed with uplifting, inspirational fare, and the film industry's patriotic heart was at the same time demonstrated. The price paid for the industry's co-operation, however, was the production of films that attempted to put social reform higher on the political agenda. This had not been in the mind of the director of MOI's Films Division when he wrote in July 1942 that he welcomed films that carried "non-war propaganda", that is, where emphasis was given to "the positive virtue of British national characteristics and the democratic way of life".[23] Several film-makers found the implied complacency of this unacceptable. They believed that the experience of "the people's war" was disclosing the defects of British society and changing people's desires and expectations for the future. Through the medium of film a vision of post-war society could be articulated that would serve to sustain morale better than one that implied all was well, and that the war was being fought merely to preserve the order of 1939. Roy and John Boulting audaciously made the going in *The dawn guard*, a documentary commissioned by the MOI in 1941. Here the vision of a different and better Britain after the war was put over in the words of a member of the Home Guard. Jennings's *Fires were started*, also made for the MOI, seemed to be just about the here and now but, as Angus Calder has suggested, the film is "replete with intimations of a classless new order".[24] In Gilbert Gunn's documentary *Tyneside story* (1943) the closing shot of the ship-building yards at full-stretch is overlaid with a voice, saying: "Tyneside is busy enough today . . . but just remember what the yards looked like five years ago . . . will it be the same five years from now?" It was in the feature films of John Baxter that this notion of "the people's war" as a war not just of the people but *for* the people was most explicit. He began with *Love on the dole* (1941), based on Walter Greenwood's novel about the Depression years. Underlining the implied message of the film was a postscript caption which appeared at its end, signed by First Lord of the Admiralty, Albert Alexander: "Our working men and women have responded magnificently to any and every call made upon them. Their reward must be a New Britain. Never again must the unemployed become the forgotten men of peace". Baxter went on to make *The common touch* (1941), *Let the people sing* (1942) and *The shipbuilders* (1943), in all of which the underlying theme was that the war was only worth fighting for if it was the means to the creation of a better, fairer society. This, too, was the sentiment of Ealing Studios' *They came to a city* (1944) where, through its characters, the author (J. B. Priestley) appealed for a future of co-operation rather than greed, envy and hate.

That films of such politically controversial potential could be made and distributed under the constraints of the wartime information regime is testimony to the relatively liberal and open-minded attitude of the MOI under Bracken's management. Far from seeing the "new order" film makers as boat-rocking dissidents who needed to be held back in the interests of the single-minded pursuit of victory, the men from the ministry actively encouraged them, in the belief that, certainly in terms of the morale of the nation, and perhaps also in terms of human justice, war aims *should* encompass the quality of life of the ordinary citizen. The Ministry's problem was that any encouragement of debate about reconstruction risked running foul of Churchill's insistence that ministers should not "deceive the people by false hopes and airy visions of Utopia and Eldorado". Finding a balance between Churchill's ban and the need to promote an optimism about the future prevented the MOI from exploiting the excitement aroused by the Beveridge Report to boost morale and counter war weariness. It cramped the BBC's style, too. Discussions with the MOI in January 1941 for a series of debates on peace aims went on for six months, coming to nothing as it became clear that, given Churchill's known views, the debate would be too confined to have any interest. The Corporation had nevertheless started the reconstruction debate, perhaps unknowingly, when it invited J. B. Priestley to give a series of *Postscripts* in 1940. In several of these talks Priestley linked the upheaval and demands of the war with the building of a better post-war society. His second series, which began in January 1941, was sharper in tone and produced complaints from the 1922 Committee and angry memoranda from the prime minister to the MOI. The BBC's courage failed it and Priestley's contract was not renewed. This produced a heated debate in the Press over the rights and wrongs of the matter; but the decision stood. The affair caused widespread belief that Priestley had been muzzled by orders from above; it also caused loss of confidence in the independence of the BBC, and damage to public optimism about the future. From the standpoint of popular morale this was unhelpful.

But reconstruction talk would not go away. On the contrary, after the Atlantic Charter (August 1941) which, on Ernest Bevin's suggestion, included a clause by which the Allies pledged themselves to the creation of post-war social security at home, and especially after the publication of the Beveridge Report in December 1942, there was no containing it. The Press, the magazines, the Army Bureau of Current Affairs, discussion forums in institutions of every kind from trades unions to Women's Institutes, and even the inveterately cautious BBC – the entire country, it seemed – was discussing reconstruction in one form or other. Its presumed relationship with popular morale made it inevitable that in the end even the reluctant prime minister would try to get some mileage out of it; this, at least in part, was the purpose of his "Four Year Plan" broadcast of 21 March 1943. The reconstruction white papers were equally expedient: while not unconnected with sectional positioning ahead of the expected return to party politics, they were undoubtedly intended to sustain the flagging war effort.

Making promises to the people was, however, like instructing, informing, exhorting and persuading: a matter of mere words. Those whose business it was to do the telling were aware, for the soundings of public feeling and opinion made it obvious, that action was more effective. People's state of mind probably had at least as much to do with present realities as with future prospects. It followed, therefore, that once survival was no longer in doubt, attention to the material conditions of life would pay dividends in the form of increased popular willingness to see the war through to a successful conclusion.

An important element in this was income. During the war real wages increased substantially. This was partly a consequence of the demand for labour and the introduction of price controls and subsidies. But as important a factor was the insistence of Ernest Bevin at the Ministry of Labour on positive discrimination to raise working-class living standards. Full employment and greater purchasing power were powerful aids to feelings of wellbeing. Bevin's success in raising the standing of the representatives of organized labour and his fairmindedness in handling industrial disputes also helped to check apathy in the workplace.

Another area where the government could intervene positively to sustain popular morale was the supply and distribution of food and essential goods. In the early months of the war it had more or less left things for the market to sort out. This had proved socially divisive: the poorer sections of the community were hardest hit by the inevitable price inflation that followed the disruption of commerce. The government learnt from this mistake, noting the rising clamour for it to intervene. Its carefully constructed policy of import controls and home production to ensure food sufficiency, and its comprehensive rationing system to ensure fairness in its distribution, won general approval. Fine tuning of the system continued through the war. In June 1942, for example, the government acted against the unfairness of the rich being able to circumvent the hardships of rationing by eating in restaurants. A maximum charge of five shillings for a meal was imposed, which meant that the restaurants could not buy on the black market and expect to remain in profit. People with money could always find some way to get extra, but for the most part the rationing regulations were observed. Moreover, by showing it was on the side of fair shares, the government helped to prevent food from becoming a morale issue; ration-books stood symbolically for the communal in everyone's day-to-day experience of the war.

Alongside the feeding of the nation, and still closer to the drive to concentrate its diet on more nutritious foods, were the measures adopted to improve the health of the nation. Priority classes (expectant and nursing mothers, children, and invalids) were allowed a milk ration of one pint a day, free or cheap, according to means. The Vitamin Welfare Scheme provided free or cheap orange juice and cod-liver oil for infants. School meals were taken by one in three of schoolchildren, and one in seven of these received them free. Seven million children were vaccinated free of charge against diphtheria. Under the Emergency Hospital Scheme, designed originally to accommodate battle and air-raid casualties, free treatment was gradually extended to more and more categories of patient, so that by the end of the war much of the nation was eligible. All this was primarily the result of the drive to maximize the use of scarce resources, but it was not unconnected with official perceptions of public morale. Mass Observation surveys had suggested that health was an important factor in people's state of mind; anything, then, which served that concern could, as a bonus, help to sustain morale.[25]

In this rather instrumental concern for the health of the nation, the government did not entirely neglect the role of those inessentials that for both body and mind, human beings privately re-classify as essential. For many people this meant tobacco and alcohol. In a period when the health risks of the habit were yet unknown, most adults smoked, and many of those would have found it difficult and depressing to have to stop or reduce their smoking. Moreover, day-to-day existence in wartime was strenuous and worrying, and for many smoking was an effective way of "calming the nerves". The government recognized that maintaining the supplies of cigarettes would have significant benefits for morale. Not only were cigarettes never rationed, therefore, but scarce shipping space was reserved to make certain that supplies did not get low. By 1943 imports were higher than they had been in 1939.

The comforting and relaxing effects of alcohol were similarly acknowledged. The War Cabinet, not least the prime minister himself, included several members whose daily consumption suggested that they, at least, felt it helped them cope with the stress of their work. Like cigarettes, beer stayed off the ration, and although the alcoholic strength was reduced, space was found in the war economy for production to be maintained, or even increased – consumption rose

25 per cent during the war. Government policy here was entirely pragmatic: if civilians were cheered by being able to smoke and drink, they would be more efficient and committed participants on the home front. In addition, the chancellor appreciated the tax yield to the Treasury resulting from the maintenance of consumption levels.

In 1939 a strict view of the requirements for victory would have given entertainment and leisure a low priority. For understandable reasons of public safety, at the start of the war the government closed down theatres, cinemas, dance halls and sports arenas. The BBC was ordered to suspend its regional services and make its single "Home Service" available for information, instruction and advice to the public. Most of this was reversed, of course, when the enemy's massive air attack failed to take place but, in any case, a more sophisticated idea of the value of entertainment in wartime began to form in government circles. Once the crisis of 1940–41 had been survived, the provision of entertainment was placed on the policy agenda. Professionals in the entertainment field found themselves permitted, indeed encouraged, simply to entertain. The explanation was straightforward enough: even the serious spirits at the MOI could appreciate that diversion and relaxation might help to revitalize the weary warriors of the home front. Besides, there were always prompts to hand. In July 1942, for example, the president of the British Film Productions Association, C. M. Woolf, argued for fewer war films. "The Public", he said "was already getting tired of this type of picture and was asking for films which took their minds off the tragedy now taking place in the world . . . They wanted some relaxation and entertainment . . . and were entitled to have it".[26] Mass Observation's investigations confirmed that light relief was needed to counter the dispiriting effects of war news and the austerity of wartime life. Whether they got it or not in the cinema depended on the MOI's Films Division, since it alone authorized the release of filmstock to the producers. Approval for comic or escapist films was forthcoming, although still with strings attached: the public's desire for entertainment might be indulged, but what was shown should be of "the highest quality and neither maudlin, morbid, nor nostalgic for the old ways and old days".[27] Under this fairly unconstraining remit the film industry was able to meet the demand that box-office figures proved was there for hours away from it all with George Formby, Tommy Trinder, The Crazy Gang, Will Hay, Frank Randle, and the like. It probably helped the case for the making of lighthearted films that Britain's ally, the United States, permitted its own film industry to produce, alongside the obviously propagandist films, musicals, comedies, thrillers, and versions of classics and historical dramas. Many of these lit up the cinema screens of blacked-out Britain, with immeasurable benefit to the people's sanity.

The official green light for entertainment was dramatically exploited at Broadcasting House. In addition to increasing its output of light music (*Music while you work*, for instance), comedy and variety (the weekly audience for shows like *ITMA* and *Hi Gang!* exceeded 16 million), the BBC won approval for a second service, eventually named the Forces Programme. This was from the start a departure from the high-minded tradition of public-service broadcasting that had characterized its pre-war output. Its content was almost entirely what later came to be called easy listening: popular music, variety and sport, with some news and advice programmes. Presenters, who included, innovatively, women, adopted an informal tone. Although originally designed for service personnel in Britain, it rapidly caught on with the general public: by 1941 six out of every ten listeners were tuned into the FP rather than the Home Service, and for the 16–20 age group, the FP was the first choice of 9 out of 10.[28] Mass Observation described it in 1942 as "a sort of tap listening, available all day as a mental background and relief".[29] This opinion lies uncomfortably with the remarkable success of the *Brains Trust*, which the BBC surprisingly chose to put out on the Forces Programme and which by 1943 had a regular weekly audience of 10 to 12 million. Five "experts" discussing eight or ten philosophical or scientific questions sent in by listeners over a time of 45 minutes, attended to by 12 million, suggests that light relief was but a part of what many people were looking for when they took a rest from the war. An understanding of this is reflected in government support for, on the one hand, ENSA (the Entertainments National Services Association), which provided (but not exclusively) light entertainment for servicemen and factory workers, and on the other, CEMA (the Council for the Encouragement of Music and the Arts), whose aim was to sustain cultural activity amidst the disruption of war. ENSA's main activity on the civilian front was putting on lunch-time variety shows in factory canteens. Over a thousand war-work factories qualified for a visit once or twice a week from teams of mostly little-known performers on the fringes of professional entertainment. ENSA also provided classical music concerts, usually in the same venues but occasionally in public buildings and concert halls. As this was much more obviously within the remit of CEMA, a (mostly friendly) rivalry grew up between the two organizations. The public gained from this, though, for the disruptions of the war, especially conscription, had physically dislocated the patterns of peacetime intercourse both for performers and their audiences. Between them ENSA and CEMA took to the people throughout Britain a wealth of cultural diversion, ranging from comic songs with ukelele accompaniment by George Formby, to the Sadler's Wells Ballet, the London Philharmonic Orchestra, the Royal Opera, and exhibitions of sculpture by Henry Moore and paintings by Graham Sutherland. Without this government support the performance arts, at least, would virtually have disappeared; their salvation was in their new official role as instruments of war.

Local authorities got the message, too. In the fourth year of the war the London County Council made its own contribution to countering insidious war weariness. Summer entertainments in the parks were given a budget of £25,000, twice the 1942 figure. The idea was to provide a substitute for the entertainments people would have enjoyed while on holiday at the seaside (by then home to tank-traps, pill-boxes and barbed-wire). Evening dances were put on, a circus itinerary was arranged, a regatta was held at Hackney, and numerous performances were given of musical comedy, opera and ballet; a marked improvement on the usual offering of a series of bandstand concerts.[30] On a more modest scale local councils in the regions also tried to enliven war's tedium. In Huddersfield, for instance, the summer of 1943 was marked by a "Holidays at Home" programme of events in Greenwood Park.[31]

Towards the end of the war the MOI produced a chart that recorded graphically the course of public morale, according to Home Intelligence Weekly Reports made from March 1941. The chart shows quite sharp fluctuations of level, apparently in relation to wartime events; thus a rise when Germany turns away from Britain and attacks Russia, a decline at the setbacks of the surrender of Singapore and the fall of Tobruk. But the overall picture is clear: morale held up through the years of tedium and deprivation as it had through the traumatic period of military defeat, threatened invasion and mass bombing. Mass Observation's reports broadly confirm this; they disclose much grumbling, some bitterness and occasional despair; but the overwhelming impression is of a willingness to see the business through, to endure the strain and the boredom, and comply with the orders and regulations which those in charge said were necessary. It is undeniable that the so-called "Dunkirk spirit" was a short-lived phenomenon, fading away as the invasion threat receded and the bombing slackened off. But when this critical period was over there was never any doubt that national solidarity, of which morale is the index, was real, and would sustain the drive to victory. In some ways, the period that followed the Emergency was a more exacting test of morale; its four years demanded the less heroic qualities of stamina and patience. It was to be expected, then, that the strain would tell. The rise in industrial conflict, the decline in industrial productivity, the persistence of profiteering and black-marketeering are indications of this. But these were blemishes on national solidarity rather than evidence of its absence. To a remarkable degree, the class society that Britain still was demonstrated a cohesion functional to modern war.

As we have seen, the instinct for survival in the face of a ruthless enemy goes a long way to explaining the behaviour of the British people during the Emergency of 1940–41. But what is the explanation for their generally good morale through the four following years?.

An important factor was the political leadership embodied in the government formed by Churchill in 1940. Churchill himself personified the spirit he hoped the people would evince, providing a model of determination, and in his speeches, inspiring others to rise to the challenge of events. But it was also important that his government was a national government, sufficiently representative of all classes to command the loyalty, or at least the acquiescence, of the large majority of the nation; the abatement of partisan politics helped to create a sense of one nation and a common purpose. A part was also played by the conscious attempts of this National Government to adopt morale-sustaining policies, particularly those that raised the material standards of life for the poorer sections of the nation, and those that sought to equalize the burdens of the war. That unemployment was gone, that feeding and health was better, that the better-off were seen to be bearing burdens, too, could only help the majority to identify with the national project. A more disputed factor of explanation is the existence of a popular sense of optimism about the future. Some reports and surveys suggest a degree of fatalism about the prospects of a better life after the war and scepticism about the promises of the politicians in that regard. But an impression is also given of widespread belief that there would be no return to the worst of the 1930s. An accumulation of words from various sources helped to sustain people in this belief: the Beveridge Report, the Press and radio debate that followed it, the documentary and feature films with a "new order" message, the white papers on reconstruction; then, in 1944, the Education Act, concrete evidence that change was on the way. Finally, perhaps the best explanation is also the simplest: the people supported the war effort because there was really no alternative. Defeatism and apathy would bring something worse, a society run to serve German needs and ends. However riven by class antagonisms British society might have been, there was a loathing for Nazism that was unifying, and there was sufficient sense of a way of life worth preserving to produce the solidarity to see off the threat Nazism posed to it.

For his monograph on the Ministry of Information, Ian McLaine chose the title *Ministry of morale* to emphasize that civilian morale was its prime duty on the home front. Any assessment of the Ministry's performance in this role must acknowledge that it ended much better than it began. "Ministry of Disinformation" was an understandable, if unfair, popular soubriquet during the Phoney War; hamstrung by the secretiveness of the service departments, it was nonetheless guilty of failing to find the common touch in its communication with the public. It learned, however, that not only was a patronizing "top-down" tone inappropriate, but that its whole policy of exhortation was misjudged, inspiring no-one and producing irritation and ridicule. To its credit it abandoned its morale campaigns. As the director of the Home Intelligence Division, Stephen Taylor, explained in October 1941: "The British public as a whole shows a high degree of common sense. Given the relevant facts, they will listen to and accept explanation when they will not accept exhortation".[32]

The Ministry's role in civilian morale nevertheless continued, and may be said in the end to have been of value. In the first place, it served the public well on the information side of its activities by acting to restrain the censorship inclinations of the government. MOI officials took a liberal position on freedom of information; that is to say, within the defined limitations of security censorship, news and views should be freely disseminated without government control or suppression. This un-Whitehall-like view derived from the fact that many of the Ministry's staff were not career civil servants but "brilliant amateurs" – writers, academics, journalists – who were recruited at the start of the war and, having no intention of staying on after the war, were "not inclined to defer to what they took to be the unreasonable requests of other departments".[33] From the standpoint of civilian morale the Ministry men were right. People wanted to know how things stood; secretiveness or mendacity in an information service conduced only to fear and uncertainty.

The Ministry of Information also helped civilian morale through the information it collected via Home Intelligence and the Wartime Social Survey. Passed on to the relevant departments, this information – on health, housing, working conditions, education, transport – enabled the government to act knowledgeably to counter incipient threats to morale, and thereby contributed to the war effort. By acting as a sort of conduit between the government and the people, the Ministry of Information helped that process by which the war became a truly people's war.

Notes

1 *Persuading the people* (HMSO, 1995), p.10. I. McLaine, *Ministry of morale. Home front morale and the Ministry of Information in World War II* (London: Allen & Unwin, 1979), p.8.

2 N. Nicolson (ed.) *Harold Nicolson: diaries and letters* 1939-45 (London: Collins, 1967), p.33.

3 T. Crosby. *The impact of civilian evacuation in the Second World War* (London: Croom Helm, 1986), p. 46.

4 McLaine, *Ministry of morale*, p.34.

5 A BBC Listener Research Report of January 1940 stated that 30 per cent of the population regularly "tuned in" to Joyce's talks. S. Nicholas, *The echo of war. Home Front propaganda and the wartime BBC* (Manchester: Manchester University Press, 1996), p.53.

6 Nicolson, *Diaries and letters* 1939-45, p.106.

7 Ibid., p.91.

8 V. Hodgson, *Few eggs and no oranges* (London: Dennis Dobson, 1976), pp.92-3.

9 Typical was a response to the Director of the National Gallery Sir Kenneth Clark's request to have the paintings from the Gallery and the Royal Collections sent to Canada: "No, bury them in caves and cellars. None must go. We are going to beat them". J. Colville, *The fringes of power*, p.169.

10 T. Harrisson, *Living through the Blitz* (London: Collins, 1976), p.135.

11 McLaine, *Ministry of morale*, p.93.

12 P. Ziegler, *London at war 1939-1945* (New York: Alfred A Knopf, 1995), p.170.

13 Quoted in I. McLaine, *Ministry of morale*, p.123.

14 Harrisson, *Living through the Blitz*, p.280.

15 A. Calder, *The myth of the Blitz* (London: Jonathan Cape, 1991), p.214.

16 McLaine, *Ministry of morale*, pp.217, 240, 255.

17 Ibid., pp.10, 240.

18 Ibid., p.281.

19 Ibid., p.231.

20 The restrictions were responsible for the withdrawal of the daily weather forecasts from the newspapers and the radio. For the millions whose activities were affected by the weather, this inconvenience had to be endured until May 1945.

21 *Persuading the people* (London: HMSO, 1995), p.14.

22 Quoted in A. Aldgate & J. Richards, *Britain can take it. The British cinema in the Second World War* (Oxford: Basil Blackwell, 1986), p.219.

23 Ibid., p.12.

24 Calder, *The myth of the Blitz*, p.244.

25 Harrisson, *Living through the Blitz*, p.283.

26 Quoted in Aldgate & Richards, *Britain can take it*, p.11.

27 Ibid., p.12.

28 Nicholas, *The echo of war*, p.53.

29 Mass Observation. A: File Report 1351.

30 Ziegler, *London at war*, pp.246-7.

31 H. Wheeler, *Huddersfield at war* (Bath: Alan Sutton, 1992), p.136.

32 McLaine, *Ministry of morale*, p.251.

33 Ibid., p.277.

Chapter Eight

જી

Adapting, enduring, escaping

In its most dreadful moments, as when the Luftwaffe was battering Britain's cities, the war was a severe test of civilian nerve and sinew. But it was also a war that went on and on, putting the people to a different sort of test, where what was wanted was endurance and stamina. Without the high drama of the Blitz this test was less obvious, and all the more insidious for that. Its character lay in a series of burdens laid on the greater part of the population: separation, deprivation, restriction. Lives were disarranged, narrowed and impoverished. Passing this test required resilience, adaptability and, not least, a mental ability to "take time off" from the war.

The first of the big separations of the war was that between children and parents. Since evacuation was entirely voluntary, it was always open to parents living in designated evacuation areas to refuse the offer of a safe haven in the reception areas for their children. It was never an easy decision. Against the distress of separation had to be put the extra risk of the violent death of their children that staying on was presumed to incur, and about which the government and (although with variable energy) local authorities were warning. A poster showing a fearful brother and sister of school age carried the words: "Mothers. Send them out of London. Give them a chance of greater safety and health". The implication was that only selfish or neglectful parents denied their children that chance. For the children, separation, if it came, was decided upon by others and was one of the mysterious impositions of war. Even for those pre-school children who were evacuated with their mothers, there was the separation from fathers and older siblings to be borne. At first, for many schoolchildren, the idea of moving to the countryside with their school-fellows and teachers was an exciting adventure; children more than adults find it difficult to imagine what the abstraction "separation" means until they actually experience it at first hand. Arrival in the reception areas was the start of that experience. It meant being allocated to a new school, placed in a new home and, most importantly, acquiring instant foster-parents: all potential sources of anxiety at the time and of unhappiness ahead. The mass of material gathered from the letters and recollections of former evacuees, however, shows that for most children this settling-in operation, and indeed, the evacuation period as a whole, was not a traumatic or even slightly negative experience. Some things were better, some were worse, but by and large, the adventure which began at the home railway station did not stop until the final return. The reasons would vary with the particular experience of individuals, but also with their own personality and outlook. Recalling her evacuation year in Cirencester, Eva Figes, twelve at the time, wrote: "I was happy away from home. I revelled in my new-found sense of independence, finding things out, being a person, riding a bike as though I had grown wings. I was not homesick". And yet, she also recalled, her foster-home was spartan, and she constantly felt hungry.[1] For Robin Mitchell, evacuated with St Paul's School, London, to Crowthorne in Berkshire, the recollection of his year, lodging in a hostel, with a beautiful mansion for a school, was lyrical: "I remember it was a great adventure. I take sentimental journeys back there each year . . . I love driving up that long path and seeing the squirrels and the trees . . . I get in touch with my boyhood".[2]

For some children, then, the ache of separation from family was compensated for by happy experiences and feelings. It must be acknowledged, however, that cases of homesickness were not uncommon, and among these were children made wretched and despairing. Some children undoubtedly did undergo appalling experiences. Since billeting was (at least, initially) compulsory, people in some reception areas exploited what freedom remained to influence the process by which children were placed. Where there were more willing foster-parents than evacuees the children's experience was generally a happy one, but often the billeting officer merely assembled the children in the village hall for prospective hosts to view and choose, as if they were auction lots. Inevitably, this meant that siblings were chosen by different hosts and became separated; that all the children had, even briefly, to endure the stress of the selection; and worse, that some children were not wanted by anyone, and ended up being dumped by the billeting officer on an unwilling host. Foster-parents might be bitterly resentful about the imposition on them of evacuees, or they might be meanly neglectful of their needs, or only interested in making a profit out of the engagement by underspending the billeting allowance or exploiting the children's labour. It was quite easy for things to go wrong, however, without such obviously unfavourable circumstances. The most common cause was a mismatching in the social backgrounds of hosts and visitors. Problems arose at every point out of differences in behaviour, attitudes, language. Children raised in city slums did not fit easily into the houses of the rural middle classes, and where such social mismatching occurred, conflict and unhappiness often followed; a slum child could not help its head lice, its scabies or its foul language, but its innocence nonetheless did little to mitigate the feelings of revulsion these socially-proscribed things drew from those who were unused to encountering them in their own homes. Well might they seem to the children cold and unwelcoming. On the other hand, there were cases, although fewer, where the children were accustomed at home to middle-class notions of feeding, hygiene and language and who found themselves in the cottages of farm labourers where all these things were different and where piped water and water closets had yet to arrive. "I miss the electric light in my bedroom, we use candles here. I miss my sink at home, we have to go outside and wash under a tap here" – 13-year-old boy from North London, evacuated to Cambridge.[3] For other children the problem was more cultural than social; many evacuees from Merseyside were of African, Caribbean or Chinese background, which for their hosts in North Wales was apparently difficult to adjust to; likewise, the many Roman Catholic children among Liverpool's evacuees were unwelcome in an area where Nonconformism dominated and where no mass was ever heard.[4] Gloria Agman from a London Jewish family found herself, at thirteen, billeted with an anti-semitic Christian family in Northampton. At some cost in personal anguish, she concealed her Jewishness by pretending to belong to the Church of England and refusing parental visits, suffering the while the constant hate-talk against some Jews who lived nearby.[5] Sometimes the sense of being outsiders dumped on unwelcoming, even hostile, communities was felt outside the foster-home; in the local schools and wherever they encountered their rural contemporaries, evacuees might suffer verbal and actual sticks and stones. It was in situations like these that separation was harder to bear; the absence of those who were one's natural protectors was sharply felt when the sense of being under attack was strong. The classic symptom of this sort of insecurity manifested itself in regression: the wave of bedwetting, about which so many of the scandalized letters reaching the Press lengthily complained, and which served to worsen host-visitor relations. But homesickness could set in without the stimulus of hostility or mistreatment. Kathy Tuffin was evacuated at the age of eight from a poor home in Bromley, Kent, to Wollfold, a mill town in Lancashire. Despite the strangeness of the place and the incomprehensibility of the local accent, she settled in reasonably well, mainly because her foster-parents were models of understanding and kindness. But the upheaval was too great: "My foster-parents were very kind. They gave me the first holiday I'd ever had. We went to Blackpool. But I only stayed nine months with them. I missed my family too much. Also, I felt self-conscious and frightened of the unknown."[6]

Other children were more resilient, finding ways of coping with the homesickness from which few were absolutely immune. Where whole schools were kept together in the reception area, the mutual support of familiars from home was a major factor in mental survival. The sense of abandonment and isolation was here largely absent; if village boys ganged up against the "vaccies", the street-wise vaccies could often show them a thing or two about defending one's patch and one's pals.

A final example will serve to show the need for caution in seeking general explanations for unhappiness among evacuees. Hilary Granger, an only child of ten, was evacuated from Nottingham with her dayschool to a Leicestershire village. At Billesdon Manor her school became, in effect, a boarding school. The building was cold and comfortless, but there Hilary found the extended family she had longed for, and the war was for her a time of happy security. As she put it: "There were a few physical hardships but no emotional ones".[7] Like Eva Figes and Robin Mitchell, she found evacuation not something to endure and cope with but rather an experience to revel in.

To some extent the plight of the unhappy evacuee was self-regulating. In many cases, once parents learnt that their offspring were unhappy they brought them home again, if their circumstances enabled them to do so. Also the take-up for the later evacuations of 1940, 1943 and 1944 was proportionately smaller than that of 1939, and the same pattern of drift back to the cities occurred once the worst of the danger seemed to have passed. But there was always a residuum of unfortunate children who, for a variety of reasons, had to stick it out: mother dead, father in the forces; mother herself evacuated with younger siblings; the family home destroyed or damaged by bombing. For these, homesickness was an ache without a cure, and had to be endured.

Like evacuation, conscription was a major disrupter of family life and personal relationships. Unlike evacuation, however, it was compulsory, and the separation of husbands, wives, sons and daughters was often for much longer periods. By 1945 there were 4,680,000 people in the armed forces, 437,000 of them women. One-third of the whole male population of working age, half of them married, was in uniform and away from home. These bald figures represent a deep well of loneliness. It meant that two-and-a-half million married women were deprived of their husbands' support and company at the very time they needed it most, when burdens and worries multiplied daily. The separation in some ways bore more hardly on the wives, because their husbands had often gone into a very dangerous environment. The fear that they would be killed, injured or taken prisoner was hard to suppress and the sense of powerlessness was enervating. The luckier ones were those whose husbands' service involved extended periods away from the battle zones or inside Britain itself, for then there was the relief of home leave and short-term passes. A Hertfordshire woman recalled that "the whole of our lives was geared to the times when Daddy might be coming home on leave", and a Romford woman remembered that every leave was "like a second honeymoon. I saved all my clothing coupons to buy myself new clothes to greet him".[8] When the husband was stationed far away, letters could act as lifelines, tangible intimations that reunion was not impossible; the invention of the airgraph, a reduced, photocopied proforma letter, overcame the difficulties of getting forces' mail from distant postings quickly to Britain.

Although spared the feeling of abandonment experienced by wives, the mothers of men taken into the armed forces had to bear the same prolonged anxiety about their safety. In Huddersfield, Mrs Joe Mallinson had seven sons, all eligible for service. When war came she gathered them together and took them to a local photographer for a keepsake photograph, because she feared that not all were likely to come through the war unscathed.[9] In her wartime diary, Clara Milburn could not conceal the strain of knowing that her son Alan, with the British Expeditionary Force in May 1940, was in constant danger:

> We decided to Spring-clean the hut in the garden and there came across the little car Alan made and the box of motor-trophies put away at the beginning of the war. This, on top of a restless night, was too much altogether, and to cry a bit relieved the tension. Mrs Gorton came then, full of sympathy, and her embrace set us both weeping.[10]

Her anxiety became supportable only when she knew her son had been taken prisoner and his letters showed he was well.

The departure of young husbands and fathers for military service had another consequence for thousands of wives and dependants: poverty. An ordinary soldier's wife received seventeen shillings (85p) a week, with additions of five shillings for the first child, three for the second, one for any others. The husband would contribute a further seven shillings to this from his weekly pay of fourteen shillings. Some employers made up the pay of their serving employees to what it had been before they were called-up, but many did not, and there was no legal obligation to do so. The inadequacy of the allowances meant real hardship for those who had no other source of income. Belatedly, in 1944, after a clamour in the Press, the government raised the allowances to a level which, though still modest, permitted a decent standard of life. Until that time servicemen's wives had to get by, often by doing "outwork" or, if the children were of school age, taking paid work outside the home.

It would be almost an understatement to say that the war played havoc with everybody's sex life. The conscription of young husbands, however, had an especially disruptive impact, coming as it did at that point in their lives when they would be naturally most sexually active. And a marital relationship was what an increasing number of young couples apparently wanted, if the boom in marriages at the start of the war is any indication. The prospect of separation would seem to have impelled many to marry at once rather than put off marriage until the war was over. In 1938 there had been 409,000 marriages; in 1939 there was an increase to 495,000; in 1940 there was a further increase to 534,000, after which the number fell back to below pre-war levels. There was thus, in the early years of the war, a record number of young married couples separated, as it were, by order of the government. From this unnatural situation arose what was known at the time as "drifting", that is, lonely wives of serving soldiers giving in to the temptation of extramarital sex. The double-standards of the time allowed for husbands, especially those in the services, to "stray" if separated from their wives; whereas wives who consorted with other men in the absence of their husbands came in for censure, again especially if those husbands were in the forces, and therefore possessed the aura of self-sacrificing patriotism. A *Woman's Own* reader who had begun to "drift" sought the advice of the magazine and received a reply that reflected the general view: "You can't do this to your husband, or even your fiancé, while he is away fighting for his country. You must break it up or wait until after the war and resolve it. You must not see this man".[11] Wartime life created opportunities for women to "drift". In the first place, the absence of husbands cleared the way for others. None were better placed to fill the gap than the hordes of young American soldiers and airmen that descended on the country from early 1942. The concentrations of US servicemen were almost overwhelming in certain localities, notably East Anglia, the South West and the North West, and few parts of Britain were without the mixed blessing of their presence. Far from home and separated from their loved ones, they were naturally, in many cases, looking for female company. They had an irresistible aura, a compound of accents that called up the good life of Hollywood's creation, the charm of the exotic, and the promise that came with generous service pay. For young wives burdened with the strain of separation and loneliness, and struggling to manage on the ungenerous British serviceman's allowance, the temptation of a flirtation with one of these exciting visitors was often hard to resist. For their part, the visitors might feel they had been encouraged not to underestimate the response of those they approached; a 1942 welcome booklet issued to American soldiers by the British Government explained: "The people will be very glad to see you, but their enthusiasm is usually of a rather shy sort and you may not be aware, at first, of the warm friendliness they feel towards you".[12] Other opportunities came because many more women were in paid work outside the home than was the case before the war, thereby entering new environments and meeting new people. Others made new acquaintances through participation in civil defence and the voluntary services. Hetty Fowler and her husband were both in full-time jobs, she in the Ambulance Service, he in the Fire Service. Although they were not separated in the sense of living miles apart, in reality, working opposite shifts, they scarcely saw one another for long periods. She made new friends. Her reminiscence, while illustrating the impact of separation, also

170

alludes to another powerful solvent of moral ties elicited by the war, a heightened sense of mortality:

> We were thrown together in war and we all thought we hadn't much longer to live, so why not get what we could out of life? You're dancing with a man, he thinks you're rather nice and you think, well, nobody's told me that for years and you rather like it.[13]

Other women, on the other hand, underwent agonies of guilt. One whose husband was with the army in the East wrote to *Everywoman* about the man she'd met at a dance: "I'm not excusing myself, but I drifted until I became unfaithful to my husband. Now I'm horrified. I've given the man up – but what shall I say to my husband? I'm not really an unfaithful type of woman at all!" She was advised to say nothing and to stop feeling guilty – the war was to blame.[14]

Saying nothing was not always possible, however. Illicit affairs, notwithstanding the greater knowledge of contraception that occurred between the wars, produced a proportion of unintended pregnancies. As Calder notes, statistics of irregularly-conceived children born to married women are rare, but where they exist they show a large increase. In Birmingham, there was a three-fold increase between 1940 and 1945, half of the women having husbands in the services.[15] Secret adoption of the child was not possible because the husband's consent was required by the adopting agencies. A rise in the divorce rate, another statistical feature of the war, was doubtless in part a product of the home truths that had eventually to be told.

Children were in many ways the main sufferers from the disruption of family life that the war brought about. Most did not have to experience the upheaval of evacuation. But the war affected their lives in other ways that were damaging. The reduction of adult influence and care almost inevitably followed the state's need for the labour or services of every active person. Fathers and elder brothers were conscripted, mothers, older sisters and even grandmothers took on work in the war factories or elsewhere. Instead of a family of three or four generations, a unit of children and one or two parents became common. Many children found themselves with a busy mother as effectively the sole surviving adult to whom they could turn for support. During the war, 35 million changes of address were made in England and Wales, most of them a result of bomb damage. For many children, then, even the surroundings changed, often several times. Responsibilities were heaped prematurely on children, typically the older ones taking care of the household and younger siblings while the mother did war work. Inevitably, this ate into school time. Absenteeism from school rose significantly during the war years, with obvious impairment to the formal education of those children. Even children whose parents were not separated, or who were not forced to move from a damaged home, were likely to see less of those parents than in normal times and to be charged with adult responsibilities before they were ready for them. While most children were not traumatized or turned into delinquents out on the streets, many lived with feelings of impermanence and insecurity.

At an altogether more mundane level than the anguish of separation, the war was the bringer of restriction, limitation and confinement, wherever one lived, whoever one was. People might have known what to expect when the 1918 Defence of the Realm Act reappeared as the Emergency Powers (Defence) Bill and was enacted on 24 August 1939. This Act gave the government virtually unlimited powers over the lives of every person, and the orders and prohibitions began at once. Charles Ritchie, a Canadian diplomat in London wrote: "Living in London is like being an inmate of a reformatory school. Everywhere you turn you run into some regulation designed for your protection".[16] One of the most disruptive and irritating of the early orders, flowing from the pre-war plans that assumed the enemy would attempt a massive and immediate knockout blow, was that restricting the way artificial light might be used after dark. The "blackout", as it had already come to be called in the pre-war exercises, was not a difficult notion to get across to the public, especially at the start of the war, when people had an exaggerated idea of the enemy's navigational and aiming skills. But it was resented as the spoiler of social life. Mass Observation's reports show twice as many complaints about the blackout than about any other subject, even after the changes at the end of 1939 to the total blackout with which the war had started.[17] It was not that there was a demand for the lifting of controls. On the contrary, there was strong opposition to the introduction of "glimmer lighting", and individuals who infringed the blackout could expect angry confrontations with neighbours, fearful that their area was more likely to be a target. But the blackout did impair the quality of life in a number of ways. It was a time-wasting chore simply to black out one's house, taking up to half an hour a day, depending on the number of windows and doors and the sophistication of the method adopted. Certain activities that involved night-time illumination had to be suspended altogether – no bonfires or fireworks on 5 November, no fairground lights, no Christmas illuminations, no night-time services in churches with traditional (and inaccessible) fenestration. Moving about outside was a hazardous experience: although kerbs, steps and car running-boards were painted white, and lamp-posts and tree trunks were circled with painted rings, people still fell over or walked into things that were scarcely visible. More seriously, the number of road accidents rose dramatically, and even after the restoration of limited lighting to vehicles and a 20 mph speed limit in built-up areas, the night-time roads remained dangerous.

The extra darkness lent itself to criminal activity: detection and pursuit were made more difficult. In London one gang operated around the large railway stations by pretending to be drunks, colliding with and embracing travellers and then picking their pockets in the murk.[18] On the other hand, the blackout seems to have discouraged thieves from burgling private houses, for it was less easy to identify an unoccupied house.

Most people learned to live with the blackout. Its negative impact was felt less by the young and fit, who tended to adapt and to enjoy their social life as before. But for the rest, especially for women whose men-folk were away, it carried the fear of rape or robbery. Their social life was therefore much curtailed. After-dark activities were virtually confined to the home – good news for the BBC, for radio listening greatly increased – but a serious cramping of millions of lives, already made narrow by the other burdens of the war. It is often remembered that the blackout was one of the great sources of wartime jokes – regular features of the newspapers and radio variety shows – but for many people it was no laughing matter.

It was one of the ironies – and hardships – of the war that it increased the need for people to travel, while making it more difficult to do so. Movement of people from one place to another was a concomitant of a range of wartime happenings: the evacuation, office dispersal, conscription, industrial concentration. These movements in turn created the need for additional repeated movements, as parents visited their evacuated children, workers returned home for weekend visits, service personnel took their home leave. Since transport was a significant resource, and in total war all resources needed to be mobilized in the most efficient way for victory, it was inevitable that passenger transport would have a lower priority than the needs of the military and of the war economy.

The railways' importance to those needs was acknowledged in the decision made by the government on 1 September 1939 to take over the four mainline railway companies and the London Passenger Transport Board. Over a third of a million special trains were used for the armed forces alone during the course of the war. Trains moved the British Expeditionary Force with all its materials to Southampton just before the outbreak of war; they transported the men and materials of the Norway operation to the Scottish ports of embarkation; they brought the BEF back from the southern ports after the Dunkirk evacuation; 1,100 trains carried men and materials to the ports for the journey to the desert war in North Africa; for four months from March 1944 a thousand special trains a week participated in the build-up for the Normandy landings. For over six months 1,700 goods trains were used to carry blitz rubble from London to eastern England to build the extra runways needed for the strategic bombing campaign against Germany. Throughout the war the servicing of the war industries and the distribution of imports, re-routed to the west coast ports, claimed extra railway space. Goods traffic actually rose by 50 per cent. The 70 per cent increase in passenger traffic was therefore a great strain on a railway system already busier than before the war. It was not an expanding system, moreover. 100,000 railwaymen were called up, leaving the service undermanned (to the point in 1943 where the Minister of Labour needed to direct men and women to work on the railways); many railway workshops were converted to munitions production, so that a shortage of spare parts developed; engines, wagons and carriages were not being made, so by the end of the war there was a great deal of worn-out rolling stock still rolling. In addition, the railways suffered from the bombing, much of it aimed at this vital sinew of war.

These difficulties, together with the priorities of war, brought about a reduction in the provision of passenger trains; by 1944 the mileage was only two-thirds of what it had been before the war. Southern Railway produced a poster to explain why passenger trains had to be fewer and slower; it showed how the proportion of its trains carrying goods had increased from 25 per cent to 60 per cent, while those carrying passengers had decreased from 75 per cent to 40 per cent. The corollary was that passenger trains would always be very crowded.

Crowding was, after the inevitable queuing, just the first of the discomforts of travelling by train in wartime. Delays had to be expected: passenger trains were often diverted into sidings to let military or munitions trains through, and night-time air-raid alerts obliged drivers to reduce speed to 30 mph. Lighting was much reduced, to zero during an alert, denying travellers the comfort of reading on slow journeys. For long journeys it was always wise to carry one's own refreshments: restaurant cars were rare on wartime trains and because of rationing and poor supplies, station buffets were inadequate and always crowded. The blanking-out of station names in June 1940, as part of the measures to foil invaders, was an additional source of inconvenience and confusion, especially when the journey was unfamiliar or made at night.[19] Train travel even carried danger, since trains and stations were throughout the war often targeted by the enemy. In the southeast of England, particularly, hit-and-run machine-gun attacks on trains by single aircraft were not uncommon. In all, 1,300 people were killed on the railways by enemy action, 400 of them railway staff, and 4,500 people were injured. And if all of this was not sufficient deterrent to the would-be train traveller, the cost of fares tripled. A 1943 railway poster asked: "Is your journey really necessary?", but the truth was that for millions of people, it was. Most London commuters had no alternative. And the thousands of extra journeys generated by the displacement of people during the war were scarcely a dispensable luxury. That people needed to travel, and travel more than before the war, is attested not only by the 70 per cent increase in passenger traffic but by the fact that those people were prepared to endure the hazards and hardships described above to make their journeys. Human need dictated that, for example, a soldier on a 48 hour pass, would travel home, even if the amount of time he actually had with his family was far less than that spent on the slow-moving, overcrowded and comfortless mechanism that took him to it.

Bus services were affected by many of the factors hitting the railways. Drivers, conductors and maintenance workers were called into the armed forces, seriously reducing the workforce; the manufacture of vehicles and spare parts almost ceased as the motor industry changed to production of military vehicles and armaments; rubber and petrol became scarce commodities in the civilian sector. As a result, the provision contracted. Some rural services disappeared altogether, and urban services were reduced by the removal of some routes and the ending of late-evening services. In Central London alone 800 buses had been withdrawn by the end of 1939. Getting to and from work became as wearying and time-consuming for bus travellers as for train users: the same queuing and overcrowding, the same dim lighting after dusk, the same delays and diversions caused by bombing. The effect of reduced services was also felt on social life. When the last bus left the town centre at 9 or 9.30pm, an evening at a concert, film or play might have to be cut short, unless one was willing or able to walk home. Going to church might become a problem when the Sunday bus service was withdrawn or began at 1pm. Never was the need of mental and spiritual refreshment greater, but never was it more difficult to get to where it was to be found.

The contraction of public transport coincided with the introduction of petrol rationing for the private motorist. A basic ration of four gallons per month for the smallest car, ten gallons for the largest, with supplementary supplies for essential business or domestic purposes, was rarely enough for the 10 per cent of families fortunate enough to own a car. But even this had disappeared by March 1942: in an effort to make fuel economies, the government determined to end inessential motoring by withdrawing the basic ration. The richest of the rich might turn to the black market, but effectively, motorists had to join the bus queue, swelling the numbers of those already trying to manage on the depleted bus services. For the minority who could follow the government's advice to cycle or walk there might be the bonus of improved fitness and an enhanced patriotic halo, but for the majority this was not a practical suggestion.

If not the worst of the trials of wartime life, travel was nevertheless a major source of frustration and fatigue. Its difficulties acted to impoverish and confine the lives of the greater part of the population as long as the war lasted. For the most part, people made the best of a situation they knew to be unavoidable: transport consumed scarce resources, and if the war was to be won, the "Lines behind the Lines", as the railway posters had it, had to be given over primarily to the needs of the war effort. Humour and neighbourliness was often the best relief for the stress of travel. The novelist H. E. Bates spoke for many when he told of his delight at the ending of the silence of the English railway carriage: "The making of friends has never been so easy. In the whole history of the British railways there has never been, I should think, so much conversation and friendliness per mile as now".[20] The only jarring note was struck by the scandalously selfish efforts of many of the better-off to keep their cars on the road by fair means or foul. Black-market petrol was to be had only because the demand for it was strong, whatever the price. When the basic ration was withdrawn, the same people tried to abuse the system that had allowed supplementary petrol for essential use. It is an interesting reflection of the prejudices of the media of the time that a matter affecting only ten per cent of the population was given so much attention. When entertainment celebrities Jack Hylton and Ivor Novello were prosecuted for breaking the regulations, the media showed them a sympathy that was almost unpatriotic.

The difficulty of travelling was a universal experience since most people had to make journeys of some kind. Living with the threat of bombing, however, was something that most people had to bear only intermittently, or not at all. All the same, in places where bombing was a persistent hazard, the adaptations to normal life it imposed were particularly trying. The cumulative mental strain of living in a target area was of an altogether different order to the general stresses of war, more widely experienced. No indication of this appears in the statistics relating to mental illness, but one needs no such evidence to be able to assert that living with the threat of violent death does not conduce to peace of mind.

An aspect that is difficult to separate from anxiety born of fear is the effect of loss or disruption of sleep. During the blitz periods, people living in target areas commonly slept in some form of shelter as a matter of routine. No shelter was as good for a restful night as one's own bedroom. The least bearable was the public shelter: noisy, stuffy and lacking privacy. But the domestic Anderson was hardly much better: it had privacy, but it was hard to conceal what it basically was, a cold, damp hole in the ground. The indoor Morrison was greatly superior in that respect, but its cramped space made restful sleep difficult. At times, whole communities were living without adequate sleep. Early on in the London Blitz, according to Mass Observation, "loss of sleep was the major problem, outweighing all other distresses and anxieties".[21] There were, of course, periods when bombing ceased altogether, allowing people to revert to their normal sleeping arrangements. But there were also frequent periods of intermittent raids, and even more when there were alerts but no actual raids, since all places on the bombers' path were warned of the danger. This led many to use the shelter routinely, preferring its discomforts to the risk of the further disturbance of a hasty move in the blacked-out middle of the night.

Another sleep-robber was fire-watching. From early 1941 men aged between 16 and 60 and women aged 20 to 45 could be sure that at least one night a week would be lost to this tedious and usually uneventful activity. Exemptions existed, but it was compulsory for men whose working week was less than 60 hours and women who worked less than 55 hours. Even one night a week was a real burden when it came on top of a day's work and the usual hassle of travel to and from work. Like queuing, it was dead time; the war was a great manufactory of dead time, and most people were allocated a portion of it. E. H. M. Relton expressed the general feeling about this and all the other inroads the war routine made into everyday life: "Restrictions, discomforts, official supervision that smacks of Fascism – these we suffer but do not enjoy. Nor do we discuss them. But they are felt".[22]

Food – its price, quantity, quality and variety – was a universal preoccupation at all levels of society, and it features prominently in people's recollections of the war years. That it became an issue and a major area of official regulation derived from the basic fact that, like most industrialized countries, Britain was far from self-sufficient in food and had over many years allowed a vulnerable dependency on distant sources of supply to develop. As has been shown, the government anticipated the problems that this would create in time of war by preparing a rationing system as part of its overall plan. It understood the relationship between adequacy of feeding on the one hand, and public morale and economic efficiency on the other, acting, although perhaps not quickly enough, to erect an elaborate system of allocation and subsidy, alongside a policy of import substitution to meet the national need. When food rationing was introduced in January 1940 it covered only five items: ham, bacon, butter and sugar rationed by weight, and meat rationed by price. The amounts were quite generous by most people's standards and certainly by comparison with the allowance later in the war. Ham, bacon and butter were rationed to four ounces per person per week, sugar to twelve ounces. For meat the allowance, after March 1940, was one shilling and tenpence worth for everyone older than six, and eleven pence worth for children under six. In July 1940 tea was rationed to two ounces per week, and in May 1941 cheese at one ounce per week, later increased to two. Eggs came under a system of "controlled distribution" rather than rationing as such; this was to ensure that "priority consumers" – expectant and nursing mothers, children and invalids – got enough. When dried eggs became available after the middle of 1941 the ration was equivalent to three eggs per week. For margarine, jam, treacle and syrup an allowance was made of four ounces per week. Cooking-fat and butter settled down at two ounces each per week. This system left tinned foods un-rationed, and its unfairness became a source of resentment, since those with sufficient money could simply buy up supplies when they appeared. In November 1941, therefore, the government introduced a points rationing scheme to supplement the coupon rations: 16 points per week, later raised to 20, were allowed to everyone, to use as they chose against a range of tinned items such as meat, fish or vegetables, each carrying a points value. In this way a more equitable distribution of food was achieved. Unrationed foods – fish, chicken, fruit, vegetables – were available without restriction, but this was often a purely theoretical availability. Fish supplies fluctuated wildly and there was an overall fall in the tonnage landed; the fishing industry was not immune to the manpower shortage, and some of the regular fishing grounds were no longer safe to use. As a consequence, the fish queue became one of the regular sights of the war. There were alternatives offered to customers, but whalemeat, snoek and the more despised varieties of fish did not attract much custom. The "controlled distribution" system was used to even out the supply of vegetables and fruit between the different areas of the country. This at least gave every area a fair chance, but it could not relieve the need to queue for the scarcer items. Onions, for example, would vanish for months on end and then would suddenly be available – for those prepared to queue.

Queuing for food remained one of most burdensome aspects of life right to the end of the war and beyond. And its misery fell more hardly on the elderly: standing outside for hours in all weathers needed stamina. In contrast, the servant-employing class could avoid it altogether by making it part of their employees' duties. Stocking-up was not a possible way round the problem, since food was sold in small quantities only. The reward for queuing was never guaranteed; one could queue for hours, to be disappointed as the last of the stock was sold before one reached the counter. Eating out was only a partial solution. Rising real earnings meant that more workers took meals in works canteens or British Restaurants. But even a British Restaurant was not something a serviceman's wife with young children could often afford. The well-off, on the other hand, could eat out as frequently as they chose, without having to surrender coupons. For one large group of people, queuing for unrationed goods was not possible at all. A wartime survey showed that half of all working women were responsible for doing the family's shopping. This often meant shopping in the lunch-break – because shop hours did not generally extend beyond factory hours – or joining the Saturday afternoon queues. Some employers recognized the problem and allowed their women workers shopping-time, but generally women had to manage this problem unaided, mostly by going absent from work.

Rationing achieved only a limited sort of fairness. It never set out to equalize the consumption of the whole population but rather to focus on the basics. Woolton put it thus: "Food control does not mean preventing the other fellow from getting something. It is a means of ensuring that we get all the things that are necessary". This it did. In terms of calorific and nutritional needs the people did not go short. The hardship, if such it can be called, was more to do with the dull monotony of the average wartime diet. Protein and fat requirements were adequately met, therefore, but not often in the form of beefsteak and butter. There is a good case for arguing, however, that workers in heavy industry had a poor deal, for no distinction was made in the rations as between them and people in less energy-consuming jobs. A small concession was made in August 1941, when an extra allowance of cheese was made for agricultural workers, miners and other heavy workers, whose work required them to carry their food with them. But this group could rightly feel that they were still not getting enough food for normal health and fitness. This sometimes showed itself, however, in the poor health of their wives; the tradition of women going short for their men-folk was still strong in certain sections of the community.

The austerity of wartime feeding was symbolized by the National Wholemeal Loaf, made from flour of 85 per cent extraction. Although this was nutritionally superior to white bread, its colour, texture and heaviness made it universally disliked. Manufactured foods such as sausages, biscuits, cakes and ice cream deteriorated in quality and taste because of the shortage of key ingredients, notably sugar, milk, eggs and butter. Others, such as Frank Cooper's Oxford Marmalade and Crawford's Cream Crackers, disappeared altogether. The supply of some imported foods, such as onions and oranges, became erratic and of others, such as lemons and bananas, stopped completely. When unrationed items from abroad did appear, their price put them beyond most people's pockets, and they tended to end up in the fare served by hotels and restaurants. In these circumstances many householders seriously considered for the first time giving their gardens over to food production: growing vegetables or keeping hens, rabbits, or even a pig. There was plenty of advice and encouragement to be had from the government, the newspapers and magazines. Allotment and gardening societies became revitalized; the number of allotments in England and Wales rose from 815,000 in 1939 to 1,450,000 in 1942. All this activity helped to supplement and vary the diet of millions of families. But against this benefit must be set the uncosted time expended, on top of the long and arduous week already worked, by most people capable of maintaining a productive allotment; one more burden rather than a relaxing hobby. The option was hardly open, moreover, to those who by reason of age, health or circumstances could not become amateur food producers.

Allusion has already been made to the relative ease with which those with unlimited money could side-step the problem of rationing. The limit of five shillings placed on the cost of restaurant meals in June 1942 did stop the most blatant excess, but this came two and a half years after the start of rationing, during which time the wealthy ate largely in the manner to which they were accustomed. And even after the new regulation, there were ways and means of mitigating its effects; some restaurants and hotels managed it by charging five shillings for dinner, seven and sixpence as a cover charge, and two and sixpence for dancing, thereby enabling them to keep expensive unrationed items on the menu.[23] The rich were also at an advantage in getting access to under-the-counter foods and generally the best of what retailers had. From the standpoint of the butcher or grocer, the value of the orders his richer customers placed made it worth his while looking after them. It may safely be said that for the better-off, the food problem manifested itself only as the reduction of choice and the disappearance of a few favourite items of the more exotic kind.[24]

For entirely different reasons, the austerity of wartime feeding involved little or no change for the sizeable (possibly 30 per cent) of the nation who were poor (see Chapter 3). The shockingly undernourished and ill-clad state of many of the evacuees from the cities showed that this group was already familiar with austerity. For them, the tiny official allowances of wartime were well above their normal peacetime expectations. The severe shortages of the first half of 1941, before the Lend–Lease foods and the home harvest appeared, impinged on them no more than the very rich; things were pretty much as normal on the food front. But the gradual disappearance of unemployment and the rise in real incomes enabled many in this group to eat better during the war than before it. They did better in terms of quantity and, thanks to the Ministry of Food's vigorous campaigns about food values, better in terms of the nutritional quality of what they ate. To move from the bread-and-dripping regime of the 1930s to the balanced sufficiency of the 1940s was no hardship.

The group for whom rationing did seem a hardship lay between the extremes of the rich and the poor. It was not absolute hardship, of course, but a hardship relative to expectations. If one's expectations were pitched at the level of the middle classes, rationing meant getting used to rather smaller quantities of high protein foods and fats like meat, eggs and butter, and a greater proportion of bulk foods such as bread, potatoes and root vegetables. It is perhaps a reflection of how the middle class tends to dominate the social record that so much of the agony of making that adjustment has entered the popular memory of the war.

"Make do and mend", a slogan the government adapted from the old naval expression, sought to persuade the public to tolerate the widespread shortages of everyday articles created by the move to a total war economy. Stopping or reducing the production of many consumer goods could be done without causing real hardship, even where these were not in the luxury class. Unless they were actually bombed out, people could usually make their carpets, furniture, wallpaper and cutlery, for example, last out the war, however worn or shabby they had become. The imposition of Utility standards on clothing was certainly a cause of inconvenience and disappointment; but the shortages that drove people to near-desperation were of items that got used up or could not be repaired. Many household items of a practical nature are quite close to being essential. The difficulties people experienced show that the Board of Trade drew the line between these and the inessentials too low. It would have been difficult to convince the mother of a new-born infant that feeding-bottles and rubber teats were luxuries, yet both these items became scarce, along with many other items of baby equipment such as prams, push-chairs, cots, mattresses, rubber cot-sheets and baths; or a housewife, trying to cook for a family with only one saucepan – a 1943 Board of Trade survey showed that over half the women who had tried to buy a frying-pan in a one month period had been unsuccessful, and three-quarters looking for a saucepan had failed to get one; or the factory worker trying to follow the advice to use public transport less, but finding that for a new bicycle there was a waiting list, and that even if he managed to buy one second-hand, tyres and inner-tubes were in short supply. Toothbrushes, razor-blades, teacups and plates, torch batteries – the list of everyday items that became scarce was long enough to make "Make do and mend" seem a cruel taunt. People complained not only about the drab dreariness of it all but about the frustration and the extra cost in time it involved. However, wartime surveys suggest that at root most people accepted austerity as the tiresome but necessary precondition for winning the war.

It is sometimes said that deprivation *per se* is not the real source of grief; what really hurts is relative deprivation. In austerity Britain one of the most potent sources of this was the presence of the GIs. Their obvious affluence and their access to the apparent cornucopia of their px stores, aroused mixed feelings of admiration and envy among their shabby and perforcedly plain-living hosts. "If you ask people why they dislike Americans", wrote George Orwell in January 1943, "you get first of all the answer that they are 'always boasting' and then come upon a more solid grievance ... An American private soldier gets ten shillings a day and all found, which means that the whole American Army is financially in the middle class, and fairly high up in it".[25] Orwell went on to note the resentment that came from knowing that precious shipping space was being used to import food luxuries for the GIs, and even beer, since they would not drink English beer. From this situation the more enterprising among the British drew some compensation, from the children who begged for sweets and chewing-gum to the young women who, by lavishing their charms on the visitors, tapped into an apparently limitless source of cosmetics, nylons and chocolates.[26] For most people, however, feeling like poor relations was just one more of the irritations of war that had to be lived with. And as the young visitors increasingly shared the real pain of war, in the skies over Germany or on the beaches and roads of Normandy, resentment for them came to seem unworthy and mean-spirited. The feature film *The way to the stars* (1945) struck a true note in showing how British and American airmen sharing an air base in England gradually overcame their mutual resentments through their common experience of danger and loss in the combined bombing offensives against Germany.

Taking time off from the war, so to speak, was one way of making its austerity bearable. The longer the war lasted the more people felt the need for light relief. For millions, what they had to do for the war effort was clear and established by the war's mid-point, and anything that helped to make the routine tolerable was welcome. Everyday life was unavoidably more drab and usually more tiring than before the war; the antidote was something both cheering and relaxing. Like most things, leisure pursuits were not free from the restricting effects of the war, some to the point of temporary disappearance. But others flourished and even expanded.

Radio-listening was one of these. The habit of "tuning-in" was, of course, already established in most homes before the war.[27] It was in the war years, however, that what the bbc put on for people's amusement and instruction became important to their sense of well-being and their ability to carry on. A large audience was discovered for programmes that offered an escape from the stress of the war – the listening figures for comedy shows like *Hi Gang!* and *ITMA* and for the stream of dance music on the General Forces Programme and the American Forces Network testifies to this. People turned to radio partly because of the way the war forced more of them to spend their leisure time in the home: the blackout, the reduction in transport services, the contraction of spectator sports, all encouraged this. Many spent so long out of the house at work and travelling that on their return they had little time or energy to do more than listen to the radio. Millions of working women necessarily had to spend their time at home on household chores, made more onerous by the need to "make do and mend"; for them radio-listening was a background accompaniment to cooking, cleaning and sewing. Similarly, people stranded in the often boring situation of rota duty in the civil defence services, the anti-aircraft and barrage-balloon sites, or in the barracks and bases of the armed forces, found some diversion in programmes devised in many instances for just that purpose. For the many people to whom the war brought separation and loneliness, radio was a solace. "Escaping" from the war was not the only motive, however, for turning to the radio. Many of the programmes that were for entertainment and amusement used the fact of the war as a background to the fun. *ITMA*, the most successful comedy show of the war with, at its peak, 40 per cent of the population listening every week, was essentially topical. The jokes were about ministries, bureaucracy, rationing, restrictions and Careless Talk.[28] *Music while you work* and *Workers' playtime*, again, hugely popular in the home as well as in the factory, had as their *raison d'être* the cheerful support of the work routine for the common goal. Several programmes were designed round the idea of linking people separated by the war. *Children calling home* and *Hello parents* sent messages to and from evacuees abroad. *Sandy's half-hour* (Sandy Macpherson on the theatre organ), *Greetings from (Malta, Naples, etc.)* and Vera Lynn's *Sincerely yours* used the airwaves to bring together the forces abroad and their families at home. Nor was there any escapism in the many programmes about the war, including news bulletins, which were also listened to by large audiences. The nightly *War Report*, 30 minutes of eye-witness despatches from the fronts, had an audience of between 10 and 15 million, and the 9pm news was listened to by 47 per cent to 54 per cent of the population. While it is true that documentary features about the war on the home front had, by the second year, ceased to interest great numbers of listeners, features on the campaigns, such as *A harbour called Mulberry* (on D-Day), and on post-war reconstruction, such as *The Friday discussion*, drew audiences of over eight million. Radio was even a source of practical help. Two programmes had a large following: *The kitchen front*, a daily five minutes packed with advice on stretching the food rations, tips on "best buys", recipes,[29] and health-oriented contributions from the "Radio Doctor", Charles Hill; and the consumer advice programme *Can I help you?* The pattern of wartime radio-listening, then, suggests that while radio found huge audiences for new sorts of light entertainment programmes, it was not simply a medium of mental escape, and that part of its value to its listeners was that it helped them to understand the war and come to terms with its burdens.

Reading, on the other hand, seems to have served the escapist function, above all. According to Mass Observation's 1944 survey, people were reading less overall, which, given the blackout, longer working hours, and all the other disruptions of the war, is not surprising. But within that broad picture there was one category of person who was reading more: the young mobile male. In the 1940s this phrase was almost co-terminous with "serviceman" and, indeed, that was where the big market for books was: millions of more or less bored young men in billets or camps, with time on their hands. Reading helped to fill the periods of inactivity and it did so mainly by transporting the reader into the fantasy worlds of crime, suspense and sex. One of the best-selling (500,000) novels of the war, and one that represents all these categories, was James Hadley Chase's *No orchids for Miss Blandish*, described by *The Bookseller* as of the "drunk and disorderly" genre of reading.[30] On the other hand, people who had always read a lot became more addicted to the pastime during the war: the success of Penguin Specials, radical political titles, was a remarkable indication of a strengthening interest in serious subjects. F. Lafitte's *The internment of aliens*, for example, sold nearly 50,000 copies when brought out in November 1940. Literary magazines like *Penguin New Writing* and *Horizon* flourished as never before, and volumes of new poetry sold in the thousands instead of their accustomed hundreds.[31]

Theatres and cinemas, closed at the start of the war, soon reopened and, despite the disruptions of blackout and air-raid alerts, found no difficulty in getting audiences. Live theatre in all its forms was more appreciated than in the 1930s. New plays and revues appeared, despite the difficulties caused by actors' war service and restrictions on materials for sets and costumes. Lehar's *The Merry Widow* and Shaw's *Androcles and the Lion* were typical revivals. Many of the London theatres decided to escape the Blitz by sending their productions out to the regions; to the enrichment of the entertainment-starved people of Nottingham, for example, August 1941 brought Barrie's *Dear Brutus*, with John Gielgud and Roger Livesey in the cast.

Each week during the war 25 to 30 million cinema tickets were sold: a boom time for the industry, after the worst of the bombing was over, at least. Many people went more than once a week. Cinemas started opening on Sundays. Queues formed for almost any film that was offered: it was enough to be transported by the magic lantern, almost regardless of the destination. This was in fact what most people went to the cinema for and expected to happen. It followed that the greatest box-office successes fulfilled this expectation: *Rebecca*, *Casablanca* and, most popular of all, *Gone With the Wind*. Perhaps reflecting the anticipation of ultimate victory, after late 1942 there was an increasing place in the taste of audiences for films about the war. Noel Coward's film about the Royal Navy, *In Which We Serve*, came second only to Hollywood's *Random Harvest* at the box-office in 1943. By 1944 the public seemed again to prefer to get away from the war. Coward met that need, too, with *This Happy Breed*, the most popular British film of that year. Films clearly fulfilled an important function, readily understood by the millions who braved the hazards of blackout and bombs to get their weekly "fix" of fantasy. Right through the London blitz the queues circled the cinema in Leicester Square from early morning, and most filmgoers once in, would not come out until the show was over, whatever was happening outside.[32]

Some indicators suggest that increasing numbers of people sought mental relief from the pressures of war in the riches of serious music. Wherever concerts were put on – in the lunch-time at the National Gallery, the Promenade Concerts at the Royal Albert Hall (after the destruction by bombing of the Queen's Hall), in events sponsored by CEMA and ENSA in a variety of regular and irregular locations around the country – there was invariably an excess of demand for seats over what was available. In 1940 Malcolm Sargent took the London Philharmonic Orchestra on a tour of variety theatres in the regions. Twice-nightly concerts of popular classics were given to capacity audiences in ten cities. Extra lunch-time concerts were put

on to meet the demand. At the same time gramophone clubs pro-
liferated and flourished, supported by ENSA's record-lending service.
BBC Listener Research discovered an increasing audience for its output
of classical music, in line with the general increase in radio-listening.
In October 1940 2,650,000 listeners were tuned in to the hour-long
Wednesday Symphony Concert. The BBC responded to the trend by
increasing the amount of air-time devoted to serious music. Symphony concerts were extended to two hours; fortnightly lunch-hour
concerts were introduced; a full-length studio opera, a short opera
and a comic opera were broadcast every month; and in 1942, after a
two-year gap, the relaying of the Henry Wood Promenade Concerts
was resumed. On the popularity of the Proms, the 1943 BBC Handbook commented: "The nightly packed houses were a vivid and
tangible sign of the growing demand for good music which has been
constant throughout the country since the beginning of the war".[33]
Musical output was further extended in 1943 and 1944, adventur-
ously promoting British music and contemporary compositions. "Whatever else it may have destroyed", suggested *The Spectator*, "the war
has undoubtedly re-created music in our midst, affirming it a living
force vital to the needs of a great people".[34] Managers of concert-
halls whose staff invariably had to turn hundreds away would doubtless have agreed with these sentiments. With every seat sold for
every concert, the concert manager for the Proms admitted that only
after the move was made to the Royal Albert Hall did he begin to
realize how many people had been turned away from the much
smaller Queen's Hall. What seems clear in this remarkable upsurge
of interest in classical music was that it was not simply a case of
culture-starved melomanes reaching out for spiritual refreshment
wherever it was offered, although it was that, too, but that a new
audience was appearing where it had not before existed. One of the
characteristics of periods when everything – life itself – is threatened,
is the almost instinctive search of individuals living through them for
that which gives meaning. Turning to explore those products of art
that time and opinion has accorded great merit is the expression of
that search – in the concert-hall, in the art gallery, in the pages of
unread literary classics. Stephen Spender thought the revival in interest in the arts that he witnessed "arose spontaneously and simply,
because people felt that music, the ballet, poetry and painting were
concerned with a seriousness of living and dying with which they
themselves had suddenly been confronted".[35] It would be possible to
make excessive claims about the phenomenon. The sceptic might

read into the apparent increase in the demand for classical music, shown by the success of ENSA and CEMA concerts, only the fact that during the war there was less entertainment on offer altogether; and that a free lunch-time concert in the works canteen was, so to speak, served up on a plate with the meat and vegetables. The evidence for the emergence of a new audience is mainly anecdotal and impressionistic. It is unlikely that the mere fact of war produced a dramatic shift in popular taste; the likelihood is rather that the war was the framework within which a combination of factors – the changes to people's working lives, the reality and sense of shared experience, new and improvised arrangements for the presentation of the arts – brought more people into contact with serious music (and the other arts) or encouraged them to sample things outside their usual diet.

Herbert Morrison, under pressure to ban racing as out of keeping with austerity, refused, arguing that "within reason, public entertainments act as a lubricant, rather than a brake, on the war effort".[36] It was nevertheless much more difficult for people to watch (or take part in) sport than before the war. The languishing state of many of the big spectator sports contrasted sharply with the boom in indoor entertainment. Where they were put on, the size of the crowds suggested that there was a huge unsatisfied demand for this way of getting away from the war. The inescapable fact, however, was that much professional sport depended for its existence on the same fit young men who were quickly claimed by the armed forces. Amateur teams were depleted in precisely the same way. Furthermore, the places where sports took place had more urgent uses in time of war. Tennis courts and golf courses made useful sites for anti-aircraft batteries, searchlight posts and barrage-balloon moorings. The All-England Tennis Club at Wimbledon became a Home Guard drill ground, the Oval cricket ground a prisoner-of-war camp; the rugby ground at Twickenham was turned into allotments and civil defence centre, Kempton Park racecourse into an internment camp and Epsom racecourse into a military training area. Even where grounds were not diverted to such uses, they, like all other open spaces, were at least for a time made unfit for invading aircraft, and at the same time unusable for sport. There was still plenty of football and cricket to watch, although mostly at an inferior level. Racing was reduced to just six courses, all in England, and ran at local rather than national level. Greyhound racing was reduced to one day a week per track and operated to capacity crowds throughout the war. For a nation more or less addicted to sport, the enfeeblement of so many sporting activities was a real impoverishment of life. What there was, was devoured but, like the food ration, there was never quite enough, and the standard was mostly Utility.

No such gloom descended on the leisure activity whose exponential wartime growth made it one of the most important antidotes to war weariness: dancing. For young adults "dancing madness" was a more likely condition at this time than nervous collapse. Ballroom dancing declined, but informal dancing thrived in the big city centre dance-halls and in every possible space: village halls, works canteens, fire stations, Nissen huts on army or air bases, and in the ballrooms of grand houses taken over as officers' messes. In the Blitz winter of 1940–41 the main dance hall at Richmond was so popular the management decided to open an extra night a week.[37] The big London dance halls like the Lyceum, the Hammersmith Palais and the Paramount, Tottenham Court Road, were thronged throughout the war, regardless of the comings and goings of the Luftwaffe. Much of the impetus for the craze came from the fluctuating presence of large numbers of servicemen, stationed away from home and seeking evening company and cheer, preferably female. Wherever there was an air force base or an army camp, there was certain to be plenty of dancing. With the United States servicemen came their dance bands, large, noisy and glamorous, and new dances, which rapidly caught on with the hosts. Elsie Thompson, from Liverpool, learned the jitterbug at Burtonwood US Air Force base. Her recollection recreates the feeling of abandon and escape that everyone in their own way sought from time to time in the war's grim and enveloping drabness:

> Once you'd learned to do the jitterbug there was just nothing else for it. It was marvellous. They'd throw you over their shoulder and throw you under their knees and it was absolutely fabulous, really lovely. You'd dance your heart out and forget everything for a few hours.[38]

Notes

1 R. Inglis, *The children's war* (London: Collins, 1989), p.100.
2 Ibid., p.99.
3 Ibid., p.53.
4 A. Calder, *The myth of the Blitz* (London: Jonathan Cape, 1991), p.41.
5 B. S. Johnson, *The evacuees* (London: Gollancz, 1968), pp.34–41.

6   Inglis, *The children's war*, p.51.

7   Ibid., p.95.

8   N. Longmate, *How we lived then* (London: Hutchinson, 1971), p.83.

9   H. Wheeler, *Huddersfield at war* (Bath: Alan Sutton, 1992), p.6.

10 C. Milburn, *Mrs Milburn's diaries* (London: Fontana/Collins, 1980), p.48.

11 P. Lewis, *A people's war* (London: Thames Methuen, 1986), p.152.

12 *Persuading the people* (HMSO, 1995), p.26.

13 Lewis, *A people's war*, p.151.

14 Ibid., p.152

15 Calder, *The people's war*, p.314.

16 S. Briggs, *Keep smiling through* (London: Fontana, 1976), p.88.

17 Harold Nicolson, in a piece written for *The Spectator* on 4 February 1944 confirmed this: "When I ask my constituents what they really mind most about the war it is always the blackout which comes first in their list of evils".

18 P. Ziegler, *London at war* (New York: Alfred A. Knopf, 1995), p.70.

19 Harold Nicolson observed: "St. Pancras station on a wet midnight, and after three hours in a packed corridor, makes one realise that this is, in fact, a total war". (*The Spectator*, 2 February 1944).

20 *The Spectator*, 18 October 1940.

21 T. Harrisson, *Living through the Blitz* (London: Collins, 1976), p.102.

22 *The Spectator*, 2 April 1943.

23 Ziegler, *London at war*, p.249.

24 By September 1943 the Athenaeum was unable to supply its members with wine at dinner. Not everyone was equally deprived, however: Winston Churchill never ran out of his daily needs of sherry, claret, whisky, champagne, port and brandy. P. Fussell, *Wartime* (London: Oxford University Press, 1988), p.88.

25 S. Orwell & I. Angus (eds), *The collected essays, journalism and letters of George Orwell, vol. 2: My country right or left* (Harmondsworth: Penguin, 1970), p.321.

26 Interestingly, a Mass Observation survey showed that although most American servicemen liked Britain and the British people, "many strongly criticized the way in which children begged for sweets and the way Americans were being "done" by what some considered the low moral tone of British women". (MO file report 1656-7).

27 90 per cent of households had a radio in 1939.

28 S. Nicholas, *Echo of war* (Manchester: Manchester University Press, 1996), pp.130-1.

29 The daily *Kitchen Front* averaged 5.5 million listeners in October 1940.

30 S. Chibnall, "Pulp versus Penguins: paperbacks go to war", in *War Culture: social change and changing experience in World War Two*

Britain, P. Kirkham & D. Thoms (eds) (London: Lawrence & Wishart, 1995), p.40.

31 Calder, *The people's war*, pp.514–17.

32 Longmate, *How we lived then*, pp.400–401.

33 A. Briggs, *The war of words*, vol. 3 of *The history of broadcasting in the United Kingdom* (London: Oxford University Press, 1970), p.301.

34 *The Spectator*, 23 July 1943.

35 *World within world*, 1951, quoted in Ziegler, *London at war*, p.192.

36 Longmate, *How we lived then*, p.467.

37 Ziegler, *London at war*, p.91.

38 Lewis, *A people's war*, p.189.

Chapter Nine

✦

Time for change:
the General Election

At just short of six years, the second test of war to which Britain was subjected in the twentieth century was both longer than the first and in many ways more exacting. Though less costly in terms of death and injury, its effect inside Britain was more direct. Observers had already noted the blurring of the distinction between the soldier and the civilian in the earlier war; but the notion of a home front, as dangerous and at the same time as defined, organized and controlled as the military fronts, came fully into being only in the Second World War. The sense that the whole nation had experienced the war at the sharp end, so to speak, was strong in 1945, and this perhaps explains why it was accompanied by an equally strong urge to take stock and reflect upon the nature of British society and where it was going. Already, well before peace came formally in August, the dynamic of the popular mood was discernible. It ran in two apparently contrary directions. There was, on the one hand, a strong desire to piece together again lives disrupted by the demands of war (implying return to what had been); on the other, there were expectations, generated in part by those same disruptions, of a better life ahead (implying new departures). The General Election embraced both movements. In simply taking place it symbolized a return to normal times. In its result it pointed to the desire for change.

When the votes were counted and the results declared on 26 July it was clear that the 1945 General Election marked a sea-change in British politics. Labour was returned with 393 seats, taking 48 per cent of the popular vote, against 213 Conservatives and allies with 39.6 per cent, and 12 Liberals with 9 per cent. Overturning a

Conservative majority of over 200 seats, Labour held power with a majority for the first time, and a huge majority, at that. Subsequent analyses of the voting showed that of the three million people in the forces eligible to vote, 1,700,653 voted and that these votes were predominantly for Labour. A fifth of the electorate was voting for the first time; 61 per cent of these voted for Labour.[1] Labour increased its support among skilled workers and the middle classes, making gains in dormitory and suburban constituencies in the southeast, where it had previously had little success. The voting also showed consolidation of the Labour position in the big conurbations: it became the dominant force in large cities such as Liverpool, Manchester, Birmingham and Leeds; the West Midlands moved a full 23 per cent towards Labour, in many rural areas traditional Conservative strongholds fell to Labour, for example, six out of the seven Norfolk seats; and cathedral cities like Lincoln, York and Winchester lost their Conservative complexion. The electoral map no longer showed Labour's influence predictably tied to its traditional bases in the inner constituencies of large cities and in single-industry areas like steel or textile towns, mining villages, or the Potteries. "We are a really national Party", claimed Arthur Greenwood. "We are a cross-section of the national life, and this is something that has never happened before."[2] And the massed ranks of new Labour MPs reflected this: members of the professions outnumbered trade unionists, who had previously always constituted a majority of the parliamentary party.

The result was a surprise for many. Led by Winston Churchill, crowned with the glory of victory in war, most Conservatives understandably found it difficult to imagine that the electorate would look to others to lead the country through the difficulties of the peace; for them the "Churchill factor" was a winner. Even Labour leaders Attlee and Morrison were guilty of overestimating Churchill's electoral value to the Conservatives; their most sanguine expectation was a reduction of the Conservative majority to about 50 seats. They should have known better. For those with eyes to see and ears to hear, there was clear evidence of a swing towards Labour sufficient to carry it to power. The evidence was in the results of by-elections and public opinion polls. Tom Harrisson, the co-founder of Mass Observation, writing in early 1944, drew attention to these results and concluded: "I have no doubt that the present Conservative Party, even if led by Mr. Churchill, will not accomplish enough of itself to govern again, unless the alternatives commit suicide".[3] Under the terms of the electoral truce made at the start of the war, the three main parties had agreed not to nominate candidates for parliamentary vacancies against the candidate nominated by the party holding the seat at the time the vacancy occurred. Of the 140 vacancies that occurred during the war 65 were filled without a contest. In the 75 contested by-elections the challengers were from small parties like the ILP and the CPGB or from independents. During the course of 1941 independents came increasingly to be the unofficial proxies of the main parties, this situation being evident in the attitude local activists adopted towards the official nominee. Between March and June 1942 independents took Conservative seats at Grantham, Wallasey, Rugby and Maldon. What was significant was that when the official nominee was a Conservative the swing (between 9 and 36 per cent) was towards the challenger; whereas when the official nominee was a Labour person, as in South Poplar in August and Manchester Clayton in October, the swing was towards the candidate (13 per cent at the former, 40 per cent at the latter). At Skipton in January 1944 the local Labour party refused to support the Conservative nominee and, in defiance of the electoral truce, gave support to the challenger and eventual winner, Hugh Lawson, representing the Common Wealth Party. But the result that most revealed the depth of anti-Conservative feeling, and hope for Labour was at West Derbyshire. At the 1935 election the Conservative candidate was returned unopposed. For the February 1944 by-election the Marquess of Hartington, son of the Duke of Devonshire to whose family the seat had long been virtually a private possession, was opposed by Charlie White, who resigned from the local Labour Party to stand as an independent. White won by 4,500 votes on a platform of welfare reform that might have been written in Labour Party headquarters. The West Derbyshire by-election, and subsequent contests at Rusholme, Wolverhampton, Bilston and Chelmsford, revealed not only that the electoral truce had virtually broken down long before the formal ending of the coalition, but also that the successes of so-called independents in reality concealed a swing to Labour.

Public opinion polls had given Labour a lead of at least ten per cent from 1943 onwards. During the election campaign Gallup showed a consistently large lead for Labour even though the Conservatives narrowed the gap in the closing stages. On 18 June, Labour had 45 per cent support, the Conservatives 32 per cent; on 4 July, on the eve of polling, the figures were 47 per cent and 38.5 per cent. With indications like these, together with the pointers given by the by-elections, it is difficult to understand why there was so much astonishment over the result of the election. The explanation lies in the tendency to regard the by-election results as unreliable, for a variety of reasons: the incompleteness of the electoral roll; the absence of proper campaigning; their traditional use as a way of registering a protest; their dissimilarity from general elections, when a government is being voted for. As for the opinion polls, their very newness and consequent lack of a tested record led most politicians to be sceptical about the validity and predictive value of their findings. Even the staff of the *News Chronicle*, which published the Gallup poll, did not pay serious attention to its final pre-poll forecast, which in the event was very accurate.

Labour's victory lies in no single cause. The explanation is to be found in a combination of factors that developed and coalesced during the whole period of the war. From the standpoint of 1939 there was no likelihood of Labour coming to power with a large majority within six years. The war changed Labour's prospects for the better. In seeking to show how, we shall be looking again at the ways in which the experience of total war helped in one way or another to shape the outlook of the nation.

It is in the public reaction to the Beveridge proposals that the most revealing evidence of this process is to be found. In the discussion of the Report in Chapter 3 it was shown that it made a strong impact on the political parties and on a wide variety of organizations representing religious, intellectual, professional, business, and other interests. For present purposes, however, what needs to be emphasized is that the debate over Beveridge went far beyond the chattering classes and deep into the minds of that amorphous mass, the general public. When Beveridge himself said "one cannot make a people's war except for a people's peace", he put into words what was already in the minds of a great many people. His proposals crystallized for people the thoughts about what they really wanted after the war that had already begun to form under the stimulus not just of *Picture Post's* 1941 "Plan for Britain" and J. B. Priestley's *Postcripts*, but of the actual experience of evacuation, bombing, conscription, rationing, and the general upheaving of wartime society. As Barbara Davies, who was working at the Armstrong Whitworth factory in Coventry, and who had known real hardship in the Depression, recalled: "When the Beveridge Report came out, talking of giving us a welfare state where there would be no poverty, no-one starving, and free health care, it just seemed the sort of world we were all looking for".[4] Mollie Panter-Downes described how pre-publication leaks of the proposals had so excited public interest that on publication day Londoners:

> queued up to buy this heavy two-shilling slab of involved economics as though it were unrationed manna dropped from some heaven where the old bogey of financial want didn't exist . . . For the first time ordinary Englishmen, who had felt that the Atlantic Charter was only a lot of big words for a lot of difficult, abstract things, thought that in Sir William Beveridge's proposals for postwar social security, they saw a practical design for living".[5]

This was a subjective impression, of course, but she was not far wrong, if the evidence of opinion polls and surveys is a guide. Gallup showed that it was not just the likely beneficiaries who were enthusiastic: 75 per cent of people in the top income group, and 90 per cent of professionals and white-collar workers supported the proposals and thought they should be adopted, despite the fact that they themselves would not be gainers. The Ministry of Information's Home Intelligence unit found "almost universal approval by people of all shades of opinion and by all sections of the community". Three responses to Mass Observation reporters illustrate the feelings of the relatively poor. First, a 45-year-old man of social class D: "it will make the ordinary man think that the country at last has some regard for him as he is supposed to have regard for the country". Then, a 59-year-old man of the same class: "If it has taken a war to make a government see how urgent is the need for improving conditions of the smaller fry, then we have not fought for nothing". Finally, a 45-year-old man of social class C: "It should certainly be passed and I would not give much for the future chance of any Party that opposed it".[6] Further manifestation of the popularity of Beveridge appeared in the surge of support for the Common Wealth Party, founded five months before the Report, but discovering in it a text of biblical resonance. Common Wealth called for "Beveridge in full – Now!", a slogan which identified it as *the* party of reconstruction and which in the following two years carried it to seven by-election victories. This success, although it led nowhere (only one MP after the General Election), also showed what the public thought of the reaction of the main parties to the Beveridge Report. The division on the government's motion on the Report, in which 97 Labour MPS defied the Whips and voted against, caused James Griffiths to observe to Beveridge: "This debate, and the division, makes the return of a Labour government to power at the next election a certainty".[7] His prophecy was correct but the inference that Labour had emerged well from the episode in the eyes of the electorate was self-indulgent. Coalition constraints may well have been the explanation for the cautiousness of the Labour parliamentary leaders' welcome for Beveridge, but a negative impression was nonetheless given. The lack of whole-heartedness was noted, especially alongside the enthusiasm of Common Wealth. Certainly, the Conservatives emerged worse from the episode than Labour; a distance between the parties on the question of social reform was perceivable. The War Office's withdrawal of an Army Bureau of Current Affairs pamphlet, summarizing the plan, and the performance of Anderson and Wood in the debate saw to that. But there was also general cynicism about politicians, so that even when the main parties belatedly got their respective reconstruction acts together, they continued to encounter public disbelief. A Home Intelligence Report for December 1942, even before the debate, that is, cites one old soldier: "This new plan for social security makes me laugh, I don't forget the Land fit for Heroes of the last war".[8] Subsequent reports continued to note depression, anger and cynical pessimism about the prospects of a better post-war society. Ministry of Information official R. H. Parker, at a meeting in July 1943 with representatives of the Reconstruction Secretariat, referred to "the belief that little or nothing was being done by the government and that, in fact, the government was not particularly interested in reconstruction, or that its interest was simply simulated for political purposes".[9] Nearly a year later, in May 1944, by which time social reform committees, White Papers and even legislation had come into being, the public still doubted the government's commitment: "There is widespread suspicion of the government's attitude to the Beveridge Plan. A great many, perhaps the majority, are convinced that it will either be shelved, mutilated, or whittled away, or else an inferior substitute put forward instead".[10]

For "the government" one might here read "the politicians". The people, after all, had been taught to think of the government as the nation personified, and many might readily assume, moreover, that the coalition would continue after the war. Until the coalition was formally ended at the end of May 1945, therefore, Gallup polls on voting intentions had for the respondents an academic, unreal feel to them. Politicians claimed that they took little notice of opinion polls. But all the rhetoric and jockeying for position on reconstruction issues that the main parties indulged in from the spring of 1943 on belies this. Labour activists were a bit worried about Common Wealth appearing as a rival to Labour on the Left, the Tory Reform Committee about the Conservative Party being left behind altogether in the apparent leftward swing in public opinion. Both succeeded in moving their leaders towards commitment to measures of social reform.

Labour could take some pleasure in the gap of ten per cent that it was consistently registering in Gallup polls from the middle of 1943. What they could not confidently claim, however, was that the electorate was enthusiastic about Labour. The popular cynicism described above suggests rather that, faced with a choice of evils and assuming a real election would be essentially the usual two-party contest, then Labour was the lesser of those evils. To draw that conclusion from the choice the electors made in 1945, however, would be to ignore evidence that the mood was not wholly negative, that in voting Labour, people were voting *for* something. Opinion polls taken shortly before the election showed that a majority supported the nationalization of land, the coal mines and the railways, State control of the post-war purchase and distribution of food, and general State direction of the transition from war to peace.[11] In a Gallup poll taken immediately after the election, 30 per cent thought the result showed the British people wanted Labour to govern "along existing lines only more efficiently, whereas 56 per cent thought it wanted "to introduce sweeping changes such as nationalization". Whether they were part of the swing or not, most people accepted that Labour had a mandate for far-reaching reform; this was, so to speak, the will of the people.

Cynicism apart, then, there is still a need to explain why Labour was more attractive to voters in 1945 than its rivals. Housing, jobs and social security were the biggest worries of the people when they thought about the future, according to the reports of Home Intelligence, confirmed by Mass Observation surveys. It was clearly to Labour's advantage that the Party was historically more associated in the public mind with commitment to those issues and to social reform generally than the Conservatives and, as we have seen, the debate over the Beveridge proposals served to underline this difference between them. On social reform Labour was inherently more credible, and there was little the Conservatives could do about that. As it happened, during the election campaign Labour succeeded in playing brilliantly to this strength, while the Conservatives reinforced their image as at best lukewarm converts to social reform. In its manifesto and campaign Labour emphasized its reconstruction policies.

In promising four or five million new houses it was targeting the subject which, according to the opinion polls, was the greatest of public anxieties about the future. The Conservatives, seeing Churchill's statesmanship as a strength, gave much more emphasis to foreign policy, which, from the point of view of votes, was a tactical mistake. Domestic issues were not absent from their campaign, of course, and going on the manifestos alone the voter would have been hard put to detect a large difference between them and Labour on what was being promised. Even on the matter of controls, he would read that both parties accepted the mixed economy of coexisting public and private sectors. But the detail of the various policies for housing, jobs and health mattered less than the general impression given by the parties on these matters during the coalition years and in the election campaign. While Labour looked strong on welfare and planning, the Conservatives gave the impression that they had other priorities. Mention of welfare reform was invariably accompanied by cautions on the prior need to restore a vigorous free-enterprise economy. "Unless a sound and flourishing economy can be established," a Conservative election leaflet warned, "there is no possibility of full employment, improved conditions or the carrying out of plans for social betterment".[12] Right or wrong, this sort of statement looked like the preparation of excuses for retreating from promises made. Labour might not deliver the full extent of its promises; but it would try harder, or so it seemed.

On the question of the relative appeal of the party leaders and front bench figures, the war again seems to have been good for Labour. While it is true that Attlee lacked charisma, the combination of Attlee, Bevin, Morrison and Dalton looked impressive; and the return of Stafford Cripps to the Labour fold further enhanced the team's image. Labour's two brief periods of power between the wars had left an impression of a party lacking in sound leadership and ministerial competence. The war changed that impression decisively. Within the coalition government, Labour ministers laid to rest any doubts about their competence. Significantly for 1945, they dominated the organization of the home front. Attlee put it thus: "The work of my Labour colleagues in the government and in places of responsibility throughout the length and breadth of the land has shown that Labour can govern".[13] More humbly, Morrison admitted to the king, some months after the election: "During the coalition the Labour members learnt a great deal from the Conservatives in how to govern".[14] The Conservatives believed their greatest asset was Winston Churchill, and in the campaign they relied heavily on his huge reputation as the leader who had brought the nation through its greatest trial. Their most favoured poster was of the personality-cult genre, and carried the slogan "Help him finish the job". But the assumption that Churchill would, like Lloyd George in 1918, sweep to power on the basis of his wartime glory was false. In his prescient article of January 1944 Tom Harrisson wrote:

> Supremely popular as he is today, this is closely associated with the idea of Winston the War Leader, Bulldog of Battle, etc. Ordinary people widely assume that after the war he'll rest on his magnificent laurels. If he doesn't, many say they will withdraw support, believing him to be no man of peace, of domestic policy or human detail.[15]

As the founder of Mass Observation, Harrisson was writing in the knowledge that for at least two years before he reached this conclusion, Mass Observation reports showed public distaste for the idea of Churchill as post-war prime minister. A poll of February 1944 suggested that as many as 62 per cent of the people wanted someone other than Churchill. That was writer George Beardmore's impression, too, after overhearing working men in a teashop agreeing not to vote for Churchill: "They weren't *for* Attlee, they were *against* Churchill who in other circles is known as the Happy Warrior".[16] Although their reliance on the "Churchill factor" was natural enough, therefore, it was not the winner the Conservatives imagined it to be. At best it helped to narrow the opinion poll gap between the parties. After Churchill began active campaigning in June, the Labour lead fell from 16 per cent to 6 per cent on the eve of polling. In his tour of the country Churchill was cheered everywhere by large crowds, but when it came to voting on their future, it seems many, not without gratitude, were able to draw a line under his achievement and turn away.[17]

After the election there was naturally intensive investigation by both sides (and everyone else) into what might have brought about its extraordinary outcome. In the Labour camp the consensus was that nothing was as important as the acceptance by more of the people than ever before that the defects of British society, made more glaring during the years of war, must be addressed, and that Labour was the Party that would do the job. Some Conservative supporters privately conceded this. Churchill's private secretary John Colville, for instance, wrote in his diary during the last week of the campaign that Bracken and Beaverbrook were "firing vast salvos that mostly, I think, miss their mark. Labour propaganda is a great deal better and is launched on a rising market".[18] Among Conservatives reluctant to admit that the Party was out of touch with the public mood there was a search for more flattering explanations. One of these was a conspiracy theory, in this case that a left-wing coterie, well-placed in Fleet Street, at the BBC, in the churches and universities and, above all, in the Army Bureau of Current Affairs, had abused the opportunities presented by the suspension of party politics insidiously to implant socialist ideas and to advance the claims of socialism in the building of post-war Britain. Others sought an explanation in the relative strength of the party organizations, a line favoured by Churchill himself when he came to write his memoirs. The claim was that the Conservatives were at a disadvantage because nearly all Conservative Party agents in the constituencies had gone into the forces or war work, whereas the trade unionists who made up most of Labour's local organizers remained at home as "reserved" workers. While many Conservative constituency associations became inactive, therefore, their Labour counterparts, supposedly, were able to keep things going and get off to a running start when the election was called. It was a spurious claim; Labour had very few full-time agents before the war, which explains why there were only 16 in the services compared with the 26 Conservative agents. There were just 58 full-time Labour agents in March 1945 and in the campaign most Labour agents had no previous experience at the job. At that point, moreover, the absent 246 Conservative agents had been released from national service and were back on Party service.

Much rueful reflection was made by Conservatives upon what retrospectively appeared to be a mistaken style of campaigning. Its emphasis on scaring off the voters from Labour was blamed on Beaverbrook and Bracken, but Churchill himself arguably set the tone. In his notorious 4 June election broadcast he declared that no socialist system could be established without a political police, and that to attempt it Labour "would have to fall back on some form of Gestapo, no doubt very humanely directed in the first instance". He added that Labour's limited nationalization programme was only the start; in time they would nationalize everything. While one Labour Member's delighted view that the speech had "given us 50 seats" may be discounted as wishful thinking, there was real dismay in the Conservative camp at what looked like a damaging descent from the pinnacle by their main vote-winner.[19] And later, they judged that if

Churchill lost something in the public eye by this, Attlee's dignified response made the Labour leader the gainer.

Conservatives of the Reform Committee tendency naturally blamed the Party leadership's failure to align itself with the evident public desire for practical measures of social reform. They regarded Churchill's unconcealed lack of interest in domestic policy as a handicap. This was tellingly demonstrated by his attitude on housing, the number one issue for voters. In his election broadcasts, when he listed the tasks ahead, house-building came seventh and last. Labour, meanwhile, put the issue at the top of its agenda throughout the campaign.

Analyses of the strengths and weaknesses of the party campaigns probably miss the main point, however: most people had decided how they would vote long before the campaign started.[20] What happened between May and July may have influenced the size of Labour's victory but it did not determine the main result. The signs that Labour's time had come were already evident in 1940, when its leaders' claim to participation in government was irresistible. In government, Labour's prestige rose at the same time as the experience of "the people's war" stimulated public desire for social reform. After 1943 it was clear that the Conservatives were out of touch with the national mood and that Labour had the better claim to be entrusted with the task of rebuilding Britain.

Notes

1   D. Butler & D. Stokes, *Political change in Britain* (London: Macmillan, 1969), p.54.
2   Quoted in P. Addison, *The road to 1945* (London: Pimlico, 1994), pp.268-9.
3   T. Harrisson, "Who'll win?", *Political Quarterly* XV, 1944, pp.21-32.
4   P. Lewis, *A people's war* (London: Thames Methuen, 1986), p.230.
5   M. Panter-Downes, *London war notes 1939-1945* (London: Longman, 1972), pp.252-3.
6   P. Thomas (ed.) *Mass Observation in World War II: Post-war hopes and expectations and reaction to the Beveridge Report* (Brighton: University of Sussex Library, 1988).
7   J. Griffiths, *Pages from memory* (London: Dent, 1969), pp.71-2.
8   Home Intelligence Weekly Report, 8-15 December 1942, INF 1/292.
9   I. McLaine, *Ministry of morale. Home front morale and the Ministry of Information in World War II* (London: Allen & Unwin, 1979), p.184.

10   Ibid., p.185.
11   Addison, *The road to 1945*, p.264.
12   Quoted in K. Jefferys, *The Churchill coalition and wartime politics* (Manchester: Manchester University Press, 1991), p.197.
13   Draft of a speech to Yorkshire Regional Council of Labour, April 1944, quoted in S. Brooke, *Labour's war* (Oxford: Oxford University Press, 1992), p.319.
14   Quoted in R. Miliband, *Parliamentary socialism* (London: Merlin, 1972), p.272.
15   Harrisson, "Who'll win?", p.23.
16   G. Beardmore, *Civilians at war: Journals 1938-1946* (Oxford: Oxford University Press, 1986), p. 197.
17   When colleagues spoke angrily to Churchill about the public's ingratitude, he characteristically replied: "Oh no, I wouldn't say that. They have had a hard time". Quoted in L. Mosley, *Backs to the wall: London under fire 1939-45* (London: Weidenfeld & Nicholson, 1971), p.379.
18   J. Colville, *The fringes of power*, p.256.
19   Jefferys, *The Churchill coalition*, p.192.
20   84 per cent, according to one poll. R. McCallum & A. Readman, *The British General Election of 1945* (Oxford: Oxford University Press, 1947), p.296.

Chapter Ten

Taking stock: Britain in 1945

In the glow of victory the British people could be forgiven for believing that Britain was still a Great Power. After all, had not Britain successfully beaten off the mortal threat of German armed might virtually single-handed? Had not Britain's own forces played a significant role in the defeat of the Axis? Was not her membership of the Big Three of the Grand Alliance indicative of her status? And when the fighting stopped, were there not clear confirmations of Britain's status in the recovery of the Empire in full measure, zones of occupation in Germany and Austria, and one of the five permanent seats in the Security Council of the newly-founded United Nations Organization?

The reality behind the appearance of undiminished strength was that, quite apart from the evident gap between the USA and the USSR on the one hand, and everyone else, including Britain, on the other, the damage done by the war to Britain's economy was a serious limitation on her capacity to act like a Great Power. This reality was unpleasant for many in Britain, which is probably why coming to terms with it was to take a decade or more after the ending of the war.

It was not that there was deliberate reality-avoidance. In Britain, as elsewhere, the human urge at the ending of wars to take stock, to draw up some sort of balance-sheet of gains and losses was certainly to be seen. If there seemed some grounds for optimism about the prospects of building a better life for the majority of the people, there was no escaping the fact that the destructive effects of war had been grievous. Depending on what one chose to emphasize, Labour's legacy betokened brimming potential or austere constraint.

In one respect, at least, the price of victory was surprisingly low: the human cost in dead and injured was lighter than for the First World War, despite the second war's greater length. About 370,000 people were killed, 272,000 of them in the armed forces, 35,000 in the Merchant Navy, 63,000 civilians. Devastating though these deaths undoubtedly were for the families concerned, they did not amount to real damage to the country's productive capacity. Demographically, the effect of the war was insignificant. Over the six war years, the total population grew by 1.4 million, and the age distribution remained more or less constant.[1]

In other respects the cost of the war was measurably more threatening to the plans of the new government. External disinvestment amounted to no less than £4,198 million, or 15 per cent of the national wealth as it had stood in 1939. Just over a quarter of this disinvestment was in the form of the realization of capital assets overseas, three-quarters was the product of increased external liabilities in the form of new debts taken on by the Treasury, or old ones cancelled. The National Debt was four times the pre-war level. Many overseas markets had been lost. If Britain's balance of payments had been a cause of anxiety since the end of the previous war, the situation in 1945 was little less than alarming. From his Treasury base, Keynes issued a gloomy memorandum in August in which he said that Britain faced "an economic Dunkirk".[2] Without continuing American aid, he said, the nation would be "virtually bankrupt and the economic basis for the hopes of the public non-existent". As far as exports were concerned the prognosis was quite good: in the field of industrial exports Britain's chief rivals Germany and Japan had been laid low and would not provide competition in the foreseeable future. Also, there seemed no reason to suppose that Britain would not recover her previous position as supplier of shipping, insurance and banking services to the world: the "invisible exports" that in the past had helped maintain the balance of payments. The problem was that it would take an estimated three years to make the readjustment from war production to peacetime production. In 1945 exports were only 30 per cent of the pre-war level. Long-term solvency required a figure of 75 per cent above that pre-war level. The stopping of Lend–Lease only six days after the end of the war with Japan on 15 August greatly exacerbated the problem, for Britain was counting on the war in Asia lasting much longer, thereby providing her with the cushion of continuing Lend–Lease into the period of adjustment. Lend–Lease had undoubtedly provided Britain with short-term benefits, but its longer-term effect was to deprive her of economic power in the post-war world, while at the same time advancing the position of the USA. Keynes thought this was deliberate on the Americans' part: the US government "was very careful to take every possible precaution to see that the British were as near as possible bankrupt before any assistance was given", and they operated the scheme with the aim of "leaving the British at the end of the war . . . hopelessly insolvent".[3] A Treasury team headed by Keynes was despatched to Washington to negotiate a grant or at least a loan to help Britain over the transitional period. A loan of $3.75 billion at two per cent interest was agreed, but the negotiations were difficult: with the war over and the Churchill–Roosevelt partnership gone, the US administration and Congress were in less generous mood. Tough conditions accompanied the loan: a pledge to liberalize Britain's foreign trade and full convertibility of sterling one year after the loan came into operation. Even then, Congress delayed its approval until July 1946. The episode brought home to many in Britain not only the limits of the "special relationship" with the USA, but the reality of Britain's economic position in the year of victory.

Everything, then, would still depend on the ability of British industry to become the engine of economic growth through a great expansion of exports.

A contemporary assessment of the state of industry in 1945 would have produced a mixed picture of strengths and weaknesses enough to make prediction of future success difficult. Britain had entered the war, as was shown in Chapter 2, with a range of industries in various states of health, from those in long-term decline to those with recent growth and good prospects. The war interrupted the processes by which industries declined or grew, laying over all its own special distortions. Consequently, some industries declined more rapidly than would otherwise have been the case, others were given a temporary reprieve, yet others were stimulated into further development and expansion. Physical damage from bombing played a part in this, but more important for the longer term were the distortions introduced to skills training and investment.

Although in no way comparable to the German experience, Britain's industrial base suffered much damage from air attack. No part of the country had been safe from bombing and it was inevitable from the start that the enemy would succeed in making repeated strikes against important industrial and commercial areas and against the internal and external transport system. This is testified by the systematic targeting of the West Midlands, the ports and the merchant marine. Whether or not plant and equipment was repaired or replaced depended on where the particular industry stood on the essential–inessential continuum, for this determined its eligibility for help from the chief allocator of resources and buyer of products, the government itself. Some industries effectively had to "make do and mend", while others were given assistance.

The short-term priorities of a war for survival dictated that all resources be devoted to increasing the production of war goods. This in turn led to an overall neglect of capital investment, indeed, to the consumption of capital. In 1938, 5 per cent of the national income went into non-war capital formation; by 1945 it had fallen to –12 per cent.[4] This huge fall in capital formation was accompanied buy a fall of 13 per cent in the capital-to-labour ratio and 20 per cent in the capital-to-output ratio. These figures implied reduced efficiency in many industries as peacetime production was resumed. To them must be added the incalculable capital loss incurred by the conscription of men and women into the armed forces who might otherwise have undertaken industrial training but who instead entered the labour market unskilled. Loss of skill, moreover, resulted from the wartime policy of channelling resources away from inessential industries and towards the production of war goods. Many industries lost their skilled workers to the armed forces and ended the war with a largely unskilled, female workforce making Utility grade products for which advanced craft skills were unnecessary. For five years normal training arrangements had lapsed, and when the end of the war brought back the demand for products of greater complexity and variety, whole industries were embarking on the task with a workforce consisting of people without training, or whose training had not been appropriate to their wartime work, or who had lost much of their skill while away in the services.

The peculiarities of wartime investment had, however, given a positive stimulus to industries that were vital to the war effort and which in 1945 had great export potential. In the favoured industries, training programmes increased the numbers of key skilled workers. In addition, 25 million square metres of factory space built for munitions production was available for peacetime production, together with £100 million of machine tools.[5] Electrical power had increased by 50 per cent. Depressed areas had revived through a share of the £1,000 million government investment in armaments made during the war. Wartime expansion was accompanied by the permeation of new methods of mass production, management, design and quality control.

Through the demands of industry and the military there was a stimulation given to science and technology. In the search for solutions to military problems and the fulfilment of new industrial needs, funding was made available for teams of scientists and technologists to be formed and brought into the problem areas with unprecedented freedom to question the premisses of the policies and strategies. By 1945 the whole climate in which scientists and technologists worked, whether for the government or the major firms, had changed. Addressing the British Association in 1944, Ernest Bevin said: "I think it is true to say that science has not merely a place in industry, but does in fact dominate it now".[6] Already during the war the advance of the scientist from a former position of isolation, low status and inadequate resources, was beginning to yield dividends in fresh discoveries and in the wide application of earlier discoveries in fields such as aircraft engines and design, antibiotics, insecticides, computers and nuclear fission. Many assumed that the wartime role in the corridors of power played by leading figures in science like F. A. Lindemann, S. Zuckerman and J. D. Bernal would continue in some form after the war. Soon after the Labour Government took office, Herbert Morrison, as Lord President of the Council, commissioned the Committee on Future Scientific Policy under the chairmanship of Sir Alan Barlow. Its recommendation that a permanent advisory council on scientific policy be set up was followed by the government. But little came of it. Even at this high point of prestige for science, when the miracles of the "boffins' war" were the stuff of popular myth, Whitehall, dominated as it was by men with backgrounds in the classics and humanities, remained resistant to the idea that policy formation required a bigger input from the men of science.

For two industries, shipbuilding and cotton, the war served to check a long-term decline. Rearmament and war had the shipbuilders working to capacity, first in expanding the Royal Navy, then in repairing and replacing the vessels of both Royal and Merchant Navies that the enemy had damaged or sunk. But this was done largely without changes to technology, operational methods and personnel. Trade practices were suspended for the duration of the war but, in accordance with agreements made, were fully restored at its end. The industry would be competing with countries like Sweden and the USA, where welding had already replaced riveting, and production-line methods were in operation. It was a classic case of the sacrifice of long-term competitiveness to short-term output. In a similar way, cotton had been reprieved by the sudden demand for uniforms, parachutes and webbing, but nothing was done to invest in the automatic looms and ring-spinning techniques that were taking over in the USA and which would enable Britain to compete on world markets when the war was over.

Coal and steel were effectively brought under state control during the war. The effects of the notoriously fragmented ownership of the mines was to some degree mitigated by the creation of the Ministry of Fuel and Power in June 1942 and the subsequent centralization of coal control through Group Production Directors responsible to Area Controllers. The industry received an injection of government money from 1943, enabling the proportion of coal cut and conveyed by machinery to increase. For all that, at the end of the war coal was still an under-capitalized industry with much rundown equipment and, moreover, little progress made on its problems of bad management and worse labour relations. Like coal, steel's task in the war was, above all, to deliver more of the basic product. Such investment as went into steel was principally for increasing capacity. The government put £7 million into drop forgings and £4 million into gun forgings; ingot capacity for aluminium, vital for aircraft structures, rose from 31,000 tons in 1939 to 54,000 tons by 1943.[7] But most of this expansion was in the form of *ad hoc* extensions to plant that was already semi-obsolete. Although the industry was bigger than before the war and had a greater proportion of electric furnaces than then, the future was with purpose-built integrated mills producing steel in continuous strip, and in these Britain was under-endowed. In this respect, despite the destructive attentions of the RAF, Germany was better placed than Britain.

Inland transport was one of the sectors where the "make do and mend" approach dominated and a real running down of capital occurred. Maintenance and replacement was neglected, which was more significant at a time when ports and key railway installations were subjected to bombing. As described in Chapter 8, greatly increased traffic and the diversion of haulage from the roads to the railways exacerbated the strain on the network, engines and rolling stock. The official historian recorded the situation of the railways in 1945:

> the railways had been overloaded during the war almost to the point of breakdown ... The immediate post-war years found the

railways with heavy arrears of replacement and repair of the permanent way, locomotives and rolling-stock to be made good . . . it was to take five years or more to restore them to good working order.[8]

Road transport was in a poor shape, too. The network (if such it can be called, for no start had been made before the war to construct roads suitable for heavy haulage) had deteriorated because of bombing and reduction of maintenance, and a high proportion of the lorries and buses was aged.

The test of war, then, left inland transport in a state of near-exhaustion and in urgent need of major investment if it was to service an industrial and commercial revival.

The industries that flourished during the war, becoming not simply bigger, but more modern and competitive, were: aircraft, motor, engineering electronics, chemicals and agriculture.

It has been pointed out that few industries benefited more from government investment during the war than the aircraft industry.[9] Massive inputs of space, machine tools, research and labour enabled it to raise output dramatically. And all manner of improvements and inventions flowed from the investment: jet and turbo-propeller aircraft, stressed-metal skins, pressurised cabins, retractable undercarriages. The promise the industry represented for Britain in the international market was recognized in the War Cabinet's commissioning of an inquiry, chaired by Lord Brabazon, into the setting up of a greatly enlarged civilian industry when peace returned. As Barnett has pointed out, however, most of the machine tools that made possible the increase in output were imported from America. In terms of output per man-day, moreover, the British aircraft industry could only manage a peak of 1.19 pounds of structure weight compared with the American rate of 2.76 pounds, and the German rate of 1.5 pounds. A Whitehall memorandum of November 1944 explained: "Probably the most outstanding single cause of failing to reach a maximum production efficiency in wartime is scarcity of skilled management".[10] That same management was still in charge a year later.

For the duration of the war the motor industry was linked to the aircraft industry through the "shadow factory" scheme. Production of vehicles continued in the car plants – of army vehicles, tracked carriers and tanks rather than civilian vehicles – but in the shadow factories the mass production of aircraft and aero-engines went ahead as planned. When the war ended the car firms had the inestimable benefit of having at their disposal a wartime legacy of ample factory space and modern production lines ready for reconversion to vehicle production. In the West Midlands, for example, Rover closed its bomb-damaged works at Coventry and moved into its former shadow factory at Solihull; and in the factories where Bristol engines and Spitfires were assembled, Jaguar, Peugeot and Massey Ferguson expanded vehicle production.[11] Component-makers benefited in the same way. At Castle Bromwich, the car-body makers Fisher & Ludlow moved into the factory in which the Morris Company had made fighter-planes; at Speke near Liverpool, the tyremakers Dunlop took over the factory where the Rootes Company had made Blenheim bombers.

It is no exaggeration to say that the war's effect on the whole of the engineering group of industries was beneficial. They were permanently expanded and were the principal gainers from the spread of modern methods of mass production and management, and the enhanced role of the scientist and technologist. Infant industries such as radio, radar and computers also expanded under war needs, and the same pressure led to the creation of one virtually new industry of great potential, petrochemicals, with its off-shoots in the areas of synthetic fibres, detergents, synthetic rubber and plastics.

The post-war balance-sheet showed that no industry emerged from the war stronger than agriculture. Government policies to raise food production had at the same time modernized this most conservative of industries in several important respects. Its most striking manifestation was in the mechanization of horse power: the fourfold increase in tractors, the doubling or tripling of the numbers of disc harrows, cultivators, binders, combine harvesters and milking machines. At the same time twice as much fertilizer was being used on British farms as before the war, with significant effect on crop yields. Through the War Agricultural Committees, moreover, the whole farming community had been, as it were, re-trained in best practice. This transformation of agriculture would not, of course, have been possible without the large state subsidies and guaranteed prices, which also ensured the co-operation of the farmers. The 70-year-long depression was over and the prospects were good; for everyone had learnt the lesson about over-dependence on imported food supplies and the need to cherish the skill of the farmer.

A wartime development that affected millions of industrial workers and seemed certain to continue was the expansion of industrial welfare. This enterprise had been recognized, of course, as long ago as the early days of the factory system. But in 1939 it was still only a minority of firms that took the matter very seriously; only 1,000 firms belonged to the Industrial Welfare Society. Bevin's arrival at the Ministry of Labour gave this poor relation a much higher profile. He first insisted on the detachment of the Factory Inspectorate from the Home Office and its incorporation into his Ministry. Then in July 1940 he issued an order compelling firms with over 250 employees to appoint welfare officers. He set up three-month training courses for personnel managers. By 1944, 90 per cent of larger factories, i.e. those with over 500 employees, had some form of welfare supervision in place.[12] The practical results of Bevin's active promotion of industrial welfare were in the expansion of facilities like canteens, washrooms and sick-rooms, the appointment of medical staff, improvements in lighting, ventilation, and the like, complementing the rise in the real income of the workers in establishments on government contracts. The "cover" for many of the improvements was the introduction of women into workplaces formerly exclusive to men. Whatever the reason, however, the legacy was a positive one: new standards of worker welfare were entrenched, and the workplace could never be returned to its former crudity.

A less optimistic picture is suggested by the state of industrial relations. The pre-war legacy had been, as we have seen, more of a liability than an asset in war production. At the war's end the situation had altered in some respects and remained stubbornly tradition-bound in others. Bevin's key position at the Ministry of Labour had at least ensured that government policy was based firmly on co-operation with labour. It came to be accepted on all sides that trade union leaders should be consulted, as a matter of principle, on all issues affecting labour, and a great deal more besides; the organization and management of the economy should embrace the voice of organized labour. And as membership of trade unions rose from 6.25 million in 1939 to nearly 8 million in 1945, that voice represented an ever-increasing proportion of the nation. In effect, the trade unions became, as Bevin believed they ought to become, an estate of the realm.

The employers' organizations also came out of the war with a more influential position. Like the TUC, the British Employers' Confederation and the Federation of British Industries had been involved in the wartime tripartite consultations, and no-one doubted that this practice would continue. But the appearance of a convergence of interest between capital and labour, suggested by the patriotic commitment on both sides to increase war production, was misleading.

Behind it the basic relationship of management and workers in much of British industry remained bitterly antagonistic. As Morgan & Evans put it in a recent discussion: "Labour and capital confronted each other like armies of observation, divided, rather than united, by a common determination to win the war."[13] Although both sides accepted the mediating role of the State in a war economy of centralized planning and controls, neither relinquished its prejudices about the other, or expected their relationship to change in any fundamental way. Nor was the arrival of a Labour government at Westminster especially helpful for industrial peace. The gas, dock and bus strikes that erupted within weeks of the election suggested that for the workers, at least, nothing had changed, whoever occupied Downing Street. This did not prevent many industrialists from thinking otherwise; their instincts told them their interests were threatened by what they took to be the newly-entrenched position of labour. Their defensive posture stiffened in consequence. On the other hand, the employers' organizations had moved from their pre-war position of advocating a minimal role for the State in running the economy. In its 1944 publication *The organisation of industry*, the FBI endorsed the goal of full employment and the role of industry and government in seeking to achieve it. It accepted the need for government to produce the "framework of national economic policy, leaving the details to be filled in by working organizations provided by the industries themselves".[14]

To agree on the goal of full employment was, in 1945, to endorse present reality. Experience taught many to fear a slump, and pessimists warned of it. But for the time being, at least, there were no dole queues and work was easy to find. Regular work and regular income was the norm.

Income was, in fact, the major component in the relatively higher standard of living enjoyed by the average citizen in 1945 compared with 1939. The net income of the average working-class household enabled its members to afford a style of life measurably above that of pre-war. This situation was the product of two factors: full employment, which permitted more family members to bring in income from paid work; and the availability of overtime work, which put earnings ahead of price rises. Real wage rates had risen more slowly than the cost of living, and so the improvement in wage incomes would depend on the persistence of those factors now that the war economy had come to an end. A degree of income redistribution had come about, as the statistics for National Income show: between

1938 and 1944 wages as a proportion of all personal income increased from under 40 per cent to nearly 50 per cent. While the total paid in salaries increased by about 33 per cent and income from rents, dividends and interest by 11 per cent, that for all wages earned increased by 100 per cent.[15] If levelling-up was represented by the rise of wage income against salary and capital income, levelling-down came in the form of fiscal measures such as the Rent and Mortgage Interest Restriction Act, which froze house rents, the Excess Profits Tax and income tax. The number of manual workers paying income tax rose from less than a million to seven million during the war. While wage-earners were paying 13–17 per cent of their income in tax at the end of the war, salary-earners and *rentiers* were paying 35–44 per cent: everyone paid more tax, but some paid more than others.[16]

Full employment and higher average incomes are an important, though not the whole, explanation for the improved health of the nation, recorded in official statistics. Infant mortality rose in 1940 and 1941 but then resumed its pre-war decline, ending the war at 49 per thousand compared with 55 per thousand in 1938. Deaths from various diseases also fell: scarlet fever from 40 per million to 7 per million, diphtheria from 300 per million to 70 per million, whooping cough from 200 per million to 85 per million, and measles from 200 per million to 21 per million.[17] The rate for tuberculosis rose at the start of the war, probably because treatment was hampered by waiting lists for hospital beds and by a shortage of nurses, but by the end of the war this, too, showed a decrease on the pre-war rate. Seven out of ten men registered for military service between 1939 and 1945 were declared Grade I at the medical examination; this compared with only three out of ten in 1917–18.[18] Statistically, the war years ushered in a large increase in venereal disease, especially in the first three years, but a vigorous education and treatment campaign by the Ministry of Health had checked this by the end of the war. Neurotic illness, which might have been expected to increase, appears not to have done so.

This evidence of an overall improvement in the people's health at the end of nearly six years of all-out war is remarkable, given the fact that the medical services were over-stretched for most of this period. The demands of the armed services, and of the Emergency Hospitals set up to treat war casualties, caused shortages in the general medical resources available for the civilian population. Sick people had difficulty obtaining hospital care; the school medical services and the maternity and child welfare clinics were hampered by shortages of medical, nursing, dental and other staffs. In the public health services the number of doctors available in 1943 was 80 per cent of the 1939 figure; the school dental service was still more depleted; the numbers of general practitioners fell by 1945 to two-thirds of its pre-war strength, and one in ten was over 70 years of age. A special inquiry carried out for the government in 1943 concluded that the standard of medical service available for the civilian population was "dangerously low". That the health of the nation improved in such circumstances owed much to the interventions of government – the free vaccination schemes, the extension of the Emergency Hospital Scheme to much of the population, food subsidies and price control, the introduction of school meals and British Restaurants, subsidized milk for young children and expectant mothers, the distribution of orange juice, cod-liver oil and vitamins, campaigns to educate the public in nutrition and hygiene. In consequence, the average citizen fed better – could afford to feed better – than had been the case before the war; and the link between poor or insufficient food and bad health seemed to have been demonstrated. These interventions, although intended primarily as *ad hoc* solutions to immediate problems, established a widespread assumption that there would never be a return to the defective health provision with which the country began the war. The Beveridge Report and the National Health Service White Paper merely confirmed the existence of a consensus about the need for and expectation of a free, universal and comprehensive health service. Only the leaders of the British Medical Association raised objections, taking up defensive positions against many of the proposals of the white paper, despite the findings of their own survey of members, which showed a clear majority of doctors in favour of them. It was this opposition that caused the Conservative wing of the Coalition Government to consider a retreat from the white paper's proposals, which in turn broke the cross-party unity on the question and prevented the introduction of a legislative proposal. Once the election had been held, however, the matter was effectively decided: a Labour government would overcome all obstacles and a universal, comprehensive and free national health service would become a reality.

Beveridge had identified bad housing as one of the "Five Giants" on the road of reconstruction. The evacuation had revealed afresh how much remained to be done to solve the problem of slum housing. At the same time the war exacerbated the housing shortage; 200,000

215

homes were destroyed by bombing, 250,000 were so damaged as to be uninhabitable, many more needed repair. House-building fell away as two-thirds of construction workers were called to other duties; under 300,000 houses were built between 1939 and 1945, one-sixth of the pre-war rate. The backlog of 900,000 slum dwellings waiting to be cleared in 1939 was in 1945 only part of the problem, therefore. In the meantime, two million wartime marriages had added to the shortfall of homes needed. Even these alarming figures do not do justice to the true state of affairs in particular cities. Hull lost nearly six per cent of its houses.[19] London was especially hard hit, losing 109,000 houses, 25,000 of them in the late V-weapon raids, and suffering serious damage to a further million. There was no more pressing issue than housing in 1945. At the time of the general election a Gallup poll showed that 41 per cent of electors thought it was the most important issue, ahead of full employment (15 per cent) and social security (7 per cent). Plans and promises were made by the Coalition Government and the political parties, and a start was actually made in 1944 on the building of temporary houses, using prefabricated parts – "prefabs"; but while the war was still on, "make do and mend" more truly described the official answer to the problem. In July 1945, 76,000 people were still living in evacu-ation billets in the countryside because their homes in the cities had been destroyed or were uninhabitable.[20] By any measure, the hous-ing shortage would be one of the biggest problems a post-war gov-ernment would have to tackle. And the "homes for heroes" débâcle after the First World War was a warning precedent both of its intract-ability and its importance for the credibility of governments. As we have seen, Labour understood this and benefited electorally from the salience it accorded the issue in 1945. In doing so it recognized that "homes for heroes" symbolized the most significant part of its legacy: the popular sense that a new era was beginning that a re-ordering of social priorities would make more civilized.

Like much else in 1945 the educational system was the battered and shabby product of five lean years. Shortages of books, materials and equipment, depletion and improvisation in staffing permeated the system. Of course, everyone had been affected by austerity; but those schools that had to evacuate and re-constitute themselves in the reception areas probably had the greatest difficulty in maintain-ing a decent standard of education for their pupils. Here teachers had to cope not only with the inconvenience and discomfort of operating in buildings not designed as schools, or working a shift system in the school buildings of their hosts, but also with the behavioural problems of many of their charges, traumatized by sudden separation from home and family.

On the other hand, a snapshot of education in 1945 reveals some positive and surprising features: the number of children staying on after 14 had risen; the number successfully taking public examinations had increased; the School Certificate and Higher School Certificate pass rates remained unchanged at about 77 per cent; an age cohort 12 per cent smaller than that of 1939 was entering 13.7 per cent more candidates for these examinations.[21] These are average figures, concealing differences between one area and another, and the fact that for individual children it was a matter of chance whether or not the war brought them a substandard education. They are remarkable figures, nonetheless. Standards might have been expected to slip in the disturbed, sometimes chaotic, conditions many schools had to endure. That they were maintained was a testimony to the dedication of the teachers and administrators responsible for keeping the system going. Judged by these results they came through the test of war with flying colours. Why there was a growth in staying on and in taking public examinations is a matter for speculation. It has been suggested that a significant factor might have been the rise in average incomes during the war, which reduced the need in many families for the children to get into paid work as soon as they reached the age of 14 in order to supplement the family income.[22] If this is the explanation, it is an interesting reflection on parental attitudes, suggesting the advance of the idea, even when well-paid work was plentiful, that the value of extended education outweighed short-term gain. It was also confirmation that the demand for education had gone unsatisfied before the war and that there was public support for raising the minimum leaving-age and making secondary education available to all children.

The 1944 Education Bill embraced both these objectives. In doing so it followed the mainstream of thinking among education professionals and, by the time it was presented, at least among the majority of members, in the main political parties. It was nevertheless born more of political expediency than reforming zeal (see Chapter 3) and its defects were such as to deny to the country the most efficient use of its intellectual resources, and to its children an equal share in the financial resources allocated to schools. Brian Simon characterized the 1944 Act as "a clever exercise in manipulative politics by a past master of the art [Butler] . . . with the aid of a state bureaucracy devoted to highly conservative objectives".[23] It is clear that the grosser inequalities of the pre-war system were lessened, and the principle of education according to means replaced by that of free secondary education for all. It cannot be denied, moreover, that other important inequalities were mitigated by some of the Act's detailed clauses, such as those providing for school meals "at national nutritional standards", free transport for children living at the edges of the school catchment area, grants for clothes and equipment for children from poor families. But none of this took away the basic inequality of the tripartite system enshrined in Butler's Bill: three types of secondary school for three types of child, determined by competitive examination at the age of 11. Educational apartheid was thus built into the new system from the start. As the Report of the 1943 Norwood Committee, which provided the rationale for this part of the Bill, stated: "there should be three types of education . . . only on some such reorganization of education can the needs of the nation and the individual be met".[24] These numerically and academically unequal secondary schools were to have "parity of esteem", a gloss that ignored the status that would continue to attach to the grammar schools through their link with higher education, and the funding benefits that would go to schools retaining students beyond the minimum leaving age. As for that other educational apartheid, the divide between the state system and the independent schools, the Act had nothing to say. Mindful of the contentiousness of the issue, Butler diverted it to the attention of a committee set up in 1942 under Lord Fleming "to consider the means whereby the association between the Public Schools . . . and the general educational system of the country could be developed and extended". Because Fleming had not reported at the time of the appearance of the Education Bill in December 1943, Butler had an excuse for excluding it from substantive consideration. Brian Simon comments: "Butler stated afterwards in self-congratulation, 'the first class carriage had been shunted onto an immense siding'. This puts the matter very precisely".[25] In so far as the public schools were an important part of the existing class structure, their exclusion from the scope of what H. C. Dent described at the time as "the greatest measure of educational advance since 1870 and probably the greatest ever known", underlines the essentially conservative character of the 1944 Act.

Whether the new structure of education would be appropriate to Britain's post-war needs was doubtful. There was a general awareness at the time, sharpened by the war experience, that Britain's future economic success would depend on technical and managerial skills, and that education and training in these areas compared unfavourably with that of some other countries. And yet the Act did little to address this deficiency. Technical education was designated as appropriate to the "technical type", who often had an "uncanny insight into the intricacies of mechanism" but for whom the "subtleties of language construction" were "too delicate".[26] In other words, the technical schools would take pupils judged less able than those allocated to the grammar schools. In the secondary modern schools, meanwhile, the unselected majority of children would receive an undemanding education that would allow them to leave at 15 with no formal qualifications. If this implied a belief that what the economy required was a large unskilled workforce rather than technically specialized manpower, it was as wrong-headed as the concurrent notion that the best education for the country's future planners, managers, scientists and technologists was the traditional one offered in the grammar schools and public schools.

Appropriate or not, the reformed system implied a large increase in the education budget. A large building programme would be needed to accommodate not only the 200,000 pupils whose schools had been destroyed by bombing, but the 400,000 added by the raising of the leaving-age. Providing the extra teachers that would be needed was a problem because of the reduction of numbers entering training during the war. By the time the Act became fully operative 70,000 more teachers would be needed. A stop-gap measure was launched in 1943 by which mature candidates from other professions and from the services were given a one-year intensive training course in emergency colleges set up for the purpose by the local authorities and funded by the government. The optimists who organized the scheme were inclined to emphasize its advantages, and undoubtedly the teaching profession gained in some ways from this unorthodox infusion of new blood; but on the whole it had too much of the familiar "make do and mend" approach about it to set the right tone for this particular part of the New Jerusalem.

By comparison with the schools, the universities appear as a wartime backwater. And yet, the war was a time of upheaval for them, too, entailing considerable adjustment and adaptation. In terms of people, the sector shrank, so that at the end of the war it had only two-thirds of the number of staff and three-quarters of the number of students that it had in 1939. Science and engineering staff were combed out for work with the various ministries concerned with developments in weaponry, medicine and telecommunications. Others were channelled into cryptography and propaganda. Physics and mathematics students were recruited into crash courses in telecommunications and 6,000 bursaries were allocated to new students to study engineering, chemistry, metallurgy and radio. Vocational courses, such as were more commonly associated with the technical colleges, were set up and research took on a decidedly topical character, with numerous projects in weapons and military equipment. There was no high profile legislation on higher education during the war, but in 1944 two official reports indicated how the experience was shaping thinking about its future. The Percy Report recommended a two-fold increase in the number of graduates in engineering, and the Goodenough Committee pressed for a similar increase in medical students. Complementing these recommendations, and influential in determining the government's attitude towards future expansion of higher education, were the conclusions of the Hankey interdepartmental committee that a permanent increase of about 50 per cent of the number of students of university standard was necessary. As war gave way to peace the universities experienced a final and largely welcome change of routine: an influx of several thousand demobilized servicemen and women for whom, by courtesy of the government, degree entry-qualifications were waived. In the first autumn term of the peace, then, some among the latest cohort of 18-year-old undergraduates had the immeasurable benefit of having in their classes mature students whose world view was not a little influenced by recent matriculation in the test of war.

Histories of twentieth century Britain have invariably attached importance to the Second World War's effect on the role and status of women in society. Much of the discussion has focused on the additional opportunities for new roles in paid work that the war provided through the conscription of millions of working men into the armed forces, and on the implication of this for women's traditional role of caring for home, husband and children. This emphasis is perhaps explained by the salience of official wartime propaganda aimed at persuading women into war work, and by the subsequent prominence of media stories about women successfully doing "men's work". While it is undeniable that through choice or direction paid work was undertaken by women who would probably not otherwise have entered the job market at all, the actual numbers doing so were not huge. Between 1939 and 1943 the number of women in civilian employment rose from 4.8 million to 6.7 million, reducing to 6.2

million by June 1945. In other words, most women doing paid work during the war did not embark on it because of the war; 85 per cent of them were already in paid employment when the war came. For most women the war made no difference to this aspect of their lives. This is not to say, of course, that their lives continued unchanged. In all sorts of other ways the war brought difficulties and strains, some of which bore especially on women, and which at the war's end had influenced their situation and outlook quite as much as the experience of war work or war service.

Employment was nevertheless an important element in the way all women, those who did paid work and those who did not, came to define their role; for in this war, more than in the previous war, the question of whether or not to take on paid work was one which most women considered and indeed felt obliged to consider. Those women who were not liable to conscription, as much as those who were, were led by the circumstances of the war years to think about their role in ways that lay outside the custom of peacetime. Even where this reflection confirmed a woman's commitment to a domestic role, the very fact of having stopped to reassess attitudes that time and custom had allowed to remain unchallenged, altered her relationship with her chosen role. The possibility of alternative choices would never thereafter completely disappear.

Male conscription and the expansion of the war industries together destroyed female underemployment, and the attitudes that had sustained it in the 1930s. It was an accepted norm at all levels of society that men were as naturally the breadwinners as women were the home-makers and child-rearers. From this it followed that when paid work was in short supply, what was available should be undertaken by men. It had come to be accepted that many women needed to take paid employment while they remained single; this was certainly the norm for working-class women. When married, whether or not there were children, however, it was widely held that their proper place was at home, and that "work" should mean domestic work. In the full employment, indeed labour shortage, of the war economy such conventions had to be modified, if not abandoned. Official movement in this direction was typically cautious and incremental. The first statutory requirements on women to do war work or war service applied only to young single women; but successive widenings of the age-range followed and married women were encouraged, though not obliged, to come forward. Single women of private means and women with husbands and families, working alongside young working-class women, testified to the flexibility of the British people – employers, unions, husbands, women themselves – in their attitude towards the role of women. Or so it seemed. In two respects, sex segregation of jobs and equal pay, attitudes seem on closer examination not to have shifted in any fundamental or lasting way.

The pre-war convention that viewed women in paid work as essentially engaged in a temporary activity prior to marriage and departure for a domestic role, also assigned to them the routine work of industry and commerce, for which little or no training was needed. Employers mostly thought "investment" in female workers was economically wasteful; apprenticeships and skills-training were worthwhile only for males, with whom they could expect a long-term relationship.

Most female workers (apart from the two million or so who were in domestic service) were therefore engaged in unskilled or semi-skilled work in textiles, clothing, the food and drink industries, light metal trades, electrical goods assembly and scientific apparatus-making. In non-manual work the main opportunities were in nursing (154,000 in 1938), teaching (134,000) and the clerical grades of the civil service (28,000). What the war did was to create in existing industries opportunities for work previously restricted to men, and to open to women industries that had not employed them before. In metals, chemicals, engineering, transport, vehicle-building, energy and even shipbuilding, the barriers came down to the employment of women[27]. Most of the "no-go" areas for women were opened up.[28] At the same time, the "dilution" of skilled work was effected without gender discrimination, so that women participated in upgrading as much as men. The longer-term implications of these changes for the pattern of women's work might have been very significant were it not for the fact that they were accompanied, indeed made possible, by agreements between employers and trade unions, under the eye of the Ministry of Labour, which bound the signatories to a restoration of pre-war trade practices when the war was over. In many jobs, therefore, however well they took to the work and however competent they proved themselves to be at it, women could not, as the war drew towards its close, look forward to the prospect of career advancement or even of being retained on the payroll. "Safeguards" for the unions meant absolute insecurity for women whether they belonged to a union or not, since the unions were determined to prevent employers from reneging on the dilution agreements. A comment from a factory manager in the North of England illustrates this attitude:

> This girl has so taken to machinery that she'd like to become an apprentice and go right through the works. This of course is not possible on account of Union agreements. There's a feeling among the men at the moment women must be in the factory solely because of the war but that really women's place is in the home.[29]

Even when women did get some proper skills-training, the hostility of male workers led some employers to put the women onto un-skilled, repetitive tasks rather than face shop floor disputes.[30] In addition to the implied damage to the war effort, such evidence shows the persistence of entrenched attitudes to the role of women in employment and the likelihood that these attitudes would outlive the war. The widespread assumption that after the war jobs would once more be less plentiful naturally served to reinforce attitudes shaped by the Depression years. What women themselves thought of the issue mattered less than the fact that their male fellow-workers regarded them largely as temporary interlopers, who had better not allow the special situation of war to give them big ideas about new horizons in the world of work.

Nor was there for women any real promise in the relatively more flexible attitude of employers, compared to trade unions, in the matter of the sex segregation of jobs. The attraction to employers of eroding this segregation lay in the opportunities it gave them for getting the work done at a lower labour cost. Some of the negotiated agreements did not incorporate the principle of equal pay, so that women doing exactly the same job as the men they replaced could never match their wages. More commonly, the agreements did provide for equal pay, but there were loopholes that employers were able to use to obstruct its implementation. Women were often started on a lower rate than men, to graduate to the same rate by stages, as they acquired the necessary skills and completed a probationary period. This allowed employers to postpone indefinitely the point when a female worker was judged able to do the work "without additional assistance". If, for example, the setting of the machines in an engineering shop was forbidden to women, their work with those machines was "assisted" and therefore paid at less than the full rate. Employers also exploited that part of negotiated agreements that excluded work "commonly performed by women in the industry" from the equal pay provisions. By designating any war work offered to women as "commonly performed by women in the industry", they got it done more cheaply. It was also in their interest to widen the range of jobs so designated. To the extent that employers succeeded in this, women's job opportunities were widened, but the financial downgrading that accompanied the change made this a doubtful gain for women. Because it was also a longer-term threat to the employment of men, the trade unions took up the cause of equal pay for women; better that there was a rate for the job, whoever did it, than a situation in which women were preferred to men because their labour was cheaper. Unexpectedly then, for reasons unconnected with the justice of the matter, when women pressed their employers for equal pay or the upgrading of jobs, they found allies in the trade unions and their male fellow-workers. But even when this produced a successful outcome, as in the case of the women's pay-strike at the Rolls Royce aero-engine factory at Hillington, near Glasgow, the achieved justice was rarely unqualified. Here, a court of inquiry led to a new arrangement that attached to each machine a grade and a job-rate for its operator, male or female. However, work in the high grades was linked to men's skilled rates, in the middle grades to men's semi-skilled rates, and in the lower grades to the women's rates; since most of the women were placed on the lower grades, few derived any financial benefit from what was technically the introduction of equal pay. In white-collar jobs, the civil defence services and the armed forces, women encountered the same inequality of remuneration as on the factory shop-floor. Even as late as 1944, by which time the question of equal pay had received much public debate, parliament saw fit to defeat an amendment to the Education Bill, proposing equal pay for women teachers. It was something that the government set up a Royal Commission on Equal Pay, to report in 1946; but most women in work during the war reasonably had a sense of grievance about the persistent discrepancy between their pay and that of men. Greater availability of work and wage increases had done much to improve living standards for working-class women, but the injustice of unequal pay still rankled. As the war came to an end they had little grounds for feeling optimistic about future progress on the question.

The unprecedented demand for labour during the war produced a significant shift in employers' attitudes towards taking on part-time workers. Part-time work was particularly attractive to married women because it could be fitted in with domestic and family commitments.

With encouragement from the Ministry of Labour, employers took up the idea, coming to see the advantages for themselves: part-time workers had no statutory or customary rights, concerning job security, training, wage rises and bonuses, sick pay, paid leave and pensions. The effect of the huge wartime growth in part-time work, then, was on the one hand to open up to women a useful way of supplementing family income without serious disruption to domestic arrangements, but on the other to reinforce the sexual division of labour and the association of working women with low pay and dead-end jobs.[31] This development therefore lends weight to the view that for sexual equality at work the war was conservative, even retrogressive, in its effect.

For all that, most working women wanted to continue in paid work when the war was over. Surveys conducted late in the war bear this out. In the Amalgamated Engineering Union's 1944-5 survey, 68 per cent of the women surveyed, three-quarters of whom had entered the engineering industry during the war, said they wanted to stay on. This included 79 per cent of married women who had not been in paid work before 1939, and 86 per cent of those aged over 40.[32] The government's 1943 Social Survey found that only 20 per cent of women workers were determined to give up paid work altogether, as against 55 per cent who were resolved to stay on. Even among married women workers, more wanted to carry on working, full-time or part-time, than wanted to leave (39 per cent and 36 per cent); married women with children were yet more keen to stay on (49 per cent). Despite the fact that the government and trade unions had all along emphasized the temporary nature of the relaxation agreements, and despite the barrage of advice from all quarters urging women to turn to the task of nurturing their neglected homes and families, most women apparently found in paid employment something they did not want to give up. The simple explanation would be the increased affluence the extra income brought. And, indeed, "the money" was the most frequent response to the question "what do you value most about war work?". The feeling of independence even a small income gave to women formerly dependent entirely on their husbands' earnings is referred to over and again in the survey responses. But close behind "the money", in the value women placed on war work, was "the company", that is, the socially agreeable experience of being with others, in office or factory, as a contrast to the socially and physically restricted life of the family, especially when the latter was further cramped by poverty. Writing in 1945, the economist Gertrude Williams referred to this phenomenon in this way:

> War has shown how many women welcomed employment as a relief from the monotony and isolation of domestic work. The gossip of the shop, the companionship of fellow workers, the opportunity to see new faces and make new friends are all sources of pleasure.[33]

The evidence for women's attachment to paid work might be taken to imply a shift in their attitude towards their traditional role as full-time homeworkers once they married. Conversely, some observers have drawn attention to survey evidence that shows most people, men and women, thought that men were the main income-earners, and that wives should only take on outside commitments if these did not interfere with their home and family duties.[34] The apparent gap between the survey findings can, however, be bridged by the conclusion that most women no longer saw the roles of housewife and paid worker as mutually exclusive. With the increased availability of part-time work, especially, the dual role, trial-tested in the war, looked perfectly sustainable. Women who had coped with the double burden in wartime could manage the lightweight version that peace and the return of husbands to their former jobs would bring.

The wartime experience of women hardly amounted to a liberation from their traditional domestic roles, or to a significant change in society's attitude to those roles. Increased opportunities for routine, low-skilled work at lower rates than for men, brought no more than a modest possible variation in the lives of married women. Even this was hemmed in by the constraints imposed by inadequate nursery provision and the continuing preference of many employers for unmarried female employees. For the latter, the war certainly widened the range of occupations open to them, but it scarcely advanced sexual equality in terms of pay and career prospects.

The upheavals that many women experienced during the war in their domestic and working environment served as much to reinforce as to challenge their traditional roles, leaving at its end a dominant feeling that little had changed, after all. Social surveys and personal testimonies have provided some evidence that the new roles and responsibilities, the earning power and the geographical mobility experienced by women during the war enhanced their self-awareness and self-esteem and made them confident about their ability to take on new challenges after the war. Braybon & Summerfield cite the testimony of Mona Marshall, a nursemaid who became a steel-worker: "it made me stand on my own feet, gave me more self-confidence"; and a respondent in a 1943 Mass Observation interview: "I think the war has made a lot of difference to housewives. I don't think they'll want to go back to the old narrow life".[35] A wvs worker from Barrow wrote in a similar vein in her diary in 1942: "I wondered if people would *ever* go back to the old ways. I cannot see women settling to trivial ways – women who have done worthwhile things".[36] For women like these, whose war experience involved big changes to the roles their previous life had led them to expect, it can be readily acknowledged that the war often was a turning-point. But it needs to be borne in mind that, quite apart from those for whom the same experience was narrow, tedious and frustrating, most women lived through the war with only minor deviations from their expected roles. If it was a watershed for a few, it was a *longueur* for the many.

To describe war as a test is to imply that at its end an assessment of the candidate's "performance" can be made. This would be so whether victory or defeat was the outcome: at that level, allocating the participants in the Second World War to the pass or fail categories would only require noting who surrendered to whom. This book has not sought to explain how Britain came to be counted among the victors. Rather, it has focused on that viable social entity, in order to show how it behaved under the pressures of total war. The test was of the capacity of the nation to meet those pressures while retaining the integrity of its core values; that those values were in the process reviewed, refurbished and reinvigorated may be counted a strength, and a source of the continuing vitality of British society.

In political terms the years of war will naturally be remembered as a time of national unity, expressed in the Coalition Government and the electoral truce. This is not a misleading memory. For nearly five years the political adversaries of peacetime agreed to put aside any difference that would stand in the way of attaining the main goal of victory over the Axis powers, disbanding their pact by mutual agreement only when that victory was won in Europe and within sight in Asia. And it worked pretty much as it needed to work. Churchill's team was a ministry of all-the-talents. Only through coalition could the special strengths of these men be harnessed for the intimidating tasks that the common weal required to be undertaken. None could have succeeded, however, without the co-operation of particular sections of the people. Bevin, for instance, had to win the willing acquiescence of industrial workers in the temporary suspension of cherished working practices. By extension, the whole team owed its success to the compliance of the nation, and this, it should be noted, was achieved more by consent than compulsion. The coalition did not have seriously to worry about its internal viability or its external popularity.

A more cynical view would draw attention to features in the record that suggest a less consensual picture of wartime politics: the absence of coalition until the crisis of May 1940; the opportunism that in part moved the parties towards coalition; the persistence, after the coalition was formed, of mutual antagonism between back-benchers of the main parties; the scarce-concealed divisions in the Cabinet over issues of reconstruction during and after the debate on the Beveridge Report; the less than perfect adherence of party members in the constituencies to the spirit of the electoral truce.

Of the first of these, it is difficult to argue that the politics of the Phoney War were anything less than dysfunctional. Chamberlain's determination to keep Labour at arm's length, and Labour's opting for "constructive opposition", won little respect from the people and impeded the formulation and execution of policies necessary for the national interest. The crisis of May 1940, if not the product of, was at least made worse by the directionless and lethargic fumbling of the seven months that preceded it. Hindsight suggests that a coalition was necessary from the start. Such was Britain's political system, however, that it did not deliver what was needed quickly enough, with near-catastrophic consequences.

That there was opportunism in the actions of the party leaders cannot be denied. The Conservatives, holding power, knew that to retain it they had to get the country behind them and to achieve this they needed Labour. A coalition led by a Conservative prime minister would be a Conservative-dominated affair, it was presumed. For their part, the Labour leaders saw in the governmental role offered to them the attractive prospect of being able to influence the policy agenda, and thereby advance the interests of their supporters. In neither case, however, can the charge be sustained that these apparently sectional motives were incompatible with the pursuit of the national interest. On the contrary, the time-honoured principle of "give and take" was being activated for the common good.

Against the claim that the persistence of a degree of party politics impeded the coalition's effective prosecution of the war it may be argued that this, at least after the most critical period was passed, was no bad thing. The health of the parliamentary system depends on freedom of debate, and there was a danger that the concentration of power in the hands of the government, together with the automatic support of the majority of Members that resulted from coalition, would muffle this freedom. Lord Winterton, a Conservative front-bench critic of the government, complained in 1941 about the blandness of parliamentary proceedings: ministerial statements, invariably followed by "votes of thanks" from across the floor.[37] This was an exaggeration. There was certainly less of the cut and thrust of normal adversarial politics, but there were several major debates in 1941 and 1942 in which government strategy and economic policy was strongly criticized, and where the government's fate depended on the votes taken at the end. The fact that on each occasion the government won with very large majorities did not detract from the real sense in which the tradition was maintained whereby important matters were opened to vigorous debate in the House of Commons.

What the British political system demonstrated about itself was its adaptability to contingency. Thus, when there was a desperate need for a sinking of political differences, a form of government came into being appropriate to that need. And when the need was less urgent, when victory was within view, the system allowed a gradual disengagement from the set-up that had served its purpose well. Most remarkable of all is the way it operated to clear the way for putting supreme power into the hands of Winston Churchill in May 1940. In a famous biographical footnote, A. J. P. Taylor described Churchill as "the saviour of his country".[38] Hyperbole, perhaps, but forgivable and in any case, not unconnected with the facts of Britain's survival, in 1940–41 at least. By an almost miraculous process, the person most fitted for the role of galvanizing the British people into a supreme effort of energy and will, moved by stages from the political wilderness to the helm of the ship of state at its most critical moment. A system that could make this happen had passed a test worth passing.

The concentration of great power in the hands of one man – Churchill held the offices of both prime minister and minister of defence – theoretically posed a threat to democratic norms, and there were at the time some mumblings about a drift towards autocracy. But in reality it was generally understood and accepted that the set-up was strictly for the special circumstances of the war. In any case, Churchill himself had great respect for constitutional traditions and in particular for the sovereignty of parliament. Talk of dictatorship, actual or planned, was mistaken.

In one important sense government could be said to have moved closer to the governed during the war: the process by which interest groups and voluntary bodies participated in the shaping and execution of policy advanced rapidly. Representatives from the employers' organizations and the trade unions, in particular, were invited to offer their expertise to ministers and civil servants and to serve on public bodies. Necessity, and Bevin's presence at the Ministry of Labour, explains the prominent role accorded to trade union leaders; but few could object that democracy was ill-served when eight million trade unionists were, so to speak, given an additional voice in the corridors of power.

"Modern warfare is above all economic warfare" Adolf Hitler once stated. The source of the remark should not blind one to its insight. It had already been demonstrated in 1914–18 that the effective mobilization of economic strength was one of the keys to victory. In the end it was size of resources that determined the outcome of the Second World War. But this did not alter the importance of maximizing the potential of those resources and deploying them efficiently for the particular needs of the war at its different stages. For Britain this was how, in its economic aspect, the test of war presented itself. The war exposed the weaknesses of the British economy: antiquated plant and methods; lack of skilled workers and inadequate technical training; poor labour–employer relations; conservative and complacent management and unions. Although some industries had none of these defects, many had them in sufficient measure to impair overall performance. When account is taken of the circumstances of disruption, constraint and strain under which the resources of the nation were mobilized, however, what is remarkable is how well the economy performed. And against the flaws and failings must be set the notable fact that Britain's war economy operated largely with the consent of the mass of the people. To be sure, coercive powers were there, but they were mostly held in reserve, and what happened was much more the product of a general acceptance of the need to conform and co-operate for a common end. It must be counted a virtue and ultimately a strength that the pursuit of that end did not, for the people, mean further unfairness and exploitation; on the contrary, removal of existing injustice became part of the end itself.

When democracies are at war with autocracies they hesitate to limit basic liberties, since the very existence of such liberties is one of the most important ways in which they are to be distinguished from the enemy and why, in part, they are at war with them. They fight at a disadvantage, therefore, since the maintenance of basic liberties can impair and weaken the war effort. Britain came to terms with this problem in its own idiosyncratic way. Just as parliamentary liberties were not essentially denied, civil liberties more generally were adapted to the special circumstance of war, but within a framework of law and consent that made it clear the changes were temporary. Conscription was alien to British traditions, but it was universally accepted as necessary and, besides, it was accompanied by the right to conscientious objection. In contrast to its forerunner in the First World War, moreover, the system for dealing with appeals was liberal and humane. Defence Regulation 18B, under which internment operated, was theoretically a major erosion of civil liberties. But again, it is in its exercise that it must be judged, especially when the danger confronting the country in the early part of the war is borne in mind. As has been shown, it was undoubtedly used over-zealously at first, but amends were quickly made, in part because of the continuing existence of freedom of expression.

Even democracies, however, cannot wage total war without some form of censorship of the communication media. The temptation to influence or even control is strong for governments trying to expedite policies without the drag of public debate that an unrestrained Press and radio stimulates. In Britain the temptation was resisted, although the power was there throughout to silence those judged to be speaking against the national interest. That Defence Regulation 2D was so little used testifies not only to government restraint and the genuinely liberal outlook of the officials of the Ministry of Information, but to the generally co-operative attitude of the media. In return for the retention of the right to express opinion, the media proved to be as patriotic as could be wished for, contributing importantly to public instruction and to the sustaining of popular morale.

Any evaluation of the way the British met the physical challenge of the enemy's violent assault upon them has to encompass the paradoxical picture of, on the one hand, lapses in official foresight and preparation and, on the other, remarkable feats of adaptation and demonstrations of resilience. That the survival prospects were poor in 1940 was in no small measure attributable to the mismatch between foreign policy and military power: saying no to Hitler when the quiver was but half full. The unwise assumption that a "long game" could be played, and that this would permit any deficiencies to be made good, put the nation in a truly desperate situation. What followed demonstrated the national genius for improvisation: the Dunkirk evacuation, Beaverbrook's crash programme for fighter-plane production, the creation of the Home Guard. For all that, only a sizeable slice of good fortune prevented the catastrophe that logically ought to have occurred.

Nor were the preparations for attritive war on the home front anywhere near adequate. Had it turned out as bad as expected, the gap between provision and need would have been still wider. The evacuation was an organizational success, but everything else to do with Air Raid Precautions except, perhaps, the provision of gas-masks, was imperfect: air-raid shelters too few in number and giving low protection, little provision for fire-prevention, a fire-service impeded by fragmented command. Again, the necessary measures put right the deficiencies that planning ought to have foreseen. Adaptation was equally the hallmark of post-raid services, although the capacity of authorities to learn from the experience of others was distressingly feeble. To a far greater extent than was acceptable they chose to muddle through the problems; and to a far greater extent than was reasonable they relied on the freely-given efforts of public-spirited citizens. In some respects the selfless labour of ordinary people represents the best of Britain at war, but it was presumed upon to excess, as much in Westminster and Whitehall as in town halls across the country. This was more than officialdom deserved, since its attitude towards the public in the early part of the war was secretive, bureaucratic and mistrustful.

The obsession with morale, which the government had for much of the war, was largely a waste of nervous energy. Its conscious efforts to take care of the country's most precious resource, the people, was not without value, of course. But their effect in raising morale was probably marginal, a bonus, to be added to a sound enough base of resigned or enthusiastic commitment to the official stance towards Hitler. In retrospect it seems astonishing that this commitment was doubted; for what the test of war above all revealed about Britain was that it was a cohesive society, that the divisions and injustices within it were of less account in the end than what united it. Hitler's hope that class-division and separatism would be the Achilles heel of the British ruling establishment proved to be vain. Class divisions and class attitudes remained much as they had been in the 1930s and were no more conducive to the breakdown of society in the war than they had been before it. George Orwell, writing in 1941, put it thus: "... the English sense of national unity has never disintegrated . . . Patriotism is finally stronger than class-hatred".[39] The symbol of this feeling, the monarchy, consolidated the popular affection it had gained in the later 1930s. The fact that the king and queen had shared with ordinary citizens the dangers of the Blitz, Buckingham Palace being bombed no less than nine times during the course of the war, was an important explanation for this, together with their tireless insistence on visiting every bombed city, meeting and talking with people who had lost their relations and homes. Churchill remarked: "This war has drawn the Throne and the people more closely together than was ever before recorded"[40]. The queen admitted to being glad that the Palace had been bombed: "It makes me feel I can look the East End in the face", she said.[41] As for separatism, the Union had scarcely looked stronger. Laughing at the wrong-headed presumptions of Goebbels' propaganda, the British closed ranks and, as in 1914–18, saw the thing through.

This time there was a difference, however. Alongside an understandable sense of pride in Britain's performance, and a belief that its institutions and values were basically sound, was a widespread desire to see improvements in British society that would make it more equitable and more civilized. This was the corollary of a war that from the beginning had been presented to the people as a fight against tyranny and barbarism on behalf of civilized values. There was, then, a degree of conditionality about the patriotic commitment of the people in this war. By its end, the main features of this future society were agreed: full employment, social planning, and a redistribution of income. The test of war had proved Britain to be strong in the bonds of nationhood; but it had also helped to make clear to the nation how it should move on.

Notes

1 By comparison, Germany's dead numbered about 4.5 million and, according to recent research, in the Soviet Union possibly 40 million died.

2 "Our Overseas Financial Prospects", 14 August 1945. CP (45) 112 (CAB 129/1).

3 Quoted in R. Floud & D. McCloskey (eds), *The economic history of Britain since 1700*, vol. 3, 1939–1992, 2nd edn (Cambridge: Cambridge University Press, 1994), p.20.

4 S. Pollard, *The development of the British economy 1914–1967* (London: Edward Arnold, 1969), p.308.

5   Ibid., p.313.
6   Quoted in A. Marwick, *Britain in the century of total war* (London: Penguin, 1970), p.287.
7   Pollard, *Development of the British economy*, p.314.
8   C. I. Savage, *Inland transport* (London: HMSO, 1957), p.634, pp.638-9.
9   C. Barnett, *The audit of war* (London: Macmillan, 1986), pp.143-59.
10 Ibid., pp.146, 158.
11 D. Thoms, *War, industry and society: the Midlands 1939-45* (London: Routledge, 1989), p.169. Thoms also points out, however, that government contracts during the war enabled some relatively weak firms such as Singer and Lea-Francis to survive into the post-war period. This produced a situation of too many small, specialized and under-capitalized companies for the market to bear.
12 A. Calder, *The people's war* (London: Jonathan Cape, 1969), p.392.
13 D. Morgan & M. Evans, *The Battle for Britain: citizenship and ideology in the Second World War* (London: Routledge, 1993), p.54.
14 Quoted in C. Wrigley (ed.), *A history of British industrial relations 1939-1979* (Cheltenham: Edward Elgar, 1996), p.40.
15 Calder, *The people's war*, p.351.
16 Pollard, *The development of the British economy*, p.34.
17 CSO, *Fighting with figures*, HMSO, 1995, p.2.
18 Calder, *The people's war*, pp.28-9.
19 N. Tiratsoo, "Labour and the reconstruction of Hull, 1945-51", in *The Attlee years*, N. Tiratsoo (ed.) (London: Pinter, 1991), p.132.
20 Calder, *The people's war*, p.571.
21 Figures quoted in P. Gosden, *Education in the Second World War* (London: Methuen, 1976), pp.86-7.
22 R. Lowe, *Education and the Second World War* (London: Falmer Press, 1992), p.10.
23 B. Simon, "The 1944 Education Act: a Conservative measure?", *History of Education* 15(1), 1986, pp.31-43.
24 Quoted in Lowe, *Education and the Second World War*, p.14.
25 B. Simon, "The 1944 Education Act", p.41.
26 Norwood Report, quoted in Calder, *The people's war*, p.542.
27 See Chapter 4.
28 The most notable exception was in coalmining: no women were ordered or allowed down the pits.
29 Mass Observation, 1942. Quoted in S. Briggs, *Keep smiling through* (London: Fontana, 1976), p.174.
30 For example, the women welders at Welding Rods in Sheffield. Mass Observation, M-OA, TC 32 *Women in wartime*, Box 3, File F, Letters from Women Welders, 1942.

31 In 1944 there were 900,000 women doing part-time work. Source: K. Hancock & M. Gowing, *British war economy* (London: HMSO, 1953), p.454.

32 P. Summerfield, "Women, war and social change: women in Britain in World War II", in *Total war and social change*, A. Marwick (ed.), (London: Macmillan, 1988), p.107.

33 G. Williams, *Women and work* (London: Nicholson & Watson, 1945), p.118.

34 See H. Smith, *War and social change* (Manchester: Manchester University Press, 1986), p.225.

35 G. Braybon & P. Summerfield, *Out of the cage: women's experiences in two world wars* (London: Pandora, 1987), p.182.

36 R. Broad & S. Fleming, *Nella's last war* (Bristol: Falling Wall Press, 1981), p.229.

37 *New Statesman*, 19 April 1941.

38 A. J. P. Taylor, *English history 1914–1945* (Oxford: Oxford University Press, 1965), p.4n.

39 G. Orwell, "The lion and the unicorn", in *The collected essays, journalism and letters of George Orwell*, p.118.

40 Quoted in J. Wheeler-Bennett, *King George VI: his life and reign* (London: Macmillan, 1959), p.470.

41 Ibid., p.467.

Bibliography

Adamthwaite, A. *The making of the Second World War* (London: George Allen & Unwin, 1977).

Addison, P. *The road to 1945*, revd edn (London: Pimlico, 1994).

Aldgate, A. & J. Richards. *Britain can take it. The British cinema in the Second World War* (Oxford: Basil Blackwell, 1986).

Ayers, P. *Women at war* (Liverpool: Liver Press, 1988).

Ball, S. *The Conservative Party and British politics 1902-1951* (London: Longman, 1995).

Barker, R. *Conscience, government and war* (London: Routledge & Kegan Paul, 1982).

Barnett, C. *The audit of war* (London: Macmillan, 1986).

Beardmore, G. *Civilians at war: Journals 1938-46* (Oxford: Oxford University Press, 1986).

Beveridge, W. Social insurance and allied services, C. 6404 (HMSO, November 1942).

Bialer, U. *The shadow of the bomber* (London: The Royal Historical Society, 1980).

Blake, R. *The Conservative Party from Peel to Thatcher* (London: Fontana, 1985).

Branson, N. & M. Heinemann. *Britain in the 1930s* (London: Weidenfeld & Nicolson, 1971).

Braybon, G. & P. Summerfield. *Out of the cage: women's experiences in two world wars* (London: Pandora, 1987).

Briggs, A. *The war of words*, vol. 3 of *The history of broadcasting in the United Kingdom* (London: Oxford University Press, 1970).

Briggs, S. *Keep smiling through* (London: Fontana, 1976).

Brivati, B. & H. Jones. (eds). *What difference did the war make?* (Leicester: Leicester University Press, 1993).

Broad, R. & S. Fleming (eds). *Nella's last war* (Bristol: Falling Wall Press, 1981).

Brooke, S. *Labour's war* (Oxford: Oxford University Press, 1992).

Bullock, A. *The life and times of Ernest Bevin*, vol. 2, 1940-1945 (London: Heinemann, 1967).

Butler, D. & D. Stokes. *Political change in Britain* (London: Macmillan, 1969).

Butler, R. A. *The art of the possible* (London: Hamish Hamilton, 1971).

Calder, A. *The myth of the Blitz* (London: Jonathan Cape, 1991).

Calder, A. *The people's war: Britain 1939-45* (London: Jonathan Cape, 1969).

Calder, A. & D. Sheridan (eds). *Speak for yourself. A Mass Observation anthology 1937-1939* (Oxford: Oxford University Press, 1985).

Calvocoressi, P., G. Wint, J. Pritchard. *Total war*, 2nd edn (London: Penguin Books, 1989).

Ceadel, M. *Pacifism in Britain 1914-45* (Oxford: Oxford University Press, 1980).

Central Statistical Office. *Fighting with figures* (London: HMSO, 1995).

Chamberlain, N. *The struggle for peace* (London: Hutchinson, 1939).

Chester, D. (ed.). *Lessons of the British war economy* (Cambridge: Cambridge University Press, 1951).

Churchill, W. *The Second World War*, 6 vols. (London: Cassell, 1948-54).

Clark, R. W. *The rise of the boffins* (London: Phoenix House, 1962).

Clarke, R. *Anglo-American economic collaboration in war and peace 1942-1949* (Oxford: Oxford University Press, 1982).

Colville, J. *The fringes of power. Downing Street diaries 1939-1955*, 2 vols. (London: Sceptre, 1986).

Cooper, D. *Old men forget* (London: Rupert Hart-Davis, 1953).

Crosby, T. *The impact of civilian evacuation in the Second World War* (London: Croom Helm, 1986).

Dalton, H. *The fateful years. Memoirs 1931-45* (London: Muller, 1957).

Dilks, D. (ed.). *The diaries of Sir Alexander Cadogan 1938-1941* (London: Cassell, 1971).

Eden, A. (Lord Avon). *The Eden memoirs: the reckoning* (London: Cassell, 1965).

Feiling, K. *Neville Chamberlain* (London: Macmillan, 1939).

Floud, R. & D. McCloskey (eds). *The economic history of Britain since 1700*, vol. 3, 1939-1992 (Cambridge: Cambridge University Press, 1994).

Fraser, D. *The evolution of the welfare state* (London: Macmillan, 1973).

Fussell, P. *Wartime. Understanding and behaviour in the Second World War* (New York: Oxford University Press, 1989).

Gannon, F. *The British press and Germany 1936-1939* (Oxford: Oxford University Press, 1971).

Gooch, J. *Armies in Europe* (London: Routledge, 1980).

Gosden, P. *Education in the Second World War* (London: Methuen, 1976).

Grant, I. & N. Maddren. *The countryside at war* (London: Jupiter, 1975).

Grant, I. & N. Maddren. *The city at war* (London: Jupiter, 1975).

Graham, P. & L. Graham. *Collar the lot!* (London: Quartet, 1980).

Griffiths, J. *Pages from memory* (London: Dent, 1969).

Griffiths, R. *Fellow travellers of the Right* (London: Constable, 1980).

Hancock, K. & M. Gowing. *British war economy* (London: HMSO, 1953).

Harris, J. *William Beveridge: a biography* (Oxford: Oxford University Press, 1977).

Harrison, M. Resource Mobilization for World War II: the USA, the UK, USSR and Germany, 1938–1945. *Economic History Review*, Second Series, vol. XLI, No. 2, pp.171–92, 1988.

Harrisson, T. *Living through the Blitz* (London: Collins, 1976).

Harrisson, T. *War factory: a report* (London: Gollancz, 1943).

Harrisson, T. Who'll win? *Political Quarterly* **XV**, pp.21–32, 1944.

Harvey, J. (ed.). *The diplomatic diaries of Oliver Harvey 1937–1940* (London: Collins, 1970).

Hennessy, P. *Never again. Britain 1945–51* (London: Vintage, 1993).

HMSO. *Front Line 1940–41. The official story of the Civil Defence of Britain* (London: HMSO, 1942).

HMSO. *Persuading the people* (London: HMSO, 1995).

Hodgson, V. *Few eggs and no oranges* (London: Dennis Dobson, 1976).

Howard, M. *The Continental commitment* (London: Temple Smith, 1972).

Ingersoll, R. *Report on England* (London: Bodley Head, 1941).

Inglis, R. *The children's war* (London: Collins, 1989).

Ismay, Lord. *Memoirs* (London: Heinemann, 1960).

Jefferys, K. *The Churchill Coalition and wartime politics 1940–45* (Manchester: Manchester University Press, 1991).

Johnson, B. S. *The evacuees* (London: Gollancz, 1968).

Jones, T. *A diary with letters 1931–1954* (Oxford: Oxford University Press, 1954).

Kavanagh, D. & P. Morris. *Consensus politics from Attlee to Thatcher* (Oxford: Oxford University Press, 1989).

Kennedy, J. *The business of war* (London: Hutchinson, 1957).

Kennedy, P. *The rise and fall of the Great Powers* (London: Fontana, 1989).

Kirkham, P. & D. Thoms (eds). *War culture: social change and changing experience in World War Two* (London: Lawrence & Wishart, 1995).

Lafitte, F. *The internment of aliens* (Harmondsworth: Penguin Books, 1940).

Lamb, R. *The drift to war 1922–1939* (London: W. H. Allen, 1989).

Lamb, R. *The ghosts of peace 1935–45* (Salisbury: Michael Russell, 1987).

Lash, J. *Roosevelt and Churchill 1939–41* (London: Andre Deutsch, 1977).

Laybourn, K. *The evolution of British social policy and the welfare state* (Keele: Keele University Press, 1995).

Lewis, J. *Women in Britain since 1945* (Oxford: Basil Blackwell, 1992).

Lewis, P. *A people's war* (London: Thames Methuen, 1986).

Longmate, N. *How we lived then* (London: Hutchinson, 1971).

Lowe, R. *Education and the Second World War* (London: Falmer Press, 1992).

Macleod, R. & D. Kelly (eds). *The Ironside diaries* (London: Constable, 1962).

Marwick, A. *Britain in the century of total war* (London: Penguin Books, 1970).

McCallum, R. & A. Readman. *The British General Election of 1945* (Oxford: Oxford University Press, 1947).

McLaine, I. *Ministry of morale. Home front morale and the Ministry of Information in World War II* (London: Allen & Unwin, 1979).

Middlemas, K. *Britain in search of balance 1940-61*, vol. 1 of *Power, competition and the State* (Stanford: Hoover Institution Press, 1986).

Middlemas, K. *Diplomacy of illusion* (London: Weidenfeld & Nicolson, 1972).

Milburn, C. *Mrs Milburn's diaries* (London: Fontana, 1980).

Miliband, R. *Parliamentary socialism* (London: Merlin, 1972).

Milward, A. *War, economy and society 1939-1945* (London: Allen Lane, 1977).

Mommsen, W. (ed.). *The emergence of the welfare state in Britain and Germany* (London: Croom Helm, 1981).

Moorehead, C. *Troublesome people: enemies of war 1916-1986* (London: Hamish Hamilton, 1987).

Morgan, D. & M. Evans. *The battle for Britain: citizenship and ideology in the Second World War* (London: Routledge, 1993).

Mosley, L. *Backs to the wall: London under fire 1939-45* (London: Weidenfeld & Nicolson, 1971).

Mowat, C. *Between the wars 1918-1940* (London: Methuen, 1955).

Nicholas, S. *The echo of war. Home front propaganda and the wartime BBC* (Manchester: Manchester University Press, 1996).

Nicolson, N. (ed.). *Harold Nicolson: diaries and letters*, 2 vols *1936-39, 1939-1945* (London: Collins, 1967).

Noakes, J. (ed.). *The civilian in war* (Exeter: Exeter University Press, 1992).

Orwell, S. & I. Angus (eds). *The collected essays, journalism and Letters of George Orwell, vol. 2: my country right or left* (Harmondsworth: Penguin, 1970), p.321.

Panter-Downes, M. *London war notes 1939-1945* (London: Longman, 1972).

Parker, R. *Chamberlain and appeasement* (London: Macmillan, 1993).

Pelling, H. *Britain and the Second World War* (London: Fontana, 1970).

Pilgrim Trust. *Men without work* (London, 1938).

Pimlott, B. (ed.). *The Second World War diary of Hugh Dalton 1940-1945* (London: Jonathan Cape, 1986).

BIBLIOGRAPHY

Pollard, S. *The development of the British economy 1914-67*, 2nd edn (London: Edward Arnold, 1969).

Priestley, J. B. *Postscripts* (London, 1940).

Reynolds, D. et al. (eds). *Allies at war. The Soviet, American and British experience 1939-1945* (London: Macmillan, 1994).

Savage, C. I. *Inland transport* (London: HMSO, 1957).

Sheridan, D. (ed.). *Among you taking notes: the wartime diary of Naomi Mitchison 1939-1945* (Oxford: Oxford University Press, 1986).

Simon, B. The 1944 Education Act: a Conservative measure? *History of Education* **15**(1), pp.31-43, 1986.

Sked, A. & C. Cook. (eds). *Crisis and controversy: essays in honour of A. J. P. Taylor* (London: Macmillan, 1976).

Smith, H. (ed.). *War and social change* (Manchester: Manchester University Press, 1986).

Stevenson, J. *British society 1914-45* (London: Penguin Books, 1984).

Summerfield, P. Women, war and social change: women in Britain in World War II. In *Total war and social change*, A. Marwick (ed.) (London: Macmillan, 1988).

Taylor, A. J. P. *English history 1914-45* (Oxford: Oxford University Press, 1965).

Thomas, P. (ed.). *Mass Observation in World War II. Post-war hopes and expectations and reaction to the Beveridge Report* (Brighton: University of Sussex Library, 1988).

Thompson, L. *1940: a year of legend and history* (London: Collins, 1966).

Thoms, D. C. *War, industry and society: the Midlands 1939-45* (London: Routledge, 1989).

Thorne, C. *The approach of war 1938-39* (London: Macmillan, 1967).

Tiratsoo, N. (ed.). *The Attlee years* (London: Pinter, 1991).

Titmuss, R. *Problems of social policy* (London: HMSO, 1950).

Watt, D. *How war came* (London: Mandarin, 1990).

Wheeler, H. *Huddersfield at war* (Bath: Alan Sutton, 1992).

Wheeler-Bennett, J. *King George VI: his life and reign* (London: Macmillan, 1959).

Williams, G. *Women and work* (London: Nicholson & Watson, 1945).

Wilson, H. *A new deal for coal* (London: Contact, 1945).

Winter, J. (ed.). *War and economic development* (Cambridge: Cambridge University Press, 1975).

Woodward, L. *British foreign policy in the Second World War* (London: HMSO, 1962).

Wright, G. *The experience of total war 1939-1945* (New York: Harper Row, 1968).

Wrigley, C. (ed.). *A history of British industrial relations 1939-1979* (Cheltenham: Edward Elgar, 1996).

Ziegler, P. *London at war 1939-1945* (New York: Alfred A Knopf, 1995).

Index

INDEX

Printed in the USA/Agawam, MA
July 6, 2015

618395.006